Jesus

HIS LIFE AND TIMES

DON BLOSSER, PH.D.
TIMOTHY J. DAILEY, PH.D.
RANDY PETERSEN
DIETRICH GRUEN

CONSULTANT: THOMAS E. SCHMIDT, PH.D.

PUBLICATIONS INTERNATIONAL, LTD.

Don Blosser holds a Ph.D. from the University of St. Andrews in Scotland and is chair of the Bible, Religion, and Philosophy departments at Goshen College where he is professor of New Testament. An ordained minister, Dr. Blosser has been a guest lecturer at colleges throughout the world, including Fuller Theological Seminary. He is the author of *Dictionary of the Literature of the Bible*, *The Coming Kingdom*, and *The Word Among Us*.

Timothy J. Dailey earned his doctorate in theology from Marquette University and also studied at the Institute of Holy Land Studies, Jerusalem, and Wheaton College. He has taught theology, biblical history, and comparative religion at various institutes in the United States and Israel, including the Biblical Resources Study Center, Jerusalem, and Jerusalem Center for Biblical Studies. He is the author of a wide variety of titles, including *Mysteries of the Bible* and *Healing Through the Power of Prayer*.

Randy Petersen studied ancient languages at Wheaton College before becoming executive editor of *Bible Newsletter* and other publications. Now a full-time freelance writer and editor, he has contributed to more than twenty books including *The Revell Bible Dictionary* and *Giving to the Giver*, as well as to a wide variety of magazines, including *Christian History*. Mr. Petersen developed and teaches a Bible survey course at his church.

Dietrich Gruen is a bivocational pastor, with an M. Div. from Bethel Theological Seminary. He is the executive director of the Middleton Outreach Ministry, with a Good Samaritan ministry to the poor. He is also executive editor of The Gruen Group, which develops small group curriculum and Bible-related products. He has collaborated on more than thirty books, including *Who's Who in the Bible* and his first solo book, *Fathers Who a Made Difference*.

Thomas E. Schmidt earned his doctoral degree at Cambridge University after completing studies at Fuller Theological Seminary and Wheaton College. He served as chair of the Religious Studies Department at Westmont College, where he regularly teaches a variety of courses, including Life and Teachings of Jesus. Dr. Schmidt is the author of a several books, including *To Tell the Mystery* and *Life and Literature of the New Testament*, and has written for a wide variety of publications, including *Bible Review, Christianity Today*, and *Journal for the Study of the New Testament*. He is a member of the Society of Biblical Literature.

Louis Weber, C.E.O.
Publications International, Ltd.
7373 North Cicero Avenue
Lincolnwood, Illinois 60712

Permission is never granted for commercial purposes.

Manufactured in U.S.A.

8 7 6 5 4 3 2 1

ISBN: 0-7853-2823-8

CONTENTS

✦ ✦ ✦

INTRODUCTION

✦ ✦ ✦

ONE OF THE EARLIEST ACCOUNTS of the life of Jesus ends with these words: "There are also many other things that Jesus did; if every one of them were written down, I suppose that the world itself could not contain the books that could be written." A slight exaggeration, perhaps. But what would that ancient writer think, living as he did in a day when a great library contained no more than a few dozen scrolls, if he knew that more than a thousand volumes would be written about just his own book, the Gospel of John? Or that one day there would exist thousands of libraries, each containing hundreds of books about Jesus and the faith he founded? Or that several hundred new books about Jesus are published every year? It may take a while to fill "the world itself," but two thousand years and millions of words after John's statement, the interest in Jesus shows no sign of diminishing.

Jesus: His Life and Times is a balanced, nontechnical, well-illustrated volume that enables a broad audience of readers to deepen their understanding of the life, times, and teachings of Jesus. But who is this Jesus we write about? To some, Jesus was a revolutionary, to others, an evangelist, or a leadership trainer, or a feminist, or a role model for a godly life. Despite the passing of nearly two thousand years, it is still possible to know much about the "real" Jesus, though there are some questions that continue to intrigue and perplex many.

The gospels themselves almost never include commentary. Instead, they leave many insights between the

The life of Jesus started in a humble setting, yet no prince or princess born with wealth, power, and glory has even approached the impact that this one person has had on humanity. His teachings are as applicable today as they were two thousand years ago; and artists, writers, and poets through the ages continue to paint and write about his life.

lines, inviting the reader to make the appropriate personal connections and responses. Still, those who read the story today often benefit from some additional information. Two thousand years have passed, languages have changed, our culture is vastly different, and most of us are unfamiliar with the background and mindset of those who knew Jesus. *Jesus: His Life and Times* is not about questions regarding authorship, histor-ical accuracy, or theology. Rather, it is a presentation of what transpired in first-century Palestine according to the information provided by the Bible and other ancient sources.

One of the important and unique contributions of this book is its illustra-tions. The paintings are more than mere enhancement of visual appeal. From ear-liest times, the story of Jesus has been conveyed in pictures and symbols, and of course the biblical narrative has inspired many great works of painting, sculpture, and architecture. During times when much of the population was illiterate, it was necessary to communicate the essentials of the Christian faith visually. This is not without some risk. Because pic-tures, like words, can convey as much about the people who produce them as the times they represent, the art-work often shows a very European dress, setting, and appearance for biblical characters, and at times the creative enterprise distorts or adds to the original intent of biblical writers. But even with these and other qualifications, pic-tures are still worth a thousand words, inviting the viewer in to details and truths that the printed word might not convey.

Jesus healed the sick, resurrected the dying, and gave hope to the hopeless. These events recorded about Jesus' life continue to have a dramatic and life-changing effect on people today.

The book is organized in three sections covering the life, times, and teachings of Jesus. In describing the life of Jesus, we begin with the familiar and fascinating story of Mary and Joseph, whose unusual courtship culminates in a Bethlehem stable, involving characters as colorful and diverse as local shepherds, visiting astrologers, a madly jealous king, and a number of angels. Following the birth of Jesus, few details are given regarding Jesus' childhood and young adulthood, and the main stream of the story resumes with the beginning of his public ministry and the gathering of disciples. As a teacher and miracle worker in Galilee, he begins to attract attention, adoration, and suspicion. Gradually the story moves toward Jerusalem and the cataclysmic events of Jesus' last week. Controversies with Jewish religious leaders concludes in open opposition and the betrayal of Jesus into the rough hands of Roman authorities. He suffers a cruel and humiliating death, but a few days later appears alive and triumphant to his followers.

The area of the Dead Sea pictured here is where a group of people called Essenes lived. They separated from the mainstream Jewish religion and waited for a political and revolutionary messiah to come. Jesus would have known about this group—in fact, some scholars speculate that John the Baptist may have been an Essene.

In the times of Jesus we provide a panorama of biblical history and events taking place after the completion of the Old Testament that have a bearing on the story of Jesus. Here we discuss the distinctive beliefs of the Jewish people, including the importance of the land itself, the temple, and the growing expectations that a political and religious messiah would lead the Jews from under foreign domination. We see their successful political struggle for independence against great odds just two hundred years before Jesus, their subsequent subjugation under the

Romans, and the ongoing tensions between Judaism and Hellenism—the Greco-Roman way of life. We learn of the origins of groups like the Pharisees and Sadducees, who opposed Jesus; the Samaritans, who were despised by the Jewish establishment; and the Essenes, who left us the Dead Sea Scrolls, among other documents, which are a long-buried glimpse into biblical times.

Although the teachings of Jesus cannot be divorced from his life, we consider them separately in order to focus on important themes that together comprise Jesus' message. His authoritative style, his pattern of teaching in parables, and the ideas conveyed "between the lines" in the story are all important factors. Common and significant subjects include the kingdom of God and Jesus' own understanding of his identity and role. Did he really think he was God and that his death would save the world? What do titles like "Messiah" and "Son of Man" mean? In this section, we also read of Jesus' teaching about how to live as one of his followers. Important subjects include true righteousness, humility, faith, dependence on God, and love for one's neighbor. Finally, we consider the tension, or balance, between Jesus' high moral and spiritual standards and his message of free grace and forgiveness from God.

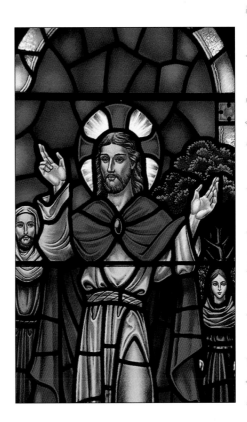

Jesus' preachings still give people guidance on how to live their lives. The tens of thousands of books available about his words attest to the fact that people still are searching for God's help in their everyday lives.

Open this book at random and point to almost any sentence, and there may be thousands, even millions, of words in print devoted to the background, meaning, and implications of that one particular statement. *Jesus: His Life and Times* is meant to help a broad range of readers to appreciate more fully, and inquire more deeply into, the fascinating life and times of Jesus.

—THOMAS E. SCHMIDT, PH.D

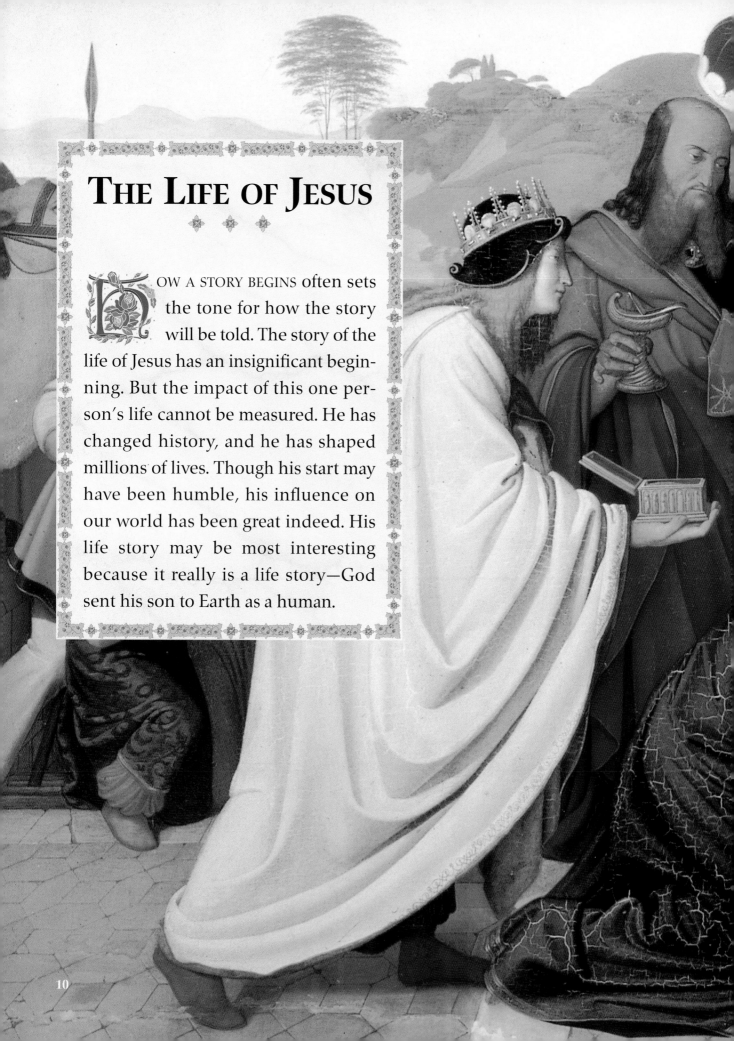

THE LIFE OF JESUS

❖ ❖ ❖

HOW A STORY BEGINS often sets the tone for how the story will be told. The story of the life of Jesus has an insignificant beginning. But the impact of this one person's life cannot be measured. He has changed history, and he has shaped millions of lives. Though his start may have been humble, his influence on our world has been great indeed. His life story may be most interesting because it really is a life story—God sent his son to Earth as a human.

THE BIRTH

✦ ✦ ✦

A YOUNG WOMAN, known simply as Mary, grew up in Nazareth. It was a small, unimpressive town. We know nothing about her parents, siblings, or background. Despite this humble beginning, she has become one of the most widely recognized people of Christendom.

Mary was a descendant of King David. But the thousand years that separated Mary from her famous royal ancestor had removed any regal status. She was a peasant woman. The Bible defines her moral and spiritual character by the brief statement that she was a virgin. That should not be surprising, for virginity was expected of all young women in that day. Serious consequences befell any who violated that moral standard.

Mary was a fortunate young woman. She was engaged to a man in the village named Joseph, and their wedding day was less than a year away. We have no reason to question her joy about this wedding. She likely had the expectation of having a happy and secure future as a loving wife and mother.

Jewish parents arranged weddings, usually when the bride was young. When Mary and Joseph reached marrying age (often midteens for the girl), they entered an official year of engagement. During this year they made plans, and the parents assembled a meager dowry. The couple began to build their relationship. They could end the engagement only by the official, legal action of a divorce. (In those days there was no returning the ring because you changed your mind!) For Mary and Joseph, it was a year of preparation, excitement, and anticipation.

Facing page: *In* The Nativity, *by Giovanni Battista Pittori, Jesus is watched over by an adoring mother, but his father, Joseph, is exhausted and asleep. In most art Joseph is a secondary figure, usually just an observer of what is going on around him.*

El Greco is noted for his originality and extravagance, as is evident in The Annunciation. *The message of the angel to Mary has dramatic importance for both God and humanity, and El Greco shows the heavenly host of angels and God (in the form of a dove) watching over this emotional conversation.*

So far the story is so routine that it would be unnoticed, except to those connected with the couple. But one day Mary's life was dramatically changed. An angel appeared, telling her that God had chosen her to give birth to the promised messiah. Angelic appearances were not common in first-century Israel, and Mary was stunned. What do you say to an angel who tells you that you are going to have a baby? Mary knew she was a virgin. Her first question showed her surprise, "How can I be pregnant? I'm not married!" Had she known all that was going to happen to her, she might have had a few more questions to ask!

An angelic announcement expressing God's honor would seem to bring joy and blessing. But for Mary there were devastating consequences. Christians sing, "The Virgin Mary had a baby boy." But do they realize what it meant for an unmarried woman of that time to be pregnant? We have created a fantasy story about how the angel appeared to Mary, how happy she was to have been chosen, how Joseph (after a few moments of doubt) quickly accepted Mary's message, and how the couple lived lives of joy fulfilling the parental role God had given them. For many this fantasy story has become the real story.

But life deals with reality, not fantasy. How did she tell her parents? "Mother and father, I have good news—I'm pregnant!" This would not have been good news to her parents. We do not know how her parents reacted. We can only imagine the shock, the sleepless nights, the pain, and the disappointment they must have felt.

What did Mary say to her fiancé? "Joseph, I'm pregnant. But I am still a virgin. I am pregnant by the Holy Spirit!" Would that be persuasive, especially since many Jews thought that God's spirit had not been active among his people since the last prophet had died three hundred years earlier? Imagine the feelings that Joseph must have had. What do you do when your bride-to-be tells you she is pregnant, and you know you aren't the father? Then she gives this explanation—"God did it." What would anyone think?

The Bible describes Joseph as a righteous, compassionate person who loved Mary. This news, however, was more than he could handle. Her angelic explanation did not convince him. He was devastated, and he considered his options. He could file morality charges against Mary, which would probably result in her death by stoning (Deuteronomy 22:20–21); he could take legal action to end the engagement and free himself from all moral or financial responsibility; or he could marry her, which would imply that he was the responsible father. But he knew he was not the father. Joseph's intense, personal pain was mixed with the love he felt for Mary. He ended the relationship without filing charges of adultery against her. He chose the most nonjudgmental option available.

A week that began with a glorious angelic visit quickly turned to despair for Mary. Her parents would not have understood what happened. Her fiancé turned against her in disbelief, leaving her alone in a hostile community. In a matter of days she was no longer the happy bride-to-be; she was labeled an adulteress. She narrowly escaped death by stoning for being pregnant before marriage. Mary must have wondered what God was doing to her.

What do you do when your world comes crashing down around you? She could no longer face the hostility

Mary left Nazareth to visit her relative Elizabeth, who was also pregnant in a miraculous way. Elizabeth was past child-bearing age, but an angel told her husband, Zechariah, that they would conceive a son and name him John. When Elizabeth heard Mary's greeting as she entered the house, the child in Elizabeth's womb leaped for joy.

The birth of John the Baptist in many ways parallels the unusual circumstances surrounding the birth of Jesus. Jacopo Tintoretto contrasts the solitude of Jesus' birth in a stable by surrounding Elizabeth, John's mother, with a group of helpful women who care for her newborn infant.

Joseph's decision to change his mind and marry Mary is explained in the Bible by the appearance of an angel. James Tissot catches the importance of this event by having the message come from a distinctly heavenly angelic being, not simply an angel in human dress.

and rejection from Joseph and the questions and disappointment of her parents. So Mary went for help to a family relative who was married to a temple priest. The angel had said that her relative Elizabeth was also pregnant. Mary went to her, perhaps hoping that she might find a sympathetic, reassuring friend.

Mary stayed to help her much older relative with her pregnancy. Mary may also have worked through her own uncertain future. Six months later, the angel appeared again, this time to Joseph. The angel confirmed what Mary had told Joseph about how she had become pregnant. To Joseph's credit, he believed the angel. He sent for Mary, pleading with her to return home. He promised they would be married as they had first planned.

But there was no happy ending in sight. Life is seldom so simple. The Roman government was demanding that a census be taken to review (probably hoping to increase) the local tax base. Joseph had to return to his family home in Bethlehem to register for the census. Mary rode a donkey, jerking along the 70-mile trip to Bethlehem. This had the impact you might expect—by the time they arrived, Mary was in labor.

Anyone who has ever tried to find a motel room at midnight on a holiday weekend can understand the crisis facing Mary and Joseph. The town was full of travelers, and there were no empty rooms in Bethlehem. Finally a sympathetic innkeeper offered a corner of his barn behind his inn. At least there they would have some privacy and shelter. Here, in a stable, Mary gave birth to her child. It certainly was not how she dreamed it would be. It certainly was not what Joseph wanted for his family. But reality does not grant our wishes. This baby, announced by an angel and conceived by the Holy Spirit, was born to a young, frightened, lonely mother in a stable on a backstreet in a small town in Palestine. This humble, poverty-level entry into the world is symbolic of the entire life of Jesus.

There is some irony in the account of Jesus' earliest days, despite the depressed surroundings. Christians tell a very sober story about Jesus' birth, yet we often miss the human side of what happened. The savior of the world was born right under the nose of the Roman army. He was born to a young couple who went to considerable inconvenience to obey a Roman order. Yet this baby began a movement that was to change the political and religious face of the world forever.

The first people to visit this new baby were several ragtag shepherds who had been tending their sheep in the hills outside Bethlehem. Shepherds barely made even the bottom rung of the first-century Palestinian social ladder. They were considered dishonest—thieves who often grazed their sheep on other people's lands. But to them, of all people, angels appeared with a message of good

The Adoration of the Shepherds *by Jusepe Ribera was a masterpiece of its time; Ribera was a very successful artist in his day. Note the slaughtered lamb, probably brought by the shepherds as a gift, at the foot of Jesus' cradle. It foretells the crucifixion of Jesus, who became the lamb who died for the sins of the world.*

The interaction of angelic beings with humans has always intrigued artists. The biblical text tells a simple story: "In that region there were shepherds living in the fields, keeping watch over their flock by night. Then an angel of the Lord stood before them, and the glory of the Lord shone around them, and they were terrified" (Luke 2:8–9). Jacopo Bassano traditionally portrays angels as very vigorous, energetic beings who cause fear among those who see them. Most shepherds in this painting are caught before they have noticed the presence of the angel.

news. A savior, the Messiah, was born in Bethlehem!

Their visit provides another insight into Mary's experience. After all she had been through, she still did not understand everything that was happening. Remember, she was just a teenager. The normal emotional experience of a first pregnancy had been intensified by the stress of the journey to Bethlehem, finding a room, and the birth of her baby. Now shepherds come with a story of angels singing. In beautiful simplicity the biblical story says Mary was quiet, wondering about everything that had happened. Mary was living out the amazing role God had given her. She may not have had the need to ask questions because an angel had told her what to expect! But even if she did accept these events as a gift from God, these changes in her life must have been unsettling.

With the pressure of Mary's delivery now past, Joseph found a room. Mary and the new baby lived in more acceptable conditions. One of the first tasks for the new parents was the presentation of the child in the temple, dedicating this gift from God back to God's service. Within a week, Mary and Joseph made the short trip to Jerusalem for this dedication service, taking with them an offering of two pigeons. This gift shows the poverty of Mary and Joseph. It was the smallest offering permitted by the law.

The welcome they received at the temple was both reassuring and troubling. An elderly priest named Simeon pronounced a blessing. This blessing surprised both Mary and Joseph with its promise of blessing for the nation because of this child. But the blessing ended with a statement of pain for Mary ("a sword will pierce your own heart"). After the presentation, Joseph and Mary returned to Bethlehem so Mary could recover her strength before going home to Nazareth.

If the shepherds caused Mary to wonder what was happening, her next visitors were truly amazing. Several astrologers from Babylon (the East) came to her room with a strange story of how they had learned of this new baby. They had been studying the skies. They may have seen in the natural rotation of the planets a special message in the heavens. The orbits of Saturn and Jupiter had come

Mary presents Jesus, as the first-born son, at the temple to be blessed by Simeon. Mary looks hesitant to give her son over to Simeon. Certainly the painter, Giovanni Bellini, knew more about the outcome of the story than Mary does at this point, so the symbolism of the stern-faced and angry-looking temple official in the background is quite dramatic.

together in a line, forming an unusually bright star within the constellation Pisces. (There are several possible astrological explanations; this is just one of several.) To astrologers, all stars and planets had meaning. Jupiter (the largest planet) was the ruler of the universe, Saturn represented the nation Palestine, while the constellation Pisces referred to the last days. This unusual meeting of Saturn and Jupiter in Pisces gave them a message: *The universal ruler of the last days has been born in Palestine.* They organized a caravan to visit this new king. They brought gifts of gold, frankincense, and myrrh.

The wise men told how Herod had helped them discover where to find Jesus. They told how Herod had also wanted to come worship the new king. Joseph became suspicious; he knew that Herod was fearful of threats to his throne. Taking Mary and the new baby, Joseph fled to Egypt, where Herod had no power. Imagine the feelings of these new parents—angelic promises and heavenly choirs could sound a bit hollow as they ran for their lives to a foreign country. The generous gift of gold by the wise men may have provided the money needed to live in exile until Herod died in March of 4 B.C. Once Herod was gone, Joseph felt it was safe to return. When the family arrived in Israel, Joseph learned that Herod's son Archelaus was the new ruler. Not trusting Archelaus either, Joseph took his family to Nazareth, and they finally settled into normal family life.

Here Jesus' family flees to Egypt. Jesus has been painted as a member of every culture, and Miguel De Berrio pictures the family of Jesus as a South American gaucho family, adding emphasis by placing a peasant hat on Mary. The protection of God against the death threats of Herod is shown by the two angels walking alongside the donkey.

HEROD THE GREAT

Herod the Great was the dominant Roman political figure in Palestine prior to the birth of Jesus. He worked his way into the Roman government through military power and political intrigue. When he was tried by the Jewish Sanhedrin for his brutality toward the Jews who opposed him, Sextus Caesar (the Roman governor in Syria) forced the court to acquit him. When the Sanhedrin acquiesced to this pressure, Sextus promptly promoted Herod to a position of leadership in Syria.

In 40 B.C., Herod was given the title "King of the Jews" and was told to subdue that region of the empire. Three years later he conquered Jerusalem, executed the Jewish leaders, and imposed Roman rule on the Jewish people through brute military force.

A prolific builder, Herod built the New Testament temple in Jerusalem, plus government buildings, roads, aqueducts, and in other parts of the empire, houses of worship for pagan deities (infuriating the Jewish population). His building projects reflected a standard Roman pattern of solid, functional strength rather than aesthetic beauty.

In 5 B.C., when several astrologers from the East came to Jerusalem asking about the new king who had just been born, Herod took action. He had been removing all people he believed

In this Byzantine mosaic, the three wise men are following the star to find the baby Jesus. They meet with Herod, who wants to find and kill this new "King of the Jews."

might be threats to his throne, so this announcement created considerable anxiety. He instructed the wise men to find this child and report back to him, allegedly so that he could also pay homage to the new king. When the wise men did not return, Herod ordered the slaughter of all infant boys born in Bethlehem in the past two years (Matthew 2:1–12,16–18). By this time, however, Joseph, Mary, and Jesus had fled to Egypt.

Herod was a paranoid ruler who eliminated any person whom he thought might have ideas about succeeding him on the throne. His brutality was also directed at his own family. His wife

Mariamne (the favorite of his ten wives) was executed without a hearing because of suspected adultery. Her mother was killed for protesting this treatment of her daughter, as were Mariamne's two sons, Alexander and Aristobulus, plus many other family and court members who dared to question any of Herod's decisions.

Herod's oldest son, Antipater, who was his most logical successor, was executed only days before Herod's death. Herod himself died a miserable death in March, 4 B.C., of an intestinal parasite infection. Virtually no one, not even those who knew him in Rome, mourned his passing.

CHILDHOOD

✦ ✦ ✦

FOR TWELVE YEARS we know nothing about the boyhood of Jesus. Luke reports that as Jesus grew he became strong, gained wisdom, and was well liked by those around him. We can assume a variety of things—all Jewish boys had certain responsibilities. Sons were first taught by their fathers at home. Nazareth had a synagogue where the community met for worship, for town meetings, and where older children received religious instruction. At age five, boys began their study of the Scriptures. They also studied Jewish history. Culture, history, and religious beliefs were important to the identity of Jews. It was important to them that no Jew ever forget God and the history of Israel's experience with God.

There is one story that opens a window for us into the childhood of Jesus. Mary and Joseph attended weekly synagogue worship and often traveled to Jerusalem for the Passover festival. When Jesus was twelve, he joined his parents and other friends in this special religious celebration. Jesus was fascinated with the theological discussions that were held with the priests in the temple. He listened and asked questions, perhaps reflecting the idealism of a young man for whom the world was just starting to open. The Jewish pattern of education was conversational in style. Just as he had been asking questions of his father, here was another chance to ask questions and learn from the recognized teachers of his day.

After the festival was over, they began their return trip. Women and children usually started the journey in the morning. The men came later, catching up with the larger group by evening. This simple event confronted Mary and

Facing page: *Luke 2:52 says that Jesus grew in wisdom. John von Leonardshof, the artist, paints Jesus teaching in his father's carpenter shop. Teaching was central to Jesus' later ministry. Mary watches with an adoring gaze, amazed at what this young child knows.*

The innocence and idealism of the young Jesus is contrasted with the seriousness of the scholars with their sacred texts. Jesus confounded the scholars with his simple questions that called for profound answers.

Joseph with the reality of being parents of a twelve-year-old boy: Should he travel with the women and the children, or should he wait to come with his father? It was not until the first evening that they discovered Jesus had not come with either of them. Every loving parent can easily imagine the fear and anxiety they experienced. Their young son was alone in the city. This was frightening—after all, crime in Jerusalem rose significantly during the festival.

Traveling at night on the open roads was unsafe. Mary and Joseph had to wait until early the next morning to retrace the journey back to Jerusalem to begin their search for Jesus. They frantically checked all the places they had been. They tried to second-guess where a twelve-year-old boy might go on his own. Finally they found him in the temple. Mary's frustrations came out when she saw him, "Child, why have you treated us this way? We have been frantic, looking all over for you!" All parents can understand

THE LIFE OF JESUS

the fear and anger in her voice. This event tells us that Jesus was quite a normal young boy in some respects. He was growing in independence, while having a deep interest in spiritual things. Mary's life may have been as confusing as any mother today with a twelve-year-old child. She was constantly amazed at what he knew, but she didn't quite know what to make of it.

But his response must have baffled her: "Why were you searching for me? Did you not know that I must be in my Father's house?" (Luke 2:49). The Bible says, "they did not understand what he said to them" (verse 50). But despite not understanding him completely, the Bible says that Mary "treasured all these things in her heart" (verse 51). He was an obedient child, and his mother loved and treasured him. Certainly most parents do not completely understand their children, but they still love and cherish them. In this way, Mary was a typical loving parent, even if she didn't have a typical son.

This trip to Jerusalem is the last time the Bible mentions Joseph. Many people believe he died during Jesus' teen years. If this is true, Jesus (as the eldest son) would have taken responsibility for his mother and family. For the next twenty years, we know nothing of what Jesus did.

James Tissot identifies the anxiety and concern felt by Mary and Joseph after searching for three days to find the young Jesus. In the background, the rabbis seem concerned and displeased with what they have just been through. This is a foretaste of the tension between Jesus and the rabbis that erupted later in his ministry.

In paintings, Jesus is often shown helping others. In his painting, Gerrit van Honthorst shows Jesus admiring the work of Joseph, as he helps his earthly father in the normal working tasks of life.

We believe that he lived in Nazareth, working in the carpenter shop started by Joseph. Every Jewish boy was taught a trade so that he could support himself and his family. Tradition tells us that Jesus became a carpenter.

There is another event that occurred during the late childhood of Jesus that may have had some influence on him. Over the hill from Nazareth was the town of Sepphoris. The Bible does not mention this town, but we know it existed because of Roman records. For years, the town was a battleground between Rome and the Zealots (a radical guerrilla movement). When Jesus was between ten and twelve years of age, the Zealots made Sepphoris their headquarters. They used one of its buildings as a secret warehouse to store weapons for their war against Rome. Unfortunately, Rome learned about the warehouse in Sepphoris.

Finally, Rome decided to end the terrorist presence in Sepphoris. The Roman army destroyed every building and killed local citizens by the thousands, most of whom were innocent. It was Roman overkill. It failed to defeat the Zealots, and the Jewish people hated Rome for their brutality. The Romans also built the city of Tiberius on the Sea of Galilee during Jesus' youth. The additional contact with their enemy only reinforced Jewish hatred of their oppressors. These political—and perhaps personal—events would have challenged Jesus to think carefully about how to respond when tragedy strikes.

Later in his ministry, when Jesus talked about loving our enemies, he was not speaking out of a detached, philosophic vacuum. He knew the pain and the anger that comes from being oppressed and abused by a foreign government.

There are few paintings of Jesus as a boy. Herbert created a natural setting with Jesus as the faithful son. Mary has a very pensive look as she watches Jesus; perhaps she is wondering what the future will hold for him.

BAPTISM

❖ ❖ ❖

JESUS LIVED IN NAZARETH for most of his adult life. Mark 6:3 says that Jesus was a carpenter. His father, Joseph, was a carpenter, and Jesus would have learned the trade from him. First-century terms for occupations were less precise than ones we use today. The Greek word for carpenter (*tektov*) has the root meaning of artisan or skilled craftsman; it could also mean general contractor. Carpenters did much more than just work with wood; in fact, wood was very scarce. They created a variety of items for the local market. These items included tables, chairs, beds, lampstands, chests, plows, threshing boards, ox yokes, carts, wagons, and other farm implements. Carpenters often worked together on major projects. Building a house meant cutting down trees, shaping beams, building frames, and constructing doors and windows. The term "carpenter" included people who worked in all aspects of construction.

When Jesus was about thirty years old (A.D. 27), a religious revival began sweeping across Israel. A fiery, radical young preacher known as "John the Baptizer" traveled around the countryside. He preached a message of repentance and preparation for a new age.

John was a distant cousin of Jesus' and the son of Zechariah and Elizabeth. (Mary visited Elizabeth early in her pregnancy.) Zechariah was quite old when John was born. Many believe he died while John was still a young child.

John came to prepare the way for Jesus (see Matthew 11:10), preaching, "Repent, for the kingdom of heaven has

Above: *Though Joseph was called a carpenter in the Bible, he probably was not a woodworker as we know carpenters. He was more likely a skilled craftsman or artisan.* Facing page: *The baptism of Jesus is one the few settings where artists place Jesus in a position of submission to another person. In his painting, Paolo Veronese includes angelic children and a dove overhead to remind us that this experience was a statement of God's divine presence with Jesus.*

John the Baptist was a rugged individual who proclaimed judgment on Israel. John's primitive dress and the lamb in the corner of the picture symbolize the radical yet redemptive element in John's preaching. Tiziano, the artist, adds a cross to the top of John's staff, though the cross did not become a religious symbol until long after Jesus' death.

come near" (verse 11:2). John's clothing was made of camel's hair, and he ate locusts and wild honey. The location of John's ministry, his preaching, his daily rituals of purification through frequent washings, and his austere lifestyle all echo that of Elijah, a prophet of God in the Old Testament.

For more than three hundred years there had been no prophetic voice proclaiming, "Thus saith the Lord." John's appearance and message were reminders of how, historically, God had spoken directly to Israel through the prophets.

John's message called for high ethical standards. He pronounced judgment and condemnation on Israel. He also called for baptism. That message was a dramatic shift for the Jews. They had never thought of themselves as needing baptism. Baptism was for Gentiles and other pagans who were not part of the people of God—it symbolized their entry into the family of faith.

Since most Jewish people believed they were already members of God's family, they saw no need for baptism. Their status as Jews gave them a position of privilege. Many Jewish people believed that at the gates of hell God had placed a guardian angel who would turn back any Jewish person who might stray in that direction. Some

Jews believed that descent from Abraham was the passport to privilege before God. Obedience to God's commandments was not needed.

John attacked this belief with ridicule and scorn. He said to the Pharisees, "You brood of snakes! Prove by the way you live that you are really children of God. Don't justify yourselves by saying, 'We are the descendants of Abraham.' That proves nothing! God can make children of Abraham out of these stones. Every tree that does not bear good fruit will be cut down and thrown into the fire!" (Luke 3:7–9, paraphrased). Through his preaching, John symbolically excommunicated the entire nation. He stated that if

they wanted to be people of God, they had to make that choice for themselves. They needed to be baptized, making a new commitment to live righteous lives. No longer was it enough to rely on their family ancestry to save them. Amazingly, the people responded with enthusiasm. They heard John's preaching as a call from God. They came by the thousands. Many asked if John might be the promised messiah who was going to save Israel.

One day Jesus went to hear John, who was preaching along the Jordan River. Jesus asked John to baptize him.

For Palestine, the Jordan was a river of life, fed by small streams rushing down the mountains and through the center of Palestine. But in the northern portion of the country it was a small, turbulent stream. Only much further downstream did it become the lazy meandering river used by John for his baptism of the masses.

The descending dove within the trinitarian symbol (triangle and circles) is a statement of the continued presence of God with humanity. Surrounded by the stars of the heavens, it signifies that the God of glory is always present in the form of the Holy Spirit.

At first John hesitated. He said it would be right for Jesus to baptize him, but Jesus insisted. John agreed, and Jesus was baptized. It was a spiritual experience for both Jesus and John. The heavens opened (Luke 3:21), symbolizing the opening of a relationship between God in heaven and God's people on Earth. God again became accessible to humanity. Jewish tradition spoke of a number of heavenly gates that could only be opened in order. The picture of heaven opening was a meaningful image of God's openness to humanity.

The Spirit of God came as a dove, empowering Jesus for his ministry. The imagery of the dove was not new in Jewish faith. People believed the Spirit of God would come upon the Earth like a dove hovering in loving, protective care over her young. The coming of the Spirit was the way God traditionally equipped a person to do some great task. This had happened with Old Testament leaders in the past, and it happened here with the promised Servant of God.

When God spoke, he put two Old Testament texts together, Psalms 2:7 and Isaiah 42:1. "This is my beloved son" was used at the coronation of every king, representing might, majesty, and power. "In whom I am well pleased" speaks of the servant who will bear the burden of sins. The baptism of Jesus makes a divine statement about who Jesus was (son of God) and about what shape his mission would take (as a servant). That combination was not what Israel was looking for. The Jewish leadership would challenge it throughout the public ministry of Jesus; they had a different set of expectations for the messiah.

Recognizing that Christ is the Son of God for all humanity, artists have often presented Christ as having the physical characteristics of their own culture. Here Jesus is portrayed as more Western, with blond hair and light skin.

Why Jesus was baptized is an issue of some debate in Christian circles. Traditional belief is that Jesus had no sin, so John's baptism for the forgiveness of sin would not apply to him. Others say that Jesus was baptized to identify with the sinfulness of humanity—he came to save humanity from their sins.

It seems most faithful to the biblical text to see the baptism of Jesus as a commission for his ministry. He was announcing the beginning of his life's work. In baptism, Jesus identifies with the nation of Israel; he then goes on to represent it in his temptations, life, death, and resurrection. His life was a microcosm of the nation of Israel.

THE TEMPTATIONS

❖ ◆ ❖

FOLLOWING HIS BAPTISM, Jesus took over a month to be alone. While he was in the wilderness, he was visited by Satan. We are not told how Satan approached him, but Satan may not have come to Jesus in a physical form. One of the most powerful temptations we face is when we wrestle with options in decision making; when we fantasize about the way life might be. Temptations that come as an idea can be as destructive as any action we take, for ideas often lead to actions. Jesus wrestled with a series of questions in the wilderness.

Satan never challenged who Jesus was, for that had been settled. Satan began to confront Jesus with questions of method. The issue was not "Who are you?" but "What are you going to do with who you are?" This raises a concern that is still with us: Are there wrong ways to achieve good ends? Do the ends justify the means?

The mission of Jesus was to be the presence of God with humanity and to call humanity back to God. The Jewish people were expecting God to send a messiah to deliver them. They had some clear ideas about what this messiah would be like. The most popular concept was a person of charismatic power and majesty who would rally the people of Israel. He would raise an army after the manner of King David and drive out the hated Romans. Israel would then be restored to a position of world power and domination. This idea was widely accepted. Jesus had to decide, "Am I going to be like that? Is that what the will of God means?"

Above: *The Mount of Temptation, possibly where Jesus was tempted by Satan.* Facing page: *How should Satan be presented in human form? In Scripture Satan has many different descriptions. Juan de Flandes begins with a human appearance, then adds horns and lizard feet. Jesus is seated, indicating the fatigue of forty days without food. Satan is offering a rock shaped like bread, but Jesus raises his hand, rejecting the offer.*

Jesus also faced the option of making promises about how faith would bring physical health or economic prosperity. (Should he turn stones into bread and become a popular messiah, making life easy by meeting everyone's needs?) Many voices today promise that if we accept Jesus we will have peace, joy, and prosperity—all our needs will be met. Certainly there is an element of truth here, but at best it is a half-truth. Following Jesus isn't the easiest path to take, and following God's plan was not an easy road for Jesus.

Jesus also wrestled with confronting evil head-on—was there a way to take the easy path and still follow God? (Maybe people can worship God and still hold on to their possessions and their prejudices?) Perhaps he could use the divine power he felt within himself and work miracles. This would amaze people and reassure them that he was, in fact, God's messenger. (Satan suggested that perhaps he could do something really spectacular like jumping off the

Satan used the example of God feeding the Israelites with manna in the wilderness, and he urged Jesus to use his power to provide popular solutions for human needs. Jesus knew this quick-fix approach to life was not God's way, and he rejected the idea .

pinnacle of the temple; certainly that would impress people so that they would follow him.)

The struggle going on inside Jesus was very difficult because God had already done some of those things. God had saved Israel by taking on the Egyptian army (the crossing of the Red Sea during the Exodus), had fed people in the wilderness, had done many miraculous things. If, in their own history, God had accepted some of the less than perfect acts of Israel, and even used them toward a good end, why not repeat these things? Maybe this time Israel would see and would change its ways. The issues of right and wrong for Jesus were not as neatly divided as we might think. They may have carried the same kind of confusing mixed messages that we are hit with today.

Jesus knew these temptations violated the nature of God. To have followed any of these paths would have been a denial of who he was. He rejected each of them. He went back to the Scriptures to validate his decision that God's will must be done, even though he saw positive elements in each temptation. Jesus knew that to be faithful to God, he must live in harmony with God. His commitment was firm. So Satan left, temporarily accepting defeat. But a temporary setback did not end the battle. Throughout his ministry, Jesus faced these same temptations in different forms. This was not a sterile theological discussion, but an intense, gut-wrenching struggle over power, loyalty, and integrity.

While Jesus was in the wilderness, charting his ministry, the popularity of John the Baptist was creating problems for the Roman authorities. Herod Antipas was afraid John's radical preaching might stir the people to revolt against Rome. He had John arrested and imprisoned in the remote Roman military prison at Macherus, near the Dead Sea. Being in prison, however, did not silence John.

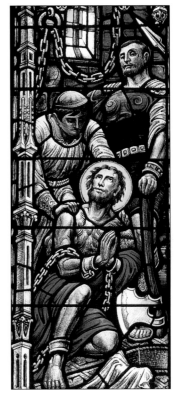

John's life ended in prison chains because he dared to challenge the Roman ruling authorities. The depth of John's faith is shown as he prays to God, even at the time of his death.

When he denounced Herod for his decision to marry Herodias (his brother's wife), Herodias became livid with anger. She manipulated Herod into having John beheaded. Then she demanded that his head be delivered to her publicly on a platter!

After John the Baptist was arrested, Jesus moved farther north into Galilee (away from Jerusalem). He began to preach there. Galilee had a more open society. There was less risk of government action against those who called for religious renewal. The early message of Jesus can be summarized in three themes: The time is fulfilled, the kingdom of God is at hand, and repent and believe the gospel (Mark 1:14–15). This message had some continuity with the preaching of John, but it also had some essential differences. John's message pointed toward the future, calling people to repent because the messiah was coming.

Jesus' call to "leave, come and follow" is emphasized by having Peter and Andrew some distance from their boats in the background. Their call was the beginning of a new direction in the ministry of Jesus, as he began forming a group of disciples who would participate with him in his ministry.

The message of Jesus brought a new element of urgency. He proclaimed that the future was now upon them.

Jesus made another important departure from John. John the Baptist had been a single voice, crying out against the sins of the world, calling for repentance. Very early in his ministry, Jesus formed a disciple group. This group was based on the traditional Jewish pattern of a teacher living with his students, teaching and preparing them for their own ministry. Forming this group did several important things. It showed that Jesus had a long-range plan for a ministry that would go far beyond his own personal impact. It also showed that he was aware of the dangers of a prophetic/messianic ministry.

There had been many radical prophetic figures in Israel, and neither Israel nor Rome had a history of looking favorably on the prophet who preached judgment or called for change within either the religious or the political system. By gathering a group of disciples around him, Jesus could be confident that the message would outlive the messenger.

The new disciple band had twelve members, patterned after the twelve sons of Israel—the patriarchal leaders of the twelve tribes of Israel. The disciples came from the common people of the day. Some were fishermen; others came from the working population. By gathering this symbolic group, Jesus was laying the foundation for a new Israel. This new nation would live in faithful obedience to the purposes of God. It is important to note, however, that these twelve were not the only people who followed Jesus.

We know the names of a cluster of women who were with Jesus throughout much of his ministry. These women are often ignored when we tell the Jesus story, but they played an important role. They provided the financial resources needed for Jesus to travel, preach, and teach. Most people are familiar with Peter, Andrew, James, John, and Judas. Less well known are Philip, Bartholomew, Matthew, Thomas, James (son of Alpheus), Thaddaeus, and Simon (of Galilee). The women who followed Jesus included Joanna (wife of Herod's steward), Mary Magdalene, Suzanna, and many others (Luke 8:1–3). The public ministry of Jesus gave new dignity to the disenfranchised social groups of his day. Women were among the prominent beneficiaries of this new acceptance.

Mary and Martha are symbols of peace and tranquility in the life of Jesus, and it was to their home Jesus turned when rest and quiet were needed. Mary sits attentively at Jesus' feet, while Martha comes with the fresh bread. The comfort Jesus felt with these two women was a refreshing contrast to the cultural separation of men and women in the first century.

BEGINNING HIS MINISTRY

❖ ❖ ❖

ESUS CAME INTO GALILEE, preaching the good news of God (Mark 1:14). With this very simple statement, Mark describes the beginning of the ministry of Jesus. It gives us some information but leaves much to the imagination. Why did Jesus choose this moment in history to begin a preaching/healing ministry that would become the defining event in Christian history? Starting a new business or launching a new product line in an established company takes months or even years of planning to ensure the greatest possible success. Politicians work very hard to find the right date, the best symbolic place, and the perfect phrases to declare their candidacy and the themes they want to promote. How did Jesus decide that the time was right, where he would begin, and the themes that would give direction and identity to his ministry?

THE IDEA

For ten years Jesus had been a carpenter in Nazareth, participating regularly in synagogue worship services (Luke 4:16) and going to the annual Jewish festivals in Jerusalem. Unfortunately, these festival experiences may not have been totally positive for this spiritually sensitive young man. People who went to the temple to worship God were confronted with quite a spectacle. Sacrifices were brought before God in forgiveness and thanksgiving, but what had started long ago as a spiritual experience had become for some only an organized ritual. The lamb was taken by a priest, who held it as another priest killed it by slitting its throat. Still another priest held a golden bowl to collect the blood, which was then handed down a

Above: *Isaiah (an influential counselor to Israel's kings) was a favorite Old Testament prophet for Jesus. This stained-glass window combines Jesus and Isaiah by dressing Jesus in the regal robes of a royal prophet, while he holds the scroll of Isaiah. The gospels report that Jesus made many references to the writings of Isaiah. Facing page: Jesus spent much of his time teaching new concepts and reteaching correct understandings of the grace of God for all humanity. By including both males and females, the artist emphasizes the fact that his teachings are for all people.*

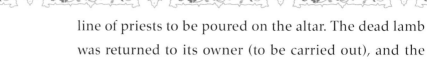

line of priests to be poured on the altar. The dead lamb was returned to its owner (to be carried out), and the golden bowl came back for the next lamb. This process was repeated again and again.

By the time of Jesus, the numbers were so large that several lines were needed to accommodate all the pilgrims who brought their lambs to God. One year the rabbis reported that more than a quarter of a million lambs were sacrificed in the temple. Imagine what the temple must have been like—crowds milling about waiting to sacrifice their lambs, the bleating of lambs being killed, the continuous flow of blood. According to the Old Testament, the smell of sacrifices was pleasing to God if it was accompanied by sincerity. Had the ritual for some become only a ritual—lacking the spiritual aspects that were needed to make it pleasing to God?

During Passover week, the Sanhedrin met in public to hold their discussions of Scripture. This had started as a stimulating interchange on God's presence, God's will, and the history of God's action on Israel's behalf. But by Jesus' day many

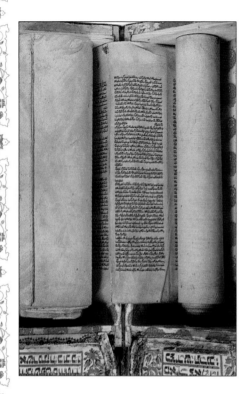

The law was the center of Jewish faith, giving the people the teachings and counsel of God. The reading of the law provided the central focus of synagogue worship. The standard form of the Torah was the scroll, as shown above.

people seemed to be caught up in debates over how far one could walk on the sabbath without violating the law, what constituted a legitimate burden, what could be eaten or not eaten, and so on. The technical had supplanted the spiritual. As Jesus listened, this must have been very painful. People are looking for mercy and hope in their lives, and this is what they are getting! From his knowledge of Scripture and these encounters in the temple, a series of themes for his public ministry emerged.

THE YEAR

The year that Jesus chose to begin his ministry carries special significance. Since the days of Moses, Israel had observed the sabbath as a day of rest and worship. After the exodus from Egypt, this period of rest also included the land. A sabbath year was introduced to the calendar. This seventh year was a special year when slaves were set free, debts were forgiven, and the land was permitted to lie untilled so that it might never lose its fertility. This was a time of religious renewal within the community. The community was to focus on God, not the material things of daily life.

Every seventh sabbath year (every forty-nine years), the Year of Jubilee was to be observed, though it is doubtful that the Jews really did observe it. Its requirements were very radical. In addition to all the normal sabbath-year observances, all land was to be returned to the original owners. The Jubilee year was to be a year of celebration, of worship and renewal. It offered hope for a new start for all Israel. These themes gradually took on messianic expectations in Israel. Many Jewish

leaders believed the messiah would come during a Jubilee year, because in that year the people were already doing spiritual things. It is likely Jesus deliberately chose the Jubilee year of A.D. 26–27 to begin his ministry. That year symbolized his own values of forgiveness, new hope, and a new start in life.

Jesus began by preaching and teaching in the small towns dotting the countryside in Galilee. Why Galilee? This was the region Jesus knew best; it was his home. Galilee was where he had worshiped in the synagogue; he knew the culture, and he understood the religious

Galilee was a land of hills, crops, and fruit, once described as flowing with milk and honey. But it is also a tight, compact land where no space can lie idle, since all the land is needed for survival. Here we see the contrast of rocky roads with gnarled shrubs in the foreground, the vineyards, and the trees on the hillside.

thoughts and hopes of the people. Galilee was also the most populous region in Palestine (possibly having more than three million people living in two hundred villages of at least fifteen thousand people each). That made it the best place to reach the most people with the least traveling. But even more important was the political and religious climate in Galilee. Some of the best roads in the ancient world went through Galilee, exposing the population to more travelers and therefore to new ideas. This created a more forward-looking community of people who were willing to listen and who had the freedom to act. Judea to the south was far more traditional and more resistant to change. Jerusalem, sitting as the political and religious center, was more active in silencing those voices that might be a threat to traditional ways of thinking.

THE FIRST HOMETOWN RESPONSE

Word of this young charismatic preacher, who was preaching with authority and leaving a compassionate trail of healed people behind him, quickly spread throughout the countryside. One might believe that the symbolism of his ministry would be obvious to those who heard him—that people would be eager to hear what he had to say. But unfortunately, this was not always the case. After a brief time of preaching in northern Galilee, Jesus returned to his home in Nazareth. As was the custom for visiting rabbis, he was asked to teach in the synagogue.

The Jewish synagogue worked with a lectionary cycle (specific passages assigned to be read during the year) of texts, so that the central Scriptures would be heard by the congregation in a regular sequence. When Jesus stood to read the text of the day, the scroll of Isaiah was handed to him, open to a servant prophecy in Isaiah 61: "The spirit of the Lord God is upon me, because the Lord has anointed me; he has sent me to bring good news to the

"The spirit of the Lord is upon me" was the theme of the first sermon Jesus preached in his hometown synagogue of Nazareth. He read from a scroll, but the artist puts the message in a modern book form, showing the contemporary application of this Isaiah text.

oppressed, to bind up the brokenhearted, to proclaim liberty to the captives, and release to the prisoners; to proclaim the year of the Lord's favor."

Jesus read the text, returned the scroll to the synagogue steward, then dropped a bombshell on the congregation: "Today," he said, "this Scripture has come true as you heard it being read!" The congregation must have gasped in disbelief. In Jewish circles, this text had become a well-respected messianic text. It described the one God would send to save Israel. Here was one of their own young men claiming to be the promised messiah. And the people questioned, "How can that be? This is Joseph's boy; his mother still lives here in town. We remember watching him grow up. The messiah! Who does he think he is?" They were amazed at what he was saying. Since synagogue teaching was done in a conversational style, one member of the congregation interrupted, asking for proof: "We have heard about these miracles that you did in Capernaum. Do some miracles for us to prove that you really are the messiah. Do that and we'll believe what you say."

This challenge sounded familiar to Jesus; it was the one posed by Satan in the wilderness: "Do miraculous things for the population, and everyone will follow." Just as Jesus said no to Satan, he said no to his home congregation. He tried to explain that God's grace is not the sole property of Israel. He told several stories from their own history, when God had healed people other than Israelites or Jews, but the synagogue erupted in anger. People do not like to be reminded of the mistakes they have made. The congregation was furious, and they started a minor

In this painting, the image of the temptation of Christ moves from the traditional desert to a wooded mountain scene, drawing from the European scenery with which the artist was familiar. He shows the struggles Jesus faced in the wilderness also happen to us where we live.

riot. This degenerated into an attempt to kill Jesus—just for something he had said! Jesus slipped through the angry crowd and left town.

Not everyone who heard Jesus liked what they heard. For some people, the message of Jesus sounded like hope; these people responded with joy and excitement. But for others, the message sounded like judgment, as he called them to repent. These people rejected both him and his message. Jesus quickly learned that proclaiming the will of God is not always easy or popular.

From Nazareth, Jesus moved about twenty miles north to the town of Capernaum. He continued to preach, teach, and heal. In Capernaum he received a much more positive community response. We have no record that Nazareth ever again asked Jesus to preach.

THE MESSAGE

Jesus most often told parables to teach the people. Parables are stories drawn from daily life that illustrate an important lesson. Jesus' parables were created to clarify the point he was making. They are stories told about events, sometimes things happening right in front of their eyes. Jesus would be walking along the road carrying on a conversation with a small group, when he would see something and say, "Look over there, see that farmer sowing his fields? That's what I mean. When you broadcast the seed, some of it falls on good ground and gives a bountiful crop. But some seed falls on the hard path by the edge of the field, and the birds eat it before it has a chance to take root. Other seed falls among the rocks

Jesus used everyday events from his world to illustrate what he was teaching. As the sower planted his fields, so our faith is lived every day. As we do routine work, we are surrounded by possibilities, obstacles, and hope for the future.

where the ground is shallow. It springs up very quickly, but since it has no root system, it dies just as quickly."

Most of what Jesus taught had been said before by Moses and the Old Testament prophets. But over the generations, the meaning of the teachings had gradually become twisted so as to fit more comfortably into the cultural expectations of the time. Jesus often started by stating what the people already believed. Then he helped them see the meaning as it had first been given. Some of the Jewish leadership argued that he was destroying the religious tradition that meant so much to them. But Jesus said, "No, I am not trying to destroy it, but to fulfill it, and to help people understand what God is trying to do in their lives."

After his death and resurrection, his followers often talked about what he had said. They brought these sayings together in a collection we now call the Sermon on the Mount. This was not a single sermon preached by Jesus on one afternoon, but a collection of Jesus' teachings on a variety of subjects. Throughout his preaching, Jesus kept telling people, "I know this is what you have been taught to believe, but I am telling you this is what God intended." Jesus brought renewal to a faith that had lost its vitality and its integrity. He called people to love God, to serve others, and to live with integrity. Common people heard and found new comfort and hope. Religious leaders of the day found it threatening to their security and their control over the people. It is no wonder different people responded differently to what they heard.

What is a legitimate level of risk? One man walks away holding the money he had been paid for the field, not knowing why he was paid so much. The other man risked all he had because he knows there is a valuable treasure in this field. Jesus spoke often of risk and of certainty, inviting people to ensure their future by risking all they have on the promises made by God.

PEOPLE JESUS MET

* * *

Above: *Jesus orders Zaccheus to come down from the tree, vividly symbolizing the way in which Jesus included those who were excluded in his day. Zaccheus goes from spectator to participant in Jesus' promise of inclusive love.* Facing page: *Veronese is known for his huge, detailed paintings of biblical feasts. This center portion of a much larger canvas shows Jesus sitting beside his mother at the wedding in Cana. In the background, just above the head of Jesus, the lamb is being carved for the marriage feast, uniting the two elements of celebration and crucifixion in the life of Jesus.*

N OUR FRANTIC WORLD, people who are able to make others feel important stand out—they are a rare commodity. A great deal can be learned by watching how people treat others—not just those they can benefit from, socially or professionally, but those whom society says have nothing to offer.

The people who appear along the way in Jesus' travels present a fascinating picture. They tell us how Jesus felt about what was important, and they tell us how he used his time and energy. The official religious leaders of the day had problems with those who were attracted to Jesus, and he quickly developed a bad reputation among these leaders by spending time with the wrong people, eating with the wrong people, and offering hope to the wrong people.

Luke (7:33–34) shows how difficult it was to escape the first-century judgmental attitudes: "John the Baptist has come eating no bread and drinking no wine, and you say, 'He has a demon'; the Son of Man has come eating and drinking, and you say, 'Look, a glutton and a drunkard, a friend of tax collectors and sinners!'" If that had been said about me or you, we would be frustrated. We might think, "You just can't win!"

The gospel accounts of Jesus' life tell stories of people who met Jesus and whose lives were changed by that encounter. Jesus attracted people, and he accepted every person.

CHILDREN (MARK 10:13–16)

Children seem to have an instinctive way of knowing about adults. Once children feel acceptance, they delight

in climbing all over that person, begging for attention. Little things, like kneeling down as we talk rather than "talking down" to them, communicate so much to children. We can see children running after Jesus just as they do today when they hear the music of the ice-cream truck on a hot afternoon.

This picture shows Jesus with children going to his side, climbing on his lap, showing their trust and security in him. Since children usually do have an innate sense of goodness, this may very well have been the way children flocked to Jesus. This painting has a special feeling because Carl Vogel von Vogelstein, the painter, often used his own children as models.

But sometimes children get in the way of busy adults, especially adults who think they should have priority. The disciples often tried to protect Jesus from the intrusion of children. When parents brought their small children to Jesus for the touch of his quiet blessing, the disciples scolded the parents for taking up his time. After all, Jesus was an important person, and important people don't have time for insignificant children.

When Jesus heard this he reprimanded his disciples, saying, "Don't ever do that again, for God has a special interest in children. They are what the kingdom of God is all about. In fact, you could do a lot better if you would learn to act more like children yourselves. If you want to be part of the community of God's people, you need to learn from their innocence."

OUTSIDERS

A Roman Soldier (Matthew 8:5–13, Luke 7:1–10): Most of the people Jesus met approached him. One of the unusual people who came looking for Jesus was a Roman centurion. Centurions were career soldiers, the backbone of the Roman military forces in Palestine. Each commanded a battalion of a hundred foot soldiers. That a Roman soldier came to Jesus asking for help demonstrates the breadth of the reputation that Jesus had developed. It says something about this soldier, too. In his concern for his servant, he violated the standard cultural feelings of his day. Jewish people did not approve of the Roman occupational forces in their country.

Jesus instantly offered to help this "enemy." The centurion, however, was conscious of the tension between the Jews and the Romans. He knew that Jewish social restrictions prevented Jews from entering the house of a Gentile. He reminded Jesus, "I am a Gentile; it is not appropriate for you to come to my house. I do not expect you to do that. I know about authority. I tell soldiers to do something, and they do it. All you need to do is say the word, and my servant will be healed." Jesus was surprised by this statement of faith. He told the crowd, "I have not seen faith like this among the Jewish people. This man is an example of what is going to happen in the future. People will come from all over the world and will find healing and acceptance. Jews and Gentiles will join together in God's presence." Turning to the centurion, he said, "Go, it is done." When the centurion returned home, he found his servant had been healed.

James Tissot had a profound religious experience in his middle years, and he devoted the remainder of his life to religious works. Committed to accuracy in detail, Tissot depicts the soldiers as hesitant about kneeling before Jesus, but the centurion is willing to crawl as a statement of Roman servitude.

Jesus was constantly confronted with the social stereotypes of his day. People were accepted or rejected because

of their gender, their race, their age, or their nationality. Yet he refused to allow these things to become factors when he talked and dealt with people. He related to everyone as a person—a full human being in the sight of God.

Women: One group that found a source of hope and redemption was women. Women played an important role in the financial support of Jesus. Many assume that God miraculously provided everything Jesus needed so that Jesus was freed of concern about food, clothing, or housing. But Jesus had to find a way to provide for himself on Earth. Luke gives the names of a number of women who provided the funding for Jesus as he traveled and taught (8:1–3). It is an interesting group: Mary Magdalene, who had a history of demonic possession (she was healed by Jesus); Joanna, whose husband worked as a steward in the house of Herod Antipas; and Suzanna, whom we know nothing about. These women freed Jesus for his ministry; they were also at the cross after the male disciples fled.

El Greco recognized that people in the biblical stories were first of all human beings, and he painted them with compassion. Mary Magdalene is a lovely, almost innocent young woman, showing none of the harshness often associated with her earlier history of demon possession. Her devotion to Jesus was strong, and here she stands sadly as Jesus is being crucified in the background.

This unusual response of women reflects the attitude shown by Jesus toward women. One day he and his disciples were traveling through Samaria. They stopped at noon near the well just outside the small town of Sychar. Jesus waited at the well while the disciples went to buy food. While he was waiting, an unnamed woman came from the town to draw water. Jesus asked her for a drink. Jews and Samaritans did not normally talk to each other, and they certainly would not drink from the same container. So the woman was surprised that this Jewish man would ask her for a drink. Jesus, ignoring cultural prejudices, began a conversation with her.

The way the story is normally told is of a promiscuous woman who had gone from one husband to another (she had had five husbands). By this time, her morality had sunk so low that she was not even married to the man she was living with. But if we look closer, the woman actually appears in a very different light.

In the first century, women could not divorce. Only men had that right (and Jesus scolded them for doing it thoughtlessly). So it would be more accurate to describe this woman as one who had been married, but five times her husbands had rejected her. The present "husband" did not have enough respect for her to have a ceremony. If we look at this woman not as an immoral sinner but rather as a person who has been abused and rejected, the story goes in a much more positive direction.

Jesus recognized her situation and sympathized with her. The woman saw him as godly and immediately asked, "Where can I go to worship? My ancestors worshiped on Mount Gerizim, but you say I must go to Jerusalem. But I cannot go there because I am not Jewish!" Jesus' response gave her more hope than she'd had in years: "Believe me, worship is not a matter of geographic location, but of an intimate spiritual relationship with God. For God wants people to worship in spirit and in truth."

This is wonderful news to the woman, but with her history she is not sure she can trust what a man says—

Anton Dorph captures the quiet, intense nature of the conversation between Jesus and the woman at the well. She is young, thoughtful, and very involved in what is being said to her. The conversations of Jesus seemed to draw people more deeply into themselves, making them consider for themselves their responsibility for their own lives.

Mountains and hills often became sacred places because they were closer to God. When the Jewish leadership excluded the Samaritans from worshiping in the temple in Jerusalem, they built their own temple on Mount Gerizim.

much less a Jewish man. She tells Jesus that she will wait for the messiah to come, because she knows he will tell her the truth. Jesus answers with one of the most profound and direct statements of self-revelation made in the New Testament: "You are talking to him!"

Just then the disciples returned, and the woman went back to the city in such a rush that she left her water jar at the well. But she got the message. She told everyone she met in Sychar: "There is a man at the well who says he is the messiah."

The people rushed out to see for themselves, and they asked Jesus to stay for several days, which violated several social and cultural taboos between Jews and Samaritans. The result of this encounter at the well was that the woman found new life, and some of the people of the town came to believe that Jesus was the Messiah, the savior of the world. We can only speculate about what life was like in Sychar after Jesus left. For the Samaritan woman, the good news was that the town would no longer discriminate against her. She would no longer have to go alone at noon to draw water from the well.

This story shows Jesus at his best. He saw each person as an individual with value. He didn't see a Samaritan woman to be avoided; he saw a hurt woman. He listened to the pain behind the words that were spoken; he offered sympathy and understanding when most people would have given quick judgment. He shared himself in a way that provided hope, rather than withdrawing so that he would not be contaminated by her. Jesus modeled the acceptance and love of God that reaches across cultural lines (Jew versus Samaritan), gender lines (male versus female), and worship lines (Jerusalem versus Mount Gerizim). He crossed those lines simply by being who he was in a world that created boxes into which people were expected to fit.

Mark shows this same compassion of Jesus as he tells two stories that are intertwined. Jesus was teaching along the seashore when a man named Jairus (a leader in the local synagogue) came up to him, begging Jesus to come with him to help his young daughter, who was so sick he feared she would die. It is important to note that daughters were at the bottom of the social ladder—the least valued of all family members. However, since Jesus saw each person as having value, he went with the man to his home.

On the way they were interrupted by a woman who was considered unclean because of bleeding, so she dared not have any contact with the public. She was forced to live her whole life in seclusion. She had sought help everywhere she could, spending all the money she had on doctors, but she kept getting worse (Mark 5:26). The woman heard that Jesus was in the area, and in her desperation, she felt if she could just touch him she would be made well. So, at much risk, she made her way through the crowd. She came up behind Jesus, reached out, and grabbed the hem of his robe. Immediately she was healed. Jesus was also aware that something had happened. He

In this painting there are a variety of important symbols showing the intimate involvement of Jesus in raising Jairus' daughter. Jesus kneels down and takes the young girl's hand, both actions showing the importance Jesus accords her. Also, the dying daughter is the central focus, while the more important people (daughters being the least important in biblical times) are moved into the background.

turned and asked, "Who did that?" The disciples joked about the comment saying, "What do you expect, there are people all around you!" But the woman, who felt that she had been healed yet was terrified by what might happen to her, came forward and told Jesus what she had done. Jesus calmly reassured her that she was well. He told her to go in peace.

This reaction was certainly not what the woman expected; the average Jewish male (had he known who had touched him) would have glared at her as he gathered his robe around him to return home to change his clothes, since that robe was now contaminated. The story presents an additional dilemma: Jairus is forced to face his own prejudices. Can he allow Jesus (who is now unclean) to enter his house and touch his daughter—for that would contaminate the very person he most wanted to help! To

Hostility and rejection are in the faces of the Jewish leaders, who seem to care more for details of the law than for the life of this woman. Allowing the woman to stand indicates a sense of dignity that first-century religious leaders would not have appreciated.

save the life of his daughter, he had to change his own views about people and clean versus unclean.

Throughout his ministry, Jesus, simply by his actions, affirmed those who had been rejected and scolded those who held prejudice. This added to the tension between Jesus and the Pharisees; Jesus kept affirming those whom the Pharisees condemned, and he kept scolding the Pharisees for being so self-righteous.

This point of tension came to a head one day, just outside the temple in Jerusalem. Jesus was teaching when the Pharisees burst in, dragging a disheveled and frightened woman. "Teacher," they said, "We caught this woman in the very act of committing adultery. The law says (in case you don't remember!) that we should stone her. What do you say?"

John gives a little background for this encounter. The Pharisees were really trying to test Jesus; they didn't care about the woman. She was just a way to condemn Jesus. The Pharisees were right: Old Testament law does call for stoning a woman who is caught committing adultery.

Jesus knelt down and began to write in the sand. He then stood up and told the Pharisees: "If any of you are so perfectly righteous that you have no sin, go ahead and throw the first stone." (This was standard Jewish practice, the person bringing the charge threw the first stone.) Then Jesus bent down again and continued writing in the sand. Was he possibly making a list of the sins of which the Pharisees were also guilty? One by one, the Pharisees knew they had been backed into a corner, and they all quietly left.

The embarrassed posture of the woman caught in adultery is contrasted with the confident Jesus who comes to her defense. Anton Dorph, the artist, seems to side with the woman against the unseen people with whom Jesus is talking. He is not pointing to her in judgment, but rather he seems quite gentle with her.

Jesus looked at the woman and said, "Woman, it doesn't look like anyone is condemning you." The woman, knowing that a few moments ago she was in danger of death, looked at Jesus with gratitude and amazement. Who was this man who would side with her and protect her?

For women in the first century, prostitution was not a vocation of choice, it was about survival. Perhaps Jesus suspected what the Pharisees had done; certainly he felt sadness for this woman trapped in this demoralizing occupation. He spoke words of hope to her: "I understand. I won't condemn you, either. Your life has been given back to you. Go home, change the way you live."

There are a few stories about how Jesus interacted with his own disciples during the three years they walked with him, sharing in his ministry. These stories provide insight into the frustrations that Jesus, as the teacher, must

Jesus "held class" with his disciples whenever there was something important to talk about. He would gather the group around him and discuss what had just happened, answering their questions.

have felt as he tried to work with these men. Jesus had committed his entire life to serving people who were in need, sharing the power and love of God with those who felt they had no one to turn to.

One day Jesus overheard the disciples engaged in a rather heated argument. That evening he asked them what they had been arguing about, but they were too embarrassed to answer. They had been arguing over which one of them was the most important friend to Jesus. Once again, Jesus turned to children to teach a lesson to these adults. He told them, "If you want to be first, you do it by becoming a servant of everyone you meet. What you do for others is an indication of how you actually feel about me. How you treat children (the most insignificant members of society) shows how well you understand what the kingdom of God is all about."

The way Jesus treated children tells us a lot about God's feelings toward us as children of God. Jesus valued children, giving them attention and love. All of God's children are also assured of acceptance when we come close to God.

This made good sense to the disciples, but they did not do well at applying it to another problem that came up a few days later. They could handle the competition within the group, but when confronted with competition from another group, they reverted to their old ways of trying to be superior. They had seen a person casting out demons in the name of Jesus, but this person was not an official member of Jesus' group. The disciples told the person to stop. They reported this to Jesus, feeling rather smug about what they had done. Jesus, however, asked, "Why did you do that? People who are doing the same

Jesus found people in most unusual situations. It is not likely that Zaccheus expected Jesus to stop and talk with him when he climbed that tree. There was risk on both sides of the relationship—Jesus risked the condemnation of the crowd and Zaccheus had no idea of the way his dinner with Jesus would change his life.

thing we are doing are really team members with us. Anyone who does even a very simple thing, like sharing a cup of cold water, will be blessed by God." It took the disciples a long time to discover that in the sight of God it is not simply the social or religious group with which you identify that says who you are. It is your integrity that God sees.

A TAX COLLECTOR

Few people in Israel were hated as much as tax collectors—Jews working for the Roman government. Tax collectors betrayed their own people by working for the occupying government in their land. They were unscrupulous, often gaining enormous wealth at the expense of their own people. Also, their work kept them involved with the Gentile Romans, which rendered them unclean. In the New Testament, tax collectors are almost synonymous with sinners. The best-known tax collector was Zaccheus, who lived in Jericho. He was hated even more than most, for he had moved up the Roman bureaucracy to become a chief tax collector, a supervisor within the despised system.

As Jesus passed through Jericho on his way to Jerusalem, Zaccheus wanted to get a glimpse of this very famous person, but that was difficult because he was a very short man. So he climbed a tree to get a better view. As Jesus walked by he did a most remarkable thing—he looked up, saw Zaccheus, and told him to come down. Jesus then invited himself to Zaccheus' home for supper!

The Jews did not know what to think about this prophet of God who dared to enter the house of a collaborator with the hated Romans. The people let their feelings be known as they grumbled about this prophet going to eat with a sinner—something they were sure none of them would ever do! But they missed out on the very exciting news that came after the supper. We don't know what Zaccheus and Jesus talked about, but we do know what happened to Zaccheus from the experience. After supper he came out and made a public announcement: "I am going to give half of all I own to help care for the poor. If I have defrauded anyone, I will make restitution according to the Old Testament law, paying those people four times what they lost." To this, Jesus responded, "Today salvation has come to this house, because you are acting as all true sons of Abraham should act, you are doing the will of God, and you will be saved for it" (Luke 19:1–10, paraphrased).

Certainly Jesus knew about the social prejudices of his day—who was in and who was out. But he refused to allow that to determine how he related to people, thus giving us a clear message of how God sees people in our own day. The most religious people of his day failed to get the message because they had already made their decision about who was acceptable to God and on what basis. Fortunately for the poor, the children, the women, the Gentiles, and tax collectors like Zaccheus, Jesus kept sharing the message, "God loves all people, and he wills that all of us live together in peace and health as children of God."

"Listen! I am standing at the door, knocking; if you hear my voice and open the door, I will come in to you and eat with you, and you with me" (Revelation 3:20). Jesus knocking at the door is a statement of the Christian belief that God reaches out and asks permission to come into our lives. Faith cannot be forced upon people.

MIRACLES OF JESUS

✦ ✦ ✦

IRACLES ADD A DRAMATIC FLAVOR to human experience. They catch our attention and cause us to think about God and about ourselves. We want to believe that miracles do happen. But miracles are not always understood the same way by everyone—sometimes causing uncertainty and confusion. The ministry of Jesus is filled with these dramatic expressions of the presence of God. People came to Jesus with their personal pain and suffering, asking him to bring healing to their lives. From his first proclamation in the synagogue at Nazareth to his final days in the temple at Jerusalem, Jesus was committed to being an active expression of the powerful presence of God.

Reading the New Testament brings us face to face with the miracles of Jesus. The miracle stories have a very human dimension. They are not literary decorations given to add excitement to the stories. They provide confirmation of what Jesus was teaching about God and salvation. If we were to remove the miracle stories, Jesus' ministry would lose much of its power, and much of his teaching would lose its context. They also demonstrate the dramatic difference between Jesus and the first-century Pharisees on the meaning of faith.

The healing ministry of Jesus was the source of much tension between him and the Pharisees. These miracles documented the authority of Jesus to speak as he did about the nature of God. The miracles of Jesus open a window through which we see into the heart of God—we see

Above: *The original first-century synagogue where Jesus preached was destroyed, but another was built in its place. Synagogues were simple buildings with a table for reading the Scripture and an open platform for teaching. There was very little ornamentation, for one came to meet God, not to view the works of humans.* Facing page: *The resurrection of Lazarus was one of the most dramatic miracles of Jesus. It marked both Jesus and Lazarus as people the Jewish authorities decided to watch and destroy.*

an expression of God's love toward humanity in these events. Several of these stories are especially helpful in exploring how Jesus saw life and how he related to people who were struggling with difficult experiences.

The miracles of Jesus were certainly helpful to the people who were healed, but they also created a general level of confusion that followed Jesus almost everywhere he went. How could Jesus explain the majesty and wonder of God when he was often surrounded by crowds who thought they already knew exactly what God was doing? Miracles were simply Jesus using God's power when he came into contact with human need. For some people, these were times of healing and of celebration. For others, there was confusion, because they saw the miracles but did not understand how they happened. For a few people there was anger and frustration, because these miracles violated their beliefs about God, and they had already decided that Jesus could not be the godly person he claimed to be. These people then had to find a different explanation for the miracles of Jesus.

Throughout his ministry, Jesus had to contend with these mixed responses from the crowds. But this never deterred him from his compassionate ministry of teaching and healing.

THE POWER OF SOMEONE ELSE'S FAITH

One day, while in Capernaum, Jesus was in a small house that was so packed with people there was no room

Five loaves and two small fish— Jesus used them to feed over five thousand men, plus the women and children in the crowd. God's participation in this event is shown by the Father-God over- head and the dove hovering in the sky.

for anyone else. Four men living in the city had a friend who was paralyzed. Having heard about the wonderful things Jesus had done, they brought their friend to Jesus, believing he could help. But when they arrived at the house, it was impossible to get inside, much less get close to Jesus. After coming this far, these men were determined to get what they came for. They carried the paralyzed man up to the flat roof, removed the top covering of clay, and tore up the reeds and branches that supported the roof between the main structural beams. They made a hole large enough to lower their friend in front of Jesus.

When Jesus saw how their faith had motivated them, he turned to the paralyzed man and said, "Your sins are forgiven." This immediately caused a stir among the Jewish leaders in the room, for they believed only God had the power to forgive sins. They made this point very clear to Jesus, accusing him of blasphemy. As Jesus heard their grumbling, he confronted them with a theological dilemma: "Which is easier to do—forgive sins or heal a paralyzed person?" The Pharisees were silenced for a moment, because their theology also said that all healing (as with all forgiveness) must come from God. Having made his point, Jesus turned to the paralyzed man and told him: "Stand up, roll up your bed, and go home." The man sprang to his feet, rolled up his mattress, and walked out, to the amazement of everyone in the house.

The difficulty some people had with the healing miracles of Jesus was the belief that suffering was related to sin in the person's life. This sin-suffering relationship was deeply embedded in most ancient cultures, and it continues to be accepted by many religious people today. The Book of Job in the Old Testament is a direct challenge of this belief. Job's friends, who come to comfort him in his tragic condition, are offended by his claim that his suffer-

The Old Testament story of Job speaks to the question of why righteous people suffer. In this painting, three friends sit with Job and give him all the traditional answers, none of which provide comfort. Jesus challenged the simple answers that said all evil has a reason. Instead he urged people to stay strong in their faith even when evil or misfortune happens.

ing was unfair because he had not sinned. They admonish him by saying, "Who that was innocent ever perished?" (Job 4:7). Throughout the years, this concept that suffering is caused by sin became so sophisticated that some rabbis claimed they could identify a person's sin by looking at the nature of their suffering—"Where the sin started, the retribution also begins." In more radical cases, it was even possible for an unborn baby to participate in (and thus be guilty of) the sins of the mother.

In first-century culture, people believed diseased people were suffering because of their sins. This prevented the sick from sharing in the religious life of their community. Jesus violated these standards by touching the blind man. Jesus spat on the ground and made a paste of saliva and dirt to put on the man's eyes.

The attitude of Jesus toward this theological idea is seen in an event that happened one day as Jesus was walking along the road. A man who had been blind from birth was sitting begging for money. Jesus' disciples shared the belief in the connection between sin and suffering. When they saw the blind man, they asked, "Jesus, whose sin caused this man to be born blind—his own or his parents?" (Somebody was thought to be responsible.) Jesus, however, did not see it this way. When he looked at the man, he saw a person in need. Jesus first scolded the disciples for their insensitivity, then he said, "Let's use this situation to demonstrate the power of God's grace."

In his encounters with people, Jesus saw human need, but he refused to allow that to be the main focus of attention. Jesus did not believe that God caused this man to suffer, but he did believe the man's healing could be used to glorify God. Jesus saw people with potential, where others saw only problems to be analyzed. Jesus went over to the blind man, spat on the ground, made a tiny bit of mud from the saliva, spread it on the man's eyes, and told him to go to the nearby Pool of Siloam and wash it off. The man did as he was told, and he was healed.

This style of involving people in their own healing was typical of Jesus. His miracles were not done to a person, rather he did them with the person. He called people to act, and as they acted, their healing was realized. This suggests that if they had not joined with Jesus in their own healings the outcomes might have been different.

By the time the man came back, Jesus had moved on. The man's friends were so accustomed to seeing him as a blind beggar that they did not recognize him walking around by himself. When he convinced them of his identity, they wanted to know what had happened. He explained that a man called Jesus put mud on his eyes and told him to go wash it off. The crowd wanted to know where Jesus was, and the man had to admit he did not know. The man discovered it was not easy to get other people to celebrate with him, because his newfound sight demanded that they give up their stereotypes about illness and healing.

Former enemies, the Herodians and the Pharisees, are clustered together (though still in two distinct groups) to talk about getting rid of Jesus. How appropriate that James Tissot had these groups meet in a cemetery, since their plotting ended in Jesus' death.

When the people could not resolve their problem, they took the man to the Pharisees. They saw an even more important crisis in this event: This was the sabbath day, and since healing was a form of work, this man's sight was proof that Jesus had sinned by working on the sabbath! The Pharisees tried to discredit Jesus by saying that he could not be of God because he did not observe the sabbath. But others in the crowd challenged that assumption by saying, "If he is such a terrible sinner, how did he

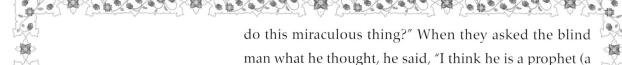

do this miraculous thing?" When they asked the blind man what he thought, he said, "I think he is a prophet (a man of God)."

That was the wrong thing to say to the Pharisees. They turned to the man's parents and asked what they thought. The poor parents were caught in the middle of their joy over what had happened to their son and their fear of what the Pharisees might do to them if they said the wrong thing. They simply reported what they knew: "He is our son. We know he was born blind. We were not there to see what happened, so we don't know. But he is an adult, he can speak for himself."

The Pharisees then called the man back and explained to him what he should believe: "We know this man is a sinner, so praise God (not him) for your healing!" It wasn't just his vision that this man gained from Jesus. This man began to "see" what was going on, and since he had very little to lose, he dared to give a short lecture: "I don't know about what you say, I just know I can see. I can tell you what happened; will that help you to believe in him, too? We are taught that God does not partici-pate in sin, and I don't know of any other case in history where a man born blind had his eyes opened. If this man were not of God, he could not have done that!"

The Pool of Siloam, pictured here, is where Jesus ordered the blind man to go to wash himself after Jesus cured him of his blindness.

To this insightful observation, the Pharisees snorted their disgust: "You were born in sin—how dare you try to teach us!" They kicked him out of the synagogue. Many people have very strange ways of dealing with new insights into God!

This story does have a happy ending. When Jesus heard what the Pharisees had done, he found the man and explained to him that he (Jesus) was the Messiah who had come into the world to help blind people see (meaning both physically and spiritually). The man thanked Jesus and believed in him. A few Pharisees overheard this conversation and asked Jesus, "Are you accusing us of being blind?" Jesus replied sadly, "Yes."

This story shows us how Jesus worked with people in need. This man's faith moved from seeing Jesus first as "a man," then as "a prophet." After the Pharisees expelled him from the synagogue, Jesus showed the man who he really was, the "Son of Man" (a term Jesus used instead of messiah), and the man believed. This story provides a delightful contrast of seeing and not seeing, of believing and not believing, of the hostility of some religious leaders and the patience of Jesus with a person whose faith is new and childlike, but growing.

After several other experiences like this, the anger of the Pharisees toward Jesus became so intense that he had to leave Jerusalem and take temporary refuge on the other side of the Jordan River. During this time, while Jesus was in Perea, he received word that his close friend Lazarus was quite ill, and that his family was asking Jesus to come visit him. Jesus did not immediately stop what he was doing and rush to Bethany where Lazarus lived. By the time Jesus arrived, Lazarus was dead and had been buried for four days. This was particularly painful for Jesus because the home of Lazarus and his two sisters, Mary and Martha, had always been a safe haven where he could relax and be among trusted friends.

Polyptych paintings were multi-panel works usually done for church altars. The number of panels often depended upon the size of the altar or space where the work would be shown. Here Lazarus is placed in the middle panel; the figures to his sides are the other people associated with his story.

When Jesus arrived at their home, Martha came running to meet him. She had always been the more active, outspoken family member. Her first words to Jesus were a combination of relief at seeing Jesus and reproach for not having come sooner. "If you had been here," she said, "all this would not have happened." Her pain was evident underneath her impulsive comment. Her brother had just died, and she knew that Jesus could have kept this from happening.

The "why" questions we all have were begging to be asked: "Why did you not come when we called you? Why did you take so long? Why did you let this happen to us?" But then she calmed down and remembered to make the appropriate faith statement: "But I know that whatever you ask, God will do for you!" In the conversation that followed, when Martha affirmed her faith in resurrection (a widely held belief in first-century Israel), Jesus told her, "I am the resurrection and the life.... everyone who lives and believes in me will never die" (John 11:25–26).

Jesus went to the tomb and asked that the stone covering the hole be moved. Martha still did not fully understand what Jesus had just said about resurrection. She scolded him for subjecting the family to the embarrassment of having to show a body that had already begun to decay and that would certainly reek. She reminded Jesus that Lazarus had been dead for four days (there was a traditional belief that the spirit of a departed person hovered over the body for three days trying to get back in). By now Lazarus was certainly dead beyond all hope of a miraculous restoration. Jesus ignored her comment. He stood at the door of the tomb and loudly called for Lazarus to come out.

Jewish bodies were buried in what was beautifully referred to as "traveling dress," a simple white garment

Facing page: *The house of Mary, Martha, and Lazarus was a place that Jesus often went when he needed time to relax and be with friends. The painter, Allori, captures the friendliness and affection that we are told Jesus had for these close friends.*

with the hands and feet wrapped in long strips of cloth wrappings. At the command of Jesus, the man who had been dead for four days came out. Jesus told the family, "Unbind him, and let him go."

We might wish to believe that bringing a person who had been dead for four days back to life would be a very persuasive act, and that all who saw it would recognize, "Here is a man of God." This was not the case, however. Many of the people who were there that day did believe in Jesus, but others went immediately to tell the Pharisees what Jesus had done this time.

The chief priests and Pharisees quickly called a meeting of the leadership. Their concern was simple: "If we allow this Jesus to continue doing these things, everyone will believe in him, and we will lose everything we have ever had." Their conclusion: "For the good of the people, it is better to have one man die than to have the whole nation be destroyed."

Christ's entrance into Jerusalem was an extravagant celebration. His popularity was enormous, and the celebration simply exploded as children ran ahead and adults stood along the street cheering. Plockhurst does paint a few old men, representing the Pharisees, who appear unhappy with the proceedings.

Based on that logic, they began to plan how they might kill Jesus. It is ironic that restoring the life of Lazarus had the direct result of leading to the death of Jesus. Jesus recognized this hostility toward him and withdrew again from public life by moving back to southern Galilee, away from the major religious center of Jerusalem.

But this is not the end of the story. In late March to early April of that same year, crowds began to gather in Jerusalem to celebrate the Passover. Jesus was the primary topic of conversation, as people wondered whether he would dare to show himself at the festival. People were aware that the chief priests had given orders that he should be arrested. Instead of going directly to Jerusalem for the Passover, Jesus stopped to visit Lazarus and his sisters in Bethany. They invited other friends in for a special dinner in honor of both Jesus and Lazarus. When the Jewish leaders heard what was going on, they went to Bethany to see for themselves. They quickly decided to add Lazarus to their death list because his presence was testimony to the power of God in Jesus. (We never do find out Lazarus' fate, though.)

The morning after the dinner, Jesus went down to Jerusalem. When the crowds heard he was coming, they cut branches of palm trees and went out to meet him with a joyful, almost riotous celebration. The chief priests knew they could not stop the crowd. They watched, saying to themselves, "The whole world is caught up with this man!" Jesus began the last week of his life with the ecstatic support of the common people. But miraculous events have a way of getting lost in yesterday's news. Within five days, this same crowd got swept up in the emotion of shouting, "Crucify him, crucify him," when asked by Pilate what he should do with Jesus, the prisoner.

This fickle crowd response is another reminder that belief in miracles does not necessarily provide for lifelong religious belief. Jesus recognized this in the wilderness when Satan urged him to take a miracle-worker approach, which would gain him instant followers. Jesus' purpose was not to gain popularity but to demonstrate the power of the kingdom that was coming soon.

Artists have only their imaginations to guide them in portraying the resurrected Jesus. Anton Dorph paints Jesus emerging from the tomb with a clean white robe, signs of new life and a new age. The painter shows the magnitude and simplicity of the story in a very simple presentation of the resurrected Christ.

JESUS FACES OPPOSITION

✦ ✦ ✦

HENEVER A PERSON challenges traditional beliefs, there is certain to be a reaction. People usually defend their beliefs from outside attacks. As Jesus looked at the first-century faith practices of the Jewish people, he saw how, over the generations, their religious practices had gradually been shifting away from God's teachings.

These were not changes introduced by evil people trying to lead Israel astray. They were the practical adjustments made in almost every religion as it adapts in order to survive persecution or demands for modernization. New problems arose that were not addressed in the original teachings, so new applications needed to be made.

Jesus challenged those interpretations that violated the original intent of the law, those changes that wound up manipulating the spirit of the law by creating layers of legal interpretations. Some of these challenges are recorded in the Sermon on the Mount. Jesus identified what the peo-

Right: *The law was given to Israel by God through Moses. It had a central place of power and reverence in the people's lives. The law represented the full authority of all the forces of heaven. To consider changing the law, or simply to challenge one of its details, was to defy God. Jesus did not challenge the law itself, but he questioned how Israel interpreted the law, and this was enough to brand him as defiant. Facing page: Jesus was best known as a rabbi (teacher). The Sermon on the Mount is a collection of the central things that Jesus taught. The common people listened eagerly to the things he said, and many believed him.*

ple had been taught to believe, then restated the original intent of the law as it was first given by God. This created a contrast between what was and what had been intended.

Not all the changes made over time were destructive; many helped Israel develop a more caring, practical faith.

On several occasions the Pharisees, who were the established teachers of the day, became so angry with what Jesus taught that they threatened to kill him. The traditional Jewish method of taking the law into your own hands was to throw stones at the person until they died, called stoning.

But some changes led the people of Israel to believe they were doing the will of God when in fact their actions violated the spirit of what God had intended.

When talking about anger, adultery, divorce, swearing oaths, retaliation, and loving enemies, Jesus began by saying, "You have heard that it was said…but I say to you…" (I know this is what you have been taught to believe, but I am telling you that this is what God intended.)

The opposition to Jesus began early in his ministry when he visited his hometown synagogue in Nazareth. The congregation was excited as they listened to this local-boy-makes-good preacher, but then he challenged their belief that they had privileged status before God. The people reacted violently, and Jesus was driven from the community.

Criticism followed from that day forward as Jesus presented his message. Throughout his ministry, the problem is seen most vividly in conflicts with two specific groups: the demon-possessed and the Pharisees. Each group had their problems with Jesus, but for very different reasons.

We so often tell the story of Jesus as though he went from town to town surrounded by people who praised him for the wonderful things he was doing, eager to have him come to their town, quick to believe what he was teaching, and instantly following him. But unfortunately that is only one side of the story, for there were also those who saw Jesus as a threat to everything they believed. He challenged them to a new way of life, but they were comfortable with the old. These people harassed Jesus, spread rumors about him, made threats against him, challenged his message, questioned his authority, and constantly tried to discredit him among the common people. Life for Jesus was not peaceful.

THE DEMON-POSSESSED

In the ancient world, there was widespread belief in the powers of spiritual beings. All of these powers were not necessarily evil, but some were. During the period between the Old and New Testaments, there was a commonly accepted belief that these powers were somehow linked with the forces of evil. Traces of belief in harmful spirits are found in the Old Testament Jewish community, but it was

The artist correctly set this miracle in an isolated place outside the city gates, for epileptics were ostracized from most social interaction. This man came to Jesus, pleaded for help, and was healed of his condition.

not until shortly before the time of Jesus that these beliefs received popular acceptance among the common people of the land.

With the infiltration of Greek and Babylonian thought into Jewish culture, the idea emerged that these evil spirits could invade either the body (causing physical problems such as paralysis or blindness) or the mind (causing various forms of mental illness). More radical beliefs also developed, including the thought that these demon powers could control the forces of nature. Thus storms and other natural catastrophes were seen as the direct results of Satanic activity.

The New Testament was written within a religious society that assumed the reality of demonic activity. Jesus was frequently put in situations of conflict with these demons. Jesus clearly had power over these evil activities. Whenever he was confronted with a demonic expression, Jesus was victorious and the demons were either destroyed, driven out of the "host person," or at least silenced.

On several occasions the Pharisees engaged Jesus in heated discussions about whether he himself might be demon-possessed. Since these demons obeyed Jesus, they contended, he must be linked with them. Perhaps they thought he was possessed by a powerful demon who could coerce other demons to obey him. Shortly after leaving Nazareth, Jesus was a guest teacher in the synagogue at Capernaum when the service was interrupted by a man possessed by a demon who shouted,

Capernaum was a town that Jesus visited often, and he was openly accepted there. This photo shows the ruins of the second-century synagogue at Capernaum; the first-century synagogue is presumably below it. Jesus was invited to speak in the first-century building on several occasions.

THE LIFE OF JESUS

"Let us alone! What have we in common with you, Jesus? Have you come to destroy us? We know who you are: the Holy One of God!" This demon recognized that Jesus' work was in complete opposition to what Satan was trying to do in the world. He also acknowledged the ultimate victory of God over evil.

The reaction of Jesus to this demon was quite startling in the face of the traditional treatment of demon-possessed people. (Elaborate exorcism rituals were performed by special people who made their living freeing others from demonic control.) Jesus simply spoke to the demon: "Be silent, and come out of him." The people who heard were amazed at the power of Jesus to issue a command and have the spirits obey him.

But on other occasions the people were less convinced. When Jesus talked about his relationship with God and how he would eventually give his life for other people, the Pharisees did not understand and dismissed what Jesus said. They responded with: "He has a demon. He is out of his mind. Why should we listen to him?"

Once, when Jesus was engaged in a philosophical discussion with the Pharisees about God, ethics, and their own identity, he questioned whether they honestly were the children of Abraham that they claimed to be, and if they were, why didn't they live by the same values by which Abraham lived? The Pharisees took a cheap shot at Jesus by reminding him that they at least knew who their fathers were—did Jesus know who was his father was? Jesus came back quickly with, "If you were really

Abraham's statement of faith was moving his entire family in response to the instructions of God. He is often used as a model of proper godly behavior. As he moved from place to place, he added to his already large flocks, herds, and other possessions.

79

children of God, you would recognize that what I am saying is from God, but since you are not of God, you do not hear what I am saying." The Pharisees lashed back: "We are right in saying you are a Samaritan, and you have a demon!" (For Jewish people these were the worst labels one could possibly put on another person: a demon-possessed half-breed!)

When Jesus dared to tell the Pharisees they were wrong, they became even more angry. They restated their charge that he had a demon. In their fury, they almost stoned him.

This conflict came to a head when the Pharisees tried to discredit what Jesus had done by spreading the rumor that Jesus was under the spell of Beelzebul, the prince of demons. Jesus asked them, "If I am under the spell of Beelzebul, under whose spell are your own exorcists working? You claim they do it in the name of God, can it not be that God is my source of power as well? Why would Satan fight against himself by casting out his own demons?"

THE PHARISEES

The demon stories in the New Testament bear witness to the power of Jesus over the forces of evil, and they frequently led to criticism of what Jesus was doing. But Jesus received a different kind of criticism from the religious community. Their criticism was about his personal life.

There were two schools of thought in the Jewish religious world. One said that the law was the supreme expression of God's will and that humanity was created to observe the law, thus giving glory to God by showing the wisdom of what God had created. These people argued that the law must be kept even in its most minute detail.

The other school said that humanity is the highest expression of God's glory, and the law was given to help

Facing page: *The Pharisees do not have a positive reputation among Christians, and that is unfortunate. There were many Pharisees who honestly engaged Jesus in conversation and who did agree with much of what he taught about God and about obedience to the law. Pictured here, Jesus is involved in an open friendly exchange with two Pharisees.*

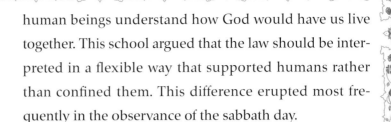

human beings understand how God would have us live together. This school argued that the law should be interpreted in a flexible way that supported humans rather than confined them. This difference erupted most frequently in the observance of the sabbath day.

The Pharisees did not agree among themselves on the issue of sabbath observance. It is important to note that the Pharisees who attacked Jesus about what he did on the sabbath represent the position of only some, not all, Pharisees. But for those Pharisees who took the conservative position of rigid sabbath observance, Jesus was a threat to their authority because he took a more relaxed approach.

The leaders of the Pharisees are upset with Jesus again, and they meet to discuss how they should handle the situation. Tissot, with his masterful setting of atmosphere, has them meeting in a dark, secluded place as they conspire.

When Jesus saw a person in need, he did not stop to check what day of the week it was. If it happened to be the sabbath, he did not ask them to wait until tomorrow. He healed them on the spot. These sabbath-day healings were a source of great tension for the Pharisees, and the problem reached critical proportions several times. Any one incident might have been accepted as an unusual circumstance, but when it happened again and again, it was more than these Pharisees could accept.

One sabbath day, Jesus was a guest teacher in a synagogue when he saw a woman in the audience who suffered from such severe arthritis that she could not stand up straight. He stopped teaching and called for her to come forward, which she did. He laid his hands on her and instantly she stood up straight, healed of her painful affliction. The synagogue leader was quite indignant, saying to the crowd, "This is not right, for there are six working days in the week, and if you want to be cured, come back on one of those days, not on the sabbath." When Jesus heard this, he spoke to the leader directly: "You hypocrite, you will without hesitation untie your donkey so that it is free to get a drink of water on the sabbath, but you would not allow this woman to be free from her bondage on the sabbath day?" Jesus was a master at confrontation.

On another sabbath day, Jesus was on his way to have dinner with a leader of the Pharisees when he passed a man who suffered from a disease in which fluid was retained in the tissues of his body, causing him great pain. A group of lawyers and Pharisees were walking with Jesus, so he asked them, "Is it legal to cure people on the sabbath or not?" When the Pharisees refused to answer, Jesus proceeded to heal the man and send him home. Then, turning to the lawyers and Pharisees, he asked, "If you had a child who fell into a well, wouldn't you immediately rescue the child, even though it was the sabbath?"

This same question about healing on the sabbath was raised by the Pharisees on another occasion. Jesus was in a synagogue when a man with a paralyzed hand entered. The Pharisees wanted to trick Jesus into "sinning" on the sabbath, so they brought the man to him. Jesus restated his earlier question, asking if they would take care of their animals on the sabbath, why couldn't they also care for others on the sabbath? He then healed the man's hand.

Confronted with this blatant disregard of "proper" sabbath observance, the Pharisees concluded that it would come down to either them or Jesus—they could not exist together. So these Pharisees began to build a conspiracy with other Jewish parties on how they might get rid of Jesus.

Images in stained glass require more color than was realistic in the biblical period. The windows are beautiful reminders of how we make Jesus into what we want him to be. It is likely that Jesus looked like a typical person in his own day.

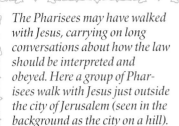

The Pharisees may have walked with Jesus, carrying on long conversations about how the law should be interpreted and obeyed. Here a group of Pharisees walk with Jesus just outside the city of Jerusalem (seen in the background as the city on a hill).

Even when faced with this hostility, Jesus refused to compromise or soften what he was doing. He continued to push the Pharisees about how they made life difficult for the common people with the way they interpreted the Scriptures. One Pharisee was shocked when Jesus did not perform a ritual washing of his hands before eating. He challenged Jesus' carelessness. Jesus used this incident to criticize the Pharisees about their legalistic spiritual pride, their greed, and their insensitivity to people. A lawyer, overhearing the comments, admonished Jesus because he felt that he also was being insulted.

Perhaps the lawyer should have kept quiet. Jesus turned to him as well, criticizing the way lawyers did their jobs—unfairly burdening the people and refusing to help them. (Lawyers in Jesus' day were experts on Jewish religious law; their title was interchangeable with scribe or Pharisee.)

After Jesus left, these lawyers and Pharisees were furious with him. They decided to cross-examine Jesus at every opportunity so that they might catch him saying something wrong.

Jesus lived with constant criticism from people who identified themselves as the keepers of the faith. One wonders how he kept his spirits up, how he could maintain a positive attitude toward the people who were asking for help.

Several times he did move away from the constant criticism that surrounded the temple and Jerusalem. He went into Galilee, where there was a more open attitude to sabbath observance. We can see the disappointment surfacing in Jesus as he responded to one critical Pharisee by saying, "Don't you realize the sabbath was made for humanity? Humanity was not created for the sabbath! Your priorities are backward."

Both in what he said and in what he did, Jesus challenged some of the central beliefs of the religious leadership. There was a price to be paid for doing that in public. Jesus faced arguments about the sabbath, questions about his sanity, personal attacks, and name-calling. Even Jesus' family members felt the intensity of the criticism that was directed at him. On at least one occasion, Jesus' mother and his brothers came to talk with him out of concern for his safety because of the Pharisees' reaction to what he was doing.

Jesus knew how it felt to face the hostility of people who are locked into one way of thinking. They could not see the freedom of knowing a God who sees people as people, all of whom need love, healing, and acceptance. Jesus chose not to compromise the nature of God and the way God wants to relate to us all. But he paid the price for his stand with his life.

James the Lesser was a disciple about whom virtually nothing is known. According to tradition, he was the son of Alphaeus and Mary, who is often mentioned as "the other Mary" in gospel accounts. Scholars assume that he was either younger or perhaps smaller in stature, thus giving him the designation "Lesser" to distinguish him from the other James, who was quite prominent.

THE FINAL DAYS

❖ ❖ ❖

ASSOVER WAS ALWAYS AN EXCITING TIME, marked by a special religious enthusiasm. Each year it raised the hopes of the Jewish population that this would be the year the messiah would come. Passover was originally a religious celebration that had expanded into part festival, part extended family reunion. Tourists flocked into Jerusalem, bringing money for food, lodging, offerings, and religious sacrifices. This created a major economic windfall for local merchants. This extra money turned these religious tourists into tempting targets for pickpockets and thieves. Because of the large numbers of people, Rome increased security by sending additional troops to guard against rebellion.

Above: *The Jewish Passover includes a symbolic meal that sets the tone for telling the story of how God led Israel out of slavery in Egypt. Each food symbolizes part of the Exodus experience. As the family eats, the story of deliverance is told once again.* Facing page: *Life was not always peaceful for the disciples as they followed Jesus. Sometimes they did not understand, and then they argued among themselves about what Jesus meant. Joergen Roed has Jesus turning away, as though asking the person viewing the painting, "Don't you understand what I am saying?"*

The Romans were not very sensitive to Jewish religious and cultural practices, so their presence was not welcome. A major religious festival, plus troops, tourists, and thieves, made Passover a highly charged event.

As if a normal Passover weren't hectic enough, this year there was the added attraction of a miracle-working, radical prophet/teacher who had been traveling around the countryside raising the hopes of the common people with his message and his miracles. At the same time, this man was creating a growing tension within the Jewish leadership because of his critical comments about their religious practices. This Passover promised to be different from all previous Passovers.

The weeks leading up to Passover held their own special intensity for the disciples. They could sense an increased urgency as Jesus spoke to the crowds, and they could feel a quickening of his pace as he went through each day. This urgency came to the surface in a conversation with Jesus as the disciples were traveling in northern Galilee near Caesarea Philippi. As they stopped along the road, Jesus asked what the people were saying about him. The disciples responded with the traditional things: "They think you are John the Baptist, others say you are Elijah, some think you are one of the prophets." (In Jewish theology, there was a tradition that said that near the end of time, the prophets would reappear proclaiming their prophetic message again. When the people heard Jesus speak, they made the connection of his message with what the previous prophetic figures had taught.) As the disciples reported what other people were saying, Jesus asked a very pointed question, "How are you hearing what I say? Who do you think I am?" Peter, always the first to speak his mind, confidently blurted out: "You are the Messiah!"

The prophet Elijah lived during a time of a major drought in Israel. He pleaded with God for rain, then climbed Mount Carmel and sat in discouragement waiting for a sign of rain. His servant stood watch and saw the small cloud appear in the distance as assurance that God had heard Elijah's prayer.

For the first time in his ministry Jesus used this opportunity to tell the disciples what it meant to be the messiah. He also gave them some idea of what they should expect in the future. He told them that the road ahead was leading to suffering, rejection, and his own death, but that he would rise again in three days. The disciples were so shocked by what Jesus was saying that they heard only "suffer…be rejected…be killed"—they completely missed his comment about resurrection. This was terrible news!

The disciples had assumed the messiah would lead a religious revival within Israel, set up a new political system in which the Jewish people would regain control of their own land, and then God would bless Israel with prosperity and peace. This scenario was exciting for the disciples because they were on the inside with Jesus, and they assumed they would be given important roles in this new kingdom.

But now Jesus was talking about persecution, suffering, and death, and he was saying it very plainly. This was not what they were expecting. The whole thing was so disturbing to Peter that he took Jesus aside and scolded him for thinking this way, reminding him, "The

Most of the conversations between Jesus and the disciples took place while walking through the countryside in Palestine, thus leading to the common idea that Jesus had an informal teaching style. Tissot's attention to detail provides a good presentation of the rugged, mountainous countryside.

messiah doesn't suffer, he rules!" Jesus immediately turned to Peter and gave him a lecture, telling him, "When you talk like that, you are thinking the way Satan thinks, not the way God thinks. I refuse to accept that way of thinking! If you want to be my follower, you won't accept it either!"

The disciples' lack of understanding must have been discouraging for Jesus. He had been preaching and teaching for nearly three years, and now, with the end of his ministry drawing near, the people closest to him still did not understand. They were still encased in their traditional ways of thinking about God, and the newness of what Jesus was saying had not yet been accepted.

Later that day Jesus gathered a small crowd around him and said to them: "If you want to follow me, you have to learn to think differently about God, about yourself, and about others. Being godly means living a new way. Don't think about yourself first, rather give of yourself for others. If you are always looking out for yourself, you

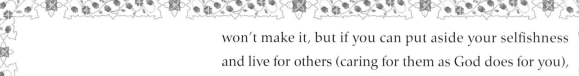

won't make it, but if you can put aside your selfishness and live for others (caring for them as God does for you), then you will be part of God's kingdom. What are you going to do once you conquer the whole world and still have nothing to live for? If you cannot accept what I am telling you as the message of God then there is little hope for you, and you will not be accepted by the messiah when he does come."

These were difficult days for Jesus. His ministry was facing a major crisis, and the future was not promising. These were equally difficult days for the disciples. Jesus had just challenged them to rethink everything they had been expecting from him. They all needed some reassurance that they were doing God's will. Days later, Jesus took Peter, James, and John to a mountain, where they shared a most unusual spiritual experience. They were joined by Moses (the supreme lawgiver for Israel) and Elijah (the first of the prophets), both of whom were believed to have a special relationship with God. They affirmed for Jesus that God would be with him in the days ahead. In this meeting, Jesus confronted the cross and his faithfulness to God. For Jesus, this was a time of recommitment to the task ahead.

Peter, James, and John were privileged to be with Jesus when he met with Moses and Elijah, in what is called the Transfiguration. Procaccini, the artist, painted a strong wind blowing to represent the presence of God in this meeting. The disciples see what is happening, but do not fully understand.

The experience on the mountain benefited the disciples also. They had followed Jesus with high expectations about how this ministry would turn out, but their faith had been challenged because Jesus was going to die. This contradicted everything they were expecting the messiah to do. Jesus told them if they wanted to follow him they had to think differently. Here, with Elijah and Moses, they had confirmation that Jesus had told them the truth. They were now ready to face the final week.

Jesus' entry into Jerusalem triggered a spontaneous demonstration of support by the common people, which hinted at what might lie ahead. There had been some question as to whether or not Jesus would attend this Passover, because the Jewish leadership had made it known they wanted him arrested.

When he arrived in the city, he went to the temple and saw the rowdy, bazaarlike, carnival atmosphere. Rigid temple regulations controlled the offerings and sacrifices: All offerings had to be in the local coins of Palestine; no foreign currency was permitted. All animals had to pass careful examination to guarantee they had no blemishes that would disqualify them as valid sacrifices.

The temple was filled with merchants who had set up stalls selling lambs and other animals; there were cages filled with doves and pigeons for the less wealthy; and moneychangers were eager to exchange Roman, Greek, or other national currencies into the Palestinian money that was required in the temple. Each of these merchants fought for the best locations around and inside the temple so that they could provide a convenient service for Jewish worshipers who had come from all over the Middle East. These zealous merchants were crowding out the legitimate worshipers, thus robbing the temple of its original God-intended purpose. But because the day was almost over, Jesus left, going a few miles out of town to Bethany and the home of Mary, Martha, and Lazarus.

The next morning, Jesus returned to the temple where the commercial atmosphere was more than he could accept. Grabbing some rope and twirling it into a whip, he

The entry of Jesus into Jerusalem was a symbolic event with an ironic twist. When a victorious military leader returned home, he led a huge military parade, he rode an impressive stallion, and people showed their gratitude by throwing robes on the street. But Jesus rode a donkey, he was followed by children and common people who had no clothes to spare, and they spread palm branches on the street and shouted "Hosanna!" The Pharisees were not amused—they saw only a religious and political threat.

stormed into the temple, upset the tables of the money-changers, opened the cages of the doves and pigeons, and untied the sheep and oxen and drove them out. He created a minor riot, shouting at the merchants to get out of the temple and telling them that they should not turn his father's house into a common marketplace.

The people in the temple were taken by surprise; they watched in shock, then they asked him what he was trying to do. He responded with a challenge: "Destroy this house and in three days I will restore it again." The disciples heard the exchange, but the comment made no sense to them then. After the resurrection, they remembered it and understood what he was talking about.

This act had consequences for Jesus in the next few days. Judas Iscariot (one of the twelve disciples) saw it as a statement of a new direction and style by Jesus. The Jewish leadership was angered by this direct challenge of the established practices of the day. Three days later, when Jesus appeared before them as a prisoner, they remembered what he had done in the temple.

For many, Jesus' dramatic behavior in the temple seems out of character. They prefer to see Jesus speaking to personal spiritual concerns—one's relationship with God. This act, instead, was a challenge to the religious abuse that had economic and social implications. It was aggressive and intentional, but it caused no personal injury. It shows the creative approach Jesus used to address the issues without attacking the people involved—the actions of the merchants were attacked.

The scene at the temple raised the tension level in Jerusalem. As Jesus continued to preach and teach in and around the temple, the events of the following days were inevitable.

Above: *One of the very last peaceful days Jesus had was an evening he spent in the home of Mary and Martha. It was the quiet before the final storm of the last week of his life. Dalsgaard's painting is a rare glimpse of the relaxed Jesus visiting with his friends.* Facing page: *When Jesus saw how the merchants and bankers were using the temple grounds, literally pushing worshipers out, he took direct and commanding action. He angrily pushed the merchants out, making a change that the temple leaders should have done years before.*

THE FINAL HOURS

* * *

ASSOVER WAS ISRAEL'S ANNUAL CELEBRATION of their deliverance by God from slavery in Egypt. This ancient tradition reenacted the night when each family had been instructed to prepare a meal of lamb and herbs, to spread some of the lamb's blood on the doorposts of their homes, and then to eat the evening meal standing up so that they would be ready to leave Egypt on a moment's notice (Exodus 12).

The anticipation, the anxiety, and the fear were intense that evening as the angel of death went through the land and "passed over" every house that had blood on the doorpost (the families of Israel). Those families without the identifying blood over the door (Egyptian families) suffered the death of the eldest son. When the Pharaoh demanded that they leave, Moses led these slave families out of Egypt toward the freedom of a new life in a new land. In Jesus' day, some twelve hundred years later, Israel continued to observe a week-long festival to remember the goodness of God in delivering them from slavery.

In the final hours of his life, Jesus gathered his disciples together for the Passover meal. As part of the evening's activities, Jesus shed his outer robe, took a basin of water, and washed the feet of the disciples—something normally done by a servant. When Jesus came to Peter, Peter objected, saying that it would be more appropriate for him (Peter) to wash the feet of Jesus. But Jesus explained that he was making a final point—his followers were to be servants of other people.

Above: *One of the last things Jesus did for his disciples was to take on the role of servant and wash his disciples' feet. Peter, who was still struggling with this new concept that Jesus was teaching, at first objected but then agreed. He did not really understanding what it all meant, however, until later.* Facing page: *We are quite familiar with the traditional Last Supper where everyone is sitting on one side of the table, but Rubens, the artist, more accurately clusters the disciples around Jesus in a more informal setting.*

Then Jesus made an announcement that mystified the disciples; he told them that he would be betrayed by a person sitting at the table with them that evening. The disciples could not imagine what he was talking about, and they looked at each other in total disbelief. Simon Peter finally mustered the courage to tell John (who was sitting next to Jesus), "Ask him who he is talking about!" Jesus turned to Judas and said, "Do what you are going to do." Judas got up and left, but the disciples did not make the connection, thinking he was leaving to get something needed for the meal.

If we know who Judas was, we can better understand what he was trying to do. Judas was the treasurer of the group, and he may have been a member of the radical Zealots, who believed the messiah would liberate Israel by driving out the Romans.

Seeing Jesus take direct action by driving the merchants out of the temple must have been exhilarating for Judas, for it told him that there was still hope that Jesus would become the messiah the Zealots were looking for, if given the right set of circumstances. Judas may have been hoping to incite Jesus to zealotlike rebellion, or he may have been frustrated by Jesus' refusal to be a military messiah. Either way, Judas was the betrayer of Jesus.

Judas went to the chief priests and promised to hand Jesus over to them in a place where they could make a quiet arrest with minimal disturbance. In payment for this

The disciples simply did not understand the intensity of the crisis facing Jesus. While they sleep, angels minister to Jesus in one of the most critical nights of his life. Here in the garden, he made the decision, while conversing with God, that he would continue the mission he had begun.

service, he was given thirty pieces of silver (the payment for the life of a servant who was accidentally killed).

While this was happening, Jesus and the disciples completed their meal in Jerusalem, then left the house to go to the Garden of Gethsemane just outside the city. When they arrived, they went to a quiet place where Jesus asked the disciples to pray that they might have the courage to face the next few days. Jesus then went a little further into the garden to pray alone.

The prayer reveals an emotional insight into the human spirit of Jesus. In this most intimate prayer conversation, Jesus asks God, "Isn't there some other way we can do this?" The prospect of death and the excruciating pain of a Roman crucifixion had to be overwhelming in Jesus' mind. But the answer came back, "No, there is no other way." The severity of this moment is impressed upon us as Jesus repeats his request to God for an alternate plan. "He went away and prayed, saying the same words" (Mark 14:39).

Then Jesus added, "If this is how it must be, I am willing to do it!"

The disciples' pathetic level of understanding is shown as Jesus went back to the place where he had asked them to pray. He found them sleeping; they had no comprehension of the life-and-death crisis facing their best friend and teacher. But they did not have to wait long to find out

The New Testament story follows the path of Jesus and all that he endured the last week of his life. But there was a second story unfolding, involving secret meetings, conferences, and furtive conversations among the official Jewish leadership as they tried to orchestrate the arrest and removal of Jesus.

Judas, with his assortment of temple guards and soldiers, arrived in the garden. Jesus, seeing what was developing, immediately stepped forward with the question, "Who are you looking for?" When they said, "Jesus of Nazareth," he responded, "I am the one you are looking for. Let these people go, they are not involved."

Jesus saw that a confrontation was developing that might easily lead to bloodshed, so he stepped forward and offered himself in order to defuse the situation and save the lives of others. But Peter pulled out a sword and sprang to the defense of Jesus, taking a swing at the first person he saw (who happened to be a servant of the high priest). When the servant ducked to avoid being killed, Peter caught the man's head with a glancing blow, cutting off his ear. Jesus reprimanded Peter for using his sword, telling him, "If I need protection, all I have to do is ask God, and I will have 70,000 angels here right now!" Jesus was arrested, put in chains, and taken to court in Jerusalem for trial.

The arrest of Jesus in the Garden of Gethsemane was a mixture of intrigue, violence, and confusion. Peter lashed out with his sword to protect Jesus, while Jesus was more concerned about protecting those around him. The artist includes half a battalion of Roman soldiers—in truth there were only a few temple soldiers.

The Jewish court process was a complicated matter, and it must have been exhausting for Jesus. Throughout the night and into the early morning hours, he was taken through a series of six preliminary hearings to determine the charges, gather evidence, and set the proceedings. This was important because his accusers needed charges that would convince the Roman government this itinerant preacher-teacher presented a major threat to the security of the nation. The final charges brought against Jesus were subversion of the nation, opposing the government by refusing payment of taxes, and claiming to be a king.

When Jesus was later brought before Pilate, Pilate looked at the charges and confronted Jesus with a very direct question: "Are you the king of the Jews?" Jesus answered, "Those are your words," implying, "I have never claimed to be a king." When he heard that, Pilate declared, "You don't have a case against this man." This interchange between Jesus and Pilate is fascinating and instructive. Throughout the process, we have the impression that Jesus is not the one on trial. He spoke rarely, once reminding the court that he had done nothing in secret so he had nothing to hide; once admonishing an officer for physically striking him (physical violence was not permitted in court); and several times responding to questions from Pilate.

Pilate tried every legal maneuver he could think of to have the case dismissed. He tried to restate the charges; he twice declared Jesus innocent; he proposed a less severe alternate sentence of whipping Jesus; he announced there was not enough evidence; he even reached back into legal history to revive a long-forgotten Roman custom of having a symbolic prisoner release at Passover. But the Jewish

After his arrest, Jesus was taken to the Roman officials so that official charges against him could be placed. The Jewish leadership was forced to cooperate with Rome, although they had an intense dislike for the Roman government, because Rome did not permit Jews to execute criminals. Only the Roman government had the authority to order capital punishment.

leadership vehemently objected to each attempt, and Pilate chose not to take a stand against the demands of the Sanhedrin, even though he often defied the Jewish leaders. Finally, in frustration, Pilate announced he was taking himself off the case. He told the Jewish leaders, "What you do now is your responsibility."

The Jewish leaders seized Jesus, the crowd erupted into a mob shouting for his crucifixion, and Jesus was led away to be executed. The point of no return had been passed; the most bizarre failure of justice in human history had developed its own momentum and was moving toward fatal reality.

The Roman army was well trained in execution by crucifixion. As with all prisoners about to be crucified, Jesus was stripped (prisoners to be crucified forfeited all rights of human dignity), his arms were wrapped around a huge post and tied, and he was whipped with leather straps that had sharp pieces of metal fastened at the ends. These metal pellets tore his skin to shreds, ripping out chunks of flesh, causing massive bleeding.

Pilate was the local Roman governor who tried to avoid taking action against Jesus by symbolically washing his hands of the whole affair. But the Jewish leaders refused to allow it, threatening to report him to Caesar if he did not do what they wanted.

Jesus was then taken to the place of execution within a formation of eight soldiers, which was led by two soldiers carrying a sign announcing the charges and the sentence (so people would know what he did and be warned not to commit the same crime). Adding insult to injury,

Jesus was forced to carry the horizontal crossbar on this public march. But he collapsed from exhaustion, and a Jewish man from Africa was pulled out of the crowd to carry the cross for him.

At the place of crucifixion, the crosspiece was laid flat on the ground, and the prisoner was nailed to it with large spikes through the wrists and the ankles. The cross was then placed upright in the ground, and the soldiers waited until the crucified victim died.

A reasonable estimate is that on average for any given day, Rome crucified dozens of people. It was their way of keeping the population under rigid control.

A Roman crucifixion was not only horribly painful, it was a very public spectacle, usually alongside a well-traveled highway, so that the pain and the humiliation of the event was seen by everyone who used that road. Some people used this occasion to jeer and ridicule, making fun of Jesus in his dying moments by mocking him with distortions of what he had said—promising to believe in him if he could convince God to save him now!

We don't often think about how people who were close to Jesus felt as he suffered. When Mary accepted the message of the angel to be the mother of the Messiah, she probably had no idea how the story would end. Here Mary says good-bye to her beloved son. Within a few hours he was dead.

For the family and a cluster of close friends who had come to this place of death, this was an experience beyond all human description. They stood in total numbness and disbelief at what was happening to someone they knew and loved. Jesus was not alone in his suffering that day outside Jerusalem.

Death by crucifixion was a slow process; people would often hang for days in the blazing sun before their bodily

No scene in religious art is as familiar as the crucifixion of Jesus. It reveals the evil of the world and shows the answer of a redeeming, loving God. The crucifixion of Jesus was a lonely experience, despite the surrounding criminals, soldiers, curious folk passing by, friends, and family. All segments of society participated in the event, and Jesus' death was a statement by God for all of humanity.

systems finally stopped. Mercifully, the death of Jesus came relatively quickly. During those hours on the cross, Jesus likely slipped in and out of consciousness. But Jesus did ask God to forgive the people who were crucifying him; he had a very short exchange with two thieves who were crucified with him; he made one brief comment to his mother; and then he asked John to take responsibility for her care.

Mark reports that Jesus was crucified at nine o'clock in the morning. Around noon a strange darkness came over the whole region and lasted for three hours, and at three o'clock in the afternoon Jesus died. The final testimony to the life of Jesus came from a most unusual source. A Roman centurion standing guard at the cross saw how Jesus died and responded with a simple, innocent faith statement: "Surely, this man was innocent!"

Jewish custom said that dead bodies should not be left in public view, and because the sabbath was coming in just three hours, things had to be done quickly. An influential community leader named Joseph, from the nearby town of Arimathea, went to Pilate and arranged for custody of the body of Jesus. He and another prominent Jewish teacher named Nicodemus, along with the women who had been at the cross, took the body, wrapped it in a temporary burial shroud, and placed it in a private tomb that had never been used before. They then returned to their homes to grieve through the most painful sabbath they had ever experienced.

The Jewish leadership, having achieved their goals, were still very nervous. They had not forgotten Jesus' prediction that he would rise after three days, even though they knew this was impossible. They asked Pilate to place guards at his temporary tomb for three days so that there could be no chance of fraud on the part of the friends of Jesus. They feared that someone would move the body of Jesus, then claim that he had been raised from the dead. Pilate agreed to their request, making a statement that Christians have repeated ever since: "You have a guard of soldiers; go make it [the tomb] as secure as you can" (Matthew 27:65). The tomb was sealed, the Roman guard was put in place, and the quiet of the sabbath fell over the land.

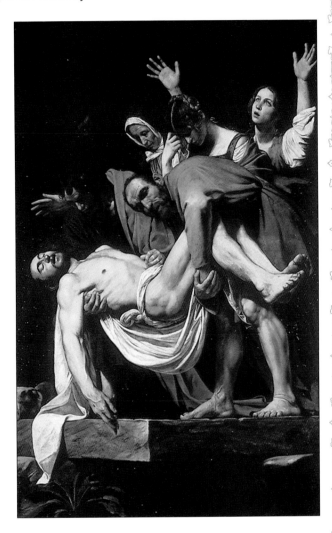

Adding insult to enormous pain, Rome expected family members to take responsibility for crucified victims. Nicodemus, a Pharisee, came to the aid of the family and assisted in doing the legal work to remove the body before the sabbath day began.

EASTER SUNDAY: A NEW BEGINNING

✦ ✦ ✦

FOR THE FAMILY AND FRIENDS OF JESUS, who were overcome with grief and fear, the sabbath day seemed to last forever, and they wondered how they could possibly get through it. How do you meditate on the Scriptures and reflect upon God's goodness when your whole world has just come crashing down around you? The disciples were hiding in secret rooms, behind locked doors, terrified that what had happened to Jesus might also happen to them. The only option seemed to be to stay in hiding and wait for the end of the sabbath so they could finish the painful task of cleaning up Jesus' body for final burial. Until the body was officially buried, they could not begin to bring closure to the events of this chilling week. How do you get on with your life when everything you have lived for in the past three years has just been ripped from your soul?

Some tasks cannot be avoided; you simply have to do them. Early Sunday morning, while the disciples were still hiding, Mary Magdalene, Mary the mother of James, and Salome went to the tomb with spices to wash the blood and dirt from Jesus' body and to wrap it for final burial. They walked slowly down the road, dreading the task that lay ahead. As they approached the garden, they remembered—the stone! How were they going to move it so they could get to Jesus' body? As the tomb came into view, they saw the stone had already been moved. Something was very wrong, and as fear began to creep over them, the women wondered what had happened.

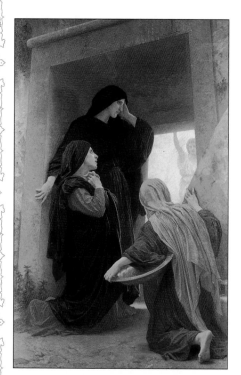

Above: *Many times during the life of Jesus, it was the women who were the most willing to act in times of crisis. Three women went to the tomb to wash and prepare Jesus' body, but Jesus had risen.* Facing page: *Despite his explanation that he would die and rise again, everyone was shocked when Jesus was resurrected. It was not until after they were sure that he was alive again that the disciples finally understood what he had been saying.*

When Mary, Salome, and Mary Magdalene went inside the tomb, they saw that Jesus' body was missing! As they stood there, numbed by fear and grief, an angel told them that Jesus had risen and that they should tell the disciples. Suddenly, the simple task of preparing the body for burial had become a very confusing and frightening experience. Nothing was as they had expected it to be, and they were badly shaken. They ran from the tomb, only to meet Jesus just outside the opening. He confirmed the instructions of the angel.

When the women told the disciples what they had seen and heard, their story was rejected as hysterical nonsense. Peter and John went to the tomb to see what had really happened, but by the time they arrived there were no angels, and the tomb was empty. They saw the empty shroud in which the body had been wrapped, and they did not know what to think. With stark simplicity, John reports that "the disciples went back to their homes" (20:10). The gospel story presents the resurrection of Jesus as a shocking intrusion into their grief. Despite all Jesus' teachings, it was so unexpected that no one knew how to handle it.

The Gospel of Matthew does tell about a conspiracy at the tomb, but it was not the disciples who were involved. The guards who had been posted at the tomb were not there when the women arrived. These Roman guards had seen the empty tomb, and they were so overwhelmed they went immediately to the chief priests and reported what had happened. For the Jewish priests, this was the worst possible turn of events, and they could not allow the public to know the truth. So they gave the guards a substantial amount of money and told them to say, "His disciples came by night and stole him away while we were asleep" (Matthew 28:13). The leaders promised to protect

Facing page: When Mary met Jesus that Sunday morning, she did not immediately recognize him. When she knew who he was, she fell at his feet in worship. Not wanting to let go of that moment, she reached out to take hold of him, but Jesus would not yet let her touch him.

the soldiers if this story got them into any trouble with their superiors. Evidently this did not happen, for Matthew reports (thirty to fifty years later when he wrote his Gospel) that this story was still being told among the Jewish people as an explanation of what happened that morning at the tomb.

While Mary Magdalene, Salome, and Mary the mother of James were the first to see Jesus after the resurrection, they were certainly not to be the last! The appearances of the resurrected Jesus were unpredictable and completely unexpected.

That Easter Sunday afternoon, a man named Cleopas and a friend were on their way home to Emmaus, grieving over the devastating events of the past four days, when a third man fell in step with them. They shared their agony over what had happened to the one whom they had believed was the redeemer of Israel. While acknowledging they had heard the women's report about the empty tomb, they rejected the story as a wild rumor because they knew that death was final.

People who met the risen Lord responded in amazing ways, even taking significant risks. Night travel was not safe in Palestine, but ignoring the risk, the two men who broke bread with Jesus ran the seven miles from Emmaus to Jerusalem to tell the disciples that they had seen Jesus.

The stranger recounted a most interesting interpretation of Old Testament texts, illustrating how the death of the messiah would fit into God's plan for human redemption. When they reached Emmaus, Cleopas and his friend invited the stranger to stay with them for supper; they had felt a strange sense of comfort while talking with him. As they sat down at the table, the stranger took the initiative: He reached for the bread and, after offering a short prayer, he broke the bread and shared it with them. This simple gesture suddenly opened their eyes. They had seen this before, and they recognized him—it was Jesus! But the instant they recognized him, he was gone. The two men jumped up from the table and raced back to Jerusalem to tell the disciples about their incredible experience, only to be told that Peter had also seen Jesus. The amazing reality

Appearances by Jesus came in unusual circumstances. He walked with two men on the road to Emmaus, then ate supper with them. When Jesus broke the bread, one of them, Cleopas, recognized him.

of the resurrection was starting to become believable—Jesus was alive, and he was out there somewhere!

While the men were talking about what was happening, Jesus himself suddenly stood in their midst. At first the disciples thought they were seeing a ghost. (Unbelievable ideas are not easily understood, even if you are confronted with visible proof!) Jesus urged them to look at him and to touch him. Still the disciples could not believe their eyes, so Jesus asked for something to eat. After accepting and eating a piece of broiled fish, Jesus explained to the disciples the meaning of everything that had happened over the past few days.

Some people are harder to convince than others. Thomas, like most of us, needed firsthand experience and proof that Jesus was alive. When Jesus met with the disciples a few days later, he told Thomas to stick his finger into the nail holes in his hands.

Jesus met with small groups of believers in quiet places. Some people wonder why Jesus did not appear to unbelievers; for they assume that a personal appearance would have so completely proven the truth about who Jesus was that it would have forever silenced the opposition. In fact, Jesus did appear to an unbeliever—his own brother James, who had been quite skeptical about what Jesus was doing during his ministry. James was converted by the experience, later becoming the leader of a community of believers in Jerusalem.

Most of these appearances were used by Jesus to educate the disciples on what they should do now that they knew he was alive, showing them that in fact he was the Messiah Israel was looking for. After a brief interlude of about six weeks, Jesus ascended back to heaven, leaving the disciples standing and looking up into the sky. They wondered what had happened, and they felt very much alone.

The task of telling the world about Jesus, of calling people to accept the message of God's love, and of spreading the word about how God's people should live in this new kingdom now fell to this small group of followers who had seen and listened to the resurrected Jesus.

The success of everything Jesus had done would now depend upon these men and women finding a way to keep the story alive. Would they remember? Would they do it right? Would they survive long enough to give direction to this new movement? Would anybody believe them? Jesus had promised they would not be left alone, but as they stood there after the ascension, wondering what to do next, they must have marveled at the wisdom of God. He entrusted the redemption of the world to such fallible human beings.

From such a beginning, history was transformed. Two thousand years later, millions alive today call themselves Christian.

Castera Bazile, a Haitian artist, places the ascension of Jesus in a contemporary Haitian setting. There are two first-century men, along with modern Haitian villagers, in the scene. Jesus is surrounded by angels for his return to heaven.

THE MEANING OF A LIFE

✦ ✦ ✦

T IS RELATIVELY EASY to tell the story of Jesus; what he said, what he did, and where he went. But when we try to explain why Jesus came and what his life means, then the answers are not quite so simple. We can agree that the life of Jesus has had great significance for humanity, but as soon as we share our various ideas on exactly why that life was so important, we find our explanations do not always agree. These different explanations about the significance of Jesus' life lead Christians into serious debates and even vehement arguments among themselves. Who was Jesus, and what is the meaning we should find in his life here on Earth?

Any teacher knows that a picture is worth a thousand words, but an experience is worth a thousand pictures. In the Old Testament, God communicated with humanity through the Torah (law) and through the preaching of the prophets. The message, however, soon became twisted into something quite different. People interpreted the revelation of God in ways that met their own needs. They did not trust that God had their best interests at heart in giving the law and in sending the prophets. In the New Testament we are told that in Jesus, God took on human form and lived among us, experiencing with us the stresses and frustrations of being human, while showing us the true nature and will of God. That sounds so simple, but it is the central point made by the Gospel of John: "In the beginning was the Word, and the Word was with God. . . . And the Word became flesh and lived among us, and we have

The story of Jesus begins with the birth of a child. There is something very special about a child being born. A new baby raises human hopes and dreams for the future. The birth of Jesus was a statement of hope, not only for Mary, but for all humanity.

The Gruenewald image of the resurrection focuses on the power and drama of the experience. Symbols of power abound as soldiers fall in fear and Christ is framed in the divine light of the sun, signifying the start of a new day and a new era.

seen his glory.... No one has ever seen God. It is God the only Son, who is close to the Father's heart, who has made him known" (John 1:1,14,18).

Those words from John are beautifully simple, but they contain a very profound truth—that in Jesus, we mortal human beings have been given a glimpse of God that was never before possible. And that is good news for all humanity.

THE TIMES OF JESUS

❖ ❖ ❖

ESUS' STORY IS ROOTED in the ancient history of the Jewish people. The Hebrew sages foretold the coming of the messiah, who would bring salvation and deliverance. But Jesus was also a person of his specific time in history—religion, world events, and the culture had an effect on the human person Jesus was. The Palestinian world of his day was very much an integral part of Jesus' life and ministry.

THE PEOPLE AND THEIR HISTORY

❖ ❖ ❖

BEHIND THE SCENES

THE EARLY HISTORY OF THE JEWS told them that they were selected by God for special favor. The patriarch Abraham and his family migrated from their home in Mesopotamia seeking the promised land, inspired by a promise from God to make from Abraham a great nation that would be a blessing to the entire world. How could one man accomplish this? Ultimately, the Jews would come to hope for a messiah from the lineage of Abraham who would bring redemption to all humankind.

The advent of the messiah, however, would not occur before a centuries-long struggle by the people of Israel, who at times persevered through trials and at other times paid a high price for disobeying God's commands. Through a long and turbulent history, hope remained that the promise to Abraham would be fulfilled.

Above: *Pierre I. Mignard strikes a balance between masculinity and sensitivity in his "Christ With the Broken Reed," which portrays a gentle, pensive Galilean who "will not break a bruised reed or quench a smoldering wick until he brings justice to victory" (Matthew 12:20). Facing page: Josef Molar's "The Departure of Abraham" depicts the Hebrew patriarch leading his family from Ur. Abraham sets his face resolutely toward the promised land.*

To understand what it means to call Jesus "Christ" or the "Messiah," it is useful to understand the struggles of his people, the Jews. Their history sets the stage for his life.

CHOSEN PEOPLE–PROMISED LAND

Sometime after 2000 B.C., a wandering band of nomads was led by the patriarch Abraham (then named Abram) across the fertile crescent of the Middle East into the land of Canaan. Abraham was seventy-five years old when he received a command and prophecy from Yahweh, whom the Hebrews would come to recognize as the One True

God: "Now the Lord said to Abram, 'Go from your country and your kindred and your father's house to the land that I will show you. I will make of you a great nation, and I will bless you, and make your name great, so that you will be a blessing. I will bless those who bless you, and the one who curses you I will curse; and in you all the families of the earth shall be blessed'" (Genesis 12:1–3).

Jan Livens captures an obedient Isaac as his agonizing yet trusting father Abraham prepares to offer him as a sacrifice on Mount Moriah according to the Lord's command. Some scholars believe that Mount Moriah is the same site where the temple, the center of Jewish sacrificial worship, was later built by Solomon.

After Abraham settled in Canaan under God's direction, his clan grew in number. But as the patriarch approached one hundred years of age, Abraham still lacked that requisite of Eastern culture—an heir to perpetuate his name. His wife Sarah laughed incredulously when she overheard the angelic messengers confirm what God had told Abraham: "Sarah shall bear you a son, and you shall name him Isaac. I will establish my covenant with him as an everlasting covenant for his offspring after him" (Genesis 17:19). Abraham's promised heir, whose name is derived from the Hebrew word for laughter, was born to Sarah soon after.

The major event of Isaac's life occurred as a young man, when his father Abraham was tested. God commanded him, "Take your son, your only son Isaac, whom you love, and go to the land of Moriah, and offer him there as a burnt offering on one of the mountains that I shall show you" (Genesis 22:2). Amazingly, Abraham was being asked to perform what seemed to be a human sacrifice after the pattern of his pagan neighbors. His unswerving faith in Yahweh, however, was evident as he went with his son to Mount Moriah. At the dramatic moment when his knife was poised above his son, God intervened and Isaac was saved. Christians see this story as foreshadowing God's sacrifice of his own son, the Messiah Jesus, and the salvation of all confirmed by his resurrection.

The divine promise that Abraham's descendants would become a great nation was confirmed to Isaac's son Jacob. He raised twelve sons, and they later moved to Egypt after reuniting with their once-rejected brother Joseph, who had become a high-ranking official under Pharaoh. But when Joseph died and a new Pharaoh arose, the Israelites were thrust into slavery. After spending almost three hundred years building the cities and monuments of Egypt, the bone-weary Israelites "groaned under their slavery, and cried out. Out of the slavery their cry for help rose up to God. God heard their groaning, and God remembered his covenant with Abraham, Isaac, and Jacob" (Exodus 2:23–24). This covenant included the promise of the land of Canaan as the enduring possession of the Israelites.

The task of leading the Hebrews out of Egypt and into the promised land fell upon Moses, a man who would become a central figure in the history of Israel. After a series of dramatic calamities culminating in the Passover, when God "passed over" the children of Israel while striking dead the firstborn sons of the Egyptians, Pharaoh was finally convinced to let the Israelites leave Egypt.

The story of the nation of Israel begins with the Exodus. With Egypt behind them, their destiny, the promised land, lay ahead. Because of their fear of the people of Canaan, however, the Israelites balked at occupying the land. God therefore made the Israelites remain in the

In this classical painting of Joseph in Egypt, the Hebrew patriarch receives his brothers, who have come to Egypt during a famine to buy grain. They are alarmed to find their sibling, whom they had earlier sold into slavery, not only alive but risen to second-in-command under Pharaoh. To show homage to Joseph, they approach him on bended knee.

THE LAW: EXCERPTS FROM LEVITICUS 19

The purpose of the Mosaic law was to instruct in the worship and service of God as well as to provide a framework for governing human relations. The strict prohibition of idolatry—a central feature of the polytheistic culture out of which the Israelites were called—is emphasized repeatedly in the Mosaic law: "Do not turn to idols or make cast images for yourselves: I am the Lord your God" (Leviticus 19:4).

The call to holiness, "Speak to all the congregation of the people of Israel and say to them: You shall be holy, for I the Lord your God am holy" (Leviticus 19:2), is mirrored in the ceremonial aspects of the law, which were intended as object lessons or illustrations of more fundamental ethical principles: "When you offer a sacrifice of well-being to the Lord, offer it in such a way that it is acceptable on your behalf. It shall be eaten on the same day you offer it, or on the next day; and anything left over until the third day shall be consumed in fire. If it is eaten at all on the third day, it is an abomination; it will not be acceptable" (Leviticus 19:5–7).

A concern for the rights of the poor and unfortunate is evident throughout the law: "You shall not strip your vineyard bare, or gather the fallen grapes of your vine-

yard; you shall leave them for the poor and the alien: I am the Lord your God" (Leviticus 19:10).

The Mosaic law also emphasizes the fundamental principles that govern human relations and provide social order: "You shall not steal; you shall not deal falsely; and you shall not lie to one another" (Leviticus 19:11).

Another fundamental principle is that of justice: "You shall not render an unjust judgment; you shall not be partial to the poor or defer to the great: with justice you shall judge your neighbor" (Leviticus 19:15).

In contrast to other known codes of law from the ancient Near East, the law of Moses is concerned not only

with relationships but also with attitudes of the heart: "You shall not hate in your heart anyone of your kin.... You shall not take vengeance or bear a grudge against any of your people, but you shall love your neighbor as yourself: I am the Lord" (Leviticus 19:17–18).

The command "love your neighbor as yourself" also demonstrates a concern for justice toward the least fortunate in society. These included widows and orphans as well as "strangers"—those foreigners who lived and worked among the Israelites. "For the Lord your God is God of gods and Lord of lords, the great God, mighty and awesome, who is not partial and takes no bribe, who executes justice for the orphan and the widow, and who loves the strangers, providing them food and clothing. You shall also love the stranger, for you were strangers in the land of Egypt" (Deuteronomy 10:17–19).

In the New Testament this command to accept those outside the Israelite nation would, after some discussion and controversy among the early Christians, contribute to the universal appeal of the gospel as Peter, Paul, and the other apostles preached the new faith to the Gentiles.

desert for forty years, until this group of Israelites died and a new generation appeared.

During this lengthy period of wandering in the desert, God gave to Moses, on Mount Sinai, a system of ceremonial and moral law intended to govern the social relations among the Israelites as well as their moral conduct and worship. This Mosaic law was designed to promote personal freedom and justice within the context of obedience to Yahweh. The appeal of the Mosaic law was great compared to the surrounding polytheistic (worship of many gods) culture, which knew only oppression by the gods.

Following the giving of the law and many years of wilderness wandering, the Israelites were permitted to enter Canaan under the leadership of Moses' lieutenant, Joshua. The highlight of the conquest of Canaan was the fall of Jericho, which stood just across the River Jordan at the gate of the land. From Jericho, in a series of stunningly successful campaigns, the Israelites captured many Canaanite cities and firmly established themselves in the land.

This painting by Raphael depicts the fall of Jericho, in which Joshua led the battle. This event allowed the Israelites into the land of Canaan, the promised land.

DYNASTY AND TEMPLE: THE LEGACY OF DAVID

After the people of Joshua's time passed away, a new generation forgot that the divine promise giving them the land of Canaan was dependent on faithfulness to God. Many Israelites "took [Canaanite] daughters as wives for themselves, and their own daughters they gave to their sons; and they worshiped their gods" (Judges 3:6).

During this time, we read that "there was no king in Israel; all the people did what was right in their own eyes"

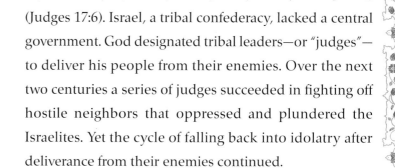

(Judges 17:6). Israel, a tribal confederacy, lacked a central government. God designated tribal leaders—or "judges"—to deliver his people from their enemies. Over the next two centuries a series of judges succeeded in fighting off hostile neighbors that oppressed and plundered the Israelites. Yet the cycle of falling back into idolatry after deliverance from their enemies continued.

Finally, the people approached Samuel, the last judge, asking him to appoint a king to unite and govern the people after the pattern of strong neighbors like the Philistines. The next day Samuel anointed a young man named Saul as king. Saul eventually gained the upper hand over the Philistines, but his reign was marked by willful disobedience against God. One day the aged Samuel sent Saul this fateful message: "The Lord has torn the kingdom of Israel from you this very day, and has given it to a neighbor of yours, who is better than you" (1 Samuel 15:28).

Israel's first king was Saul, the tall, handsome son of Kish, from the tribe of Benjamin. Chosen by God and secretly anointed by Samuel, Saul was an able leader and military commander. He later became a tragic figure whose presumption and disobedience led to his break with Samuel and rejection by God.

This neighbor was a young shepherd named David, from the town of Bethlehem and the tribe of Judah. David showed early success as a warrior, bravely killing the Philistine giant Goliath and leading Saul's army in several battles. The envy of Saul was aroused, however, when the people made David their hero, singing, "Saul has killed his thousands, and David his ten thousands" (1 Samuel 18:7). David fled from Saul and lived as a fugitive for several years until Saul's death in battle. After Saul met his end, David mourned Saul, and this attitude toward his longstanding adversary may help explain why Israel's foremost warrior-king was given the title "a man after [God's] own heart" (1 Samuel 13:14).

David took the throne about 1010 B.C. and ruled until 970 B.C. The years of his rule and those of his son Solomon are often called the Golden Age of Israel's history. After defeating the Philistines, David conquered Jerusalem, which made an ideal, centrally located capital for his united Israel. David wanted to build a sanctuary for the Lord, but God denied him permission because he had been a man of war. It would be left to Solomon to construct the most important and impressive edifice in Jerusalem: the temple.

Solomon extended the city walls to the north to create an area for the temple and other royal buildings. The temple in Jerusalem had an important and unique purpose. It was not designed as a place of public worship or prayer but to isolate the unapproachable divine Essence living within. The structure was one hundred and five feet long by thirty-five feet wide and fifty-two feet high. It was surrounded by a courtyard, in which stood an altar for sacrifices and a massive cauldron of water for purification. Only priests could enter the temple proper; other Israelites had access to the outer courtyard.

Inside the temple was another inner sanctuary called the Holy of Holies, which could only be entered by the high priest. Inside this chamber, its walls and floors overlaid with gold, was that most sacred and mysterious object of the Israelites: the ark of the covenant, symbol of the guiding presence of God.

The ark was a wooden chest overlaid with gold, about four feet long and two feet deep and wide. Images of two golden cherubim—angelic beings—stood at each end of the cover, overshadowing it with their outstretched wings. The ark contained a pot of manna (bread from heaven supplied to the Israelites during their wilderness wandering), the rod of Moses' brother Aaron, and the tablets of the Ten Commandments. After traveling with the Israelites through many turbulent times, it came to rest in the temple of Solomon, where it remained until it was plundered by the conquering Babylonians centuries later.

In the Hebrew Bible, the temple is called the "house of God" because it was the sacred place for Israel's worship of Yahweh. Because he was a man of war, King David was not permitted to build the temple, and the task of building a house of prayer and sacrifice to the Lord fell to his son Solomon.

The prosperity of Solomon's reign disguised an underlying weakness. Idolatry was reintroduced to the nation through some of Solomon's many foreign wives, and the Bible attributes the rapid demise of the nation to the influence of pagan religion. In only the next generation, ten tribes split to form the northern kingdom of Israel, while two remained as the southern kingdom of Judah, which included Jerusalem. This period of the Divided Kingdom was marked by decline and moral decay. Prophets arose to denounce idolatry, but they were ignored or persecuted by Jewish leaders.

Divine judgment loomed on the horizon. The powerful Assyrian Empire was expanding into the eastern

"By the rivers of Babylon—there we sat down and there we wept when we remembered Zion" (Psalm 137:1). The mournful longing of the Judeans for their homeland is portrayed here as they sit along the banks of the River Chebar mentioned by Ezekiel.

Mediterranean from the north. In 722 B.C., the northern kingdom fell to bloody conquest, and thousands of survivors were deported. Foreigners resettled the north, and the area became known as "Galilee of the Gentiles." One day the region would become associated with Israel's great hope, the Messiah, for Jesus would grow up and minister in the region of Galilee.

The people of the southern kingdom of Judah avoided conquest by the Assyrians, but they continued along the same path of spiritual decline as their northern neighbors. Despite the warnings of the great prophet Jeremiah, Judah continued to rebel against God and, in 586 B.C., was conquered by a new invader from the east, Babylon. Jerusalem and its temple were destroyed, and as in the case of Israel, many of the defeated Jews were deported.

The Jews exiled to Babylon were treated relatively well, and some prospered. When the Babylonians themselves were conquered less than a hundred years later, the new power, Persia, allowed the exiled Jews to return to their homeland and rebuild Jerusalem. Eventually the temple was rebuilt, and the Jews experienced a religious revival.

Under the leadership of the priest Ezra, the Jews pledged themselves to end idolatry and to study and obey God's law. They eventually developed the synagogue as a place to meet for worship, prayer, and instruction. Experts on the Scriptures became known as scribes or rabbis, and they devoted their lives to the study and practice of the law. By the time of Jesus, these religious leaders were most closely identified with the sect known as Pharisees, and so in the gospels the words *scribe, rabbi, lawyer,* and *Pharisee* are virtually interchangeable.

"For Ezra had set his heart to study the law of the Lord, and to do it, and to teach the statutes and ordinances in Israel" (Ezra 7:10). Pedro Berruguete captures the earnestness of Ezra, a priest and a scribe who brought spiritual renewal to the Jewish community in Jerusalem, which was struggling against threats to its ethnic and religious identity.

This new concern for religious purity led to one controversy that continued through the time of Jesus: the split between the Jews and the Samaritans. The Samaritans, probably a mix of Israelites who were not exiled and some foreign colonists, settled in the area north of Jerusalem and practiced a form of Judaism, eventually building their own temple on Mount Gerizim. From the perspective of the Jerusalem establishment, the population of Samaria was forever suspect as a group of racial and religious half-breeds. It is evident in the gospels that the Samaritans were at that time still a despised people.

Jeremiah pleaded with God that he not forget his people in Exile. He also prayed that God would one day allow them to return to the land of Judea.

Through all this time, through all the turmoil and rebellion and hardships experienced by the Jews, the one constant voice is the prophetic voice offering hope to a people who seem both confused and confusing. The words of Isaiah, Jeremiah, and Ezekiel ring out with the message that although God's people had rebelled and were suffering for it, they would one day know peace and prosperity again. One would come from the lineage of David to restore their fortunes and spirits, one who would proclaim:

> The spirit of the Lord God is upon me,
>   because the Lord has anointed me;
> he has sent me to bring good news to the oppressed,
>   to bind up the brokenhearted,
> to proclaim liberty to the captives,
>   and release to the prisoners;
> to proclaim the year of the Lord's favor,
>   and the day of vengeance of our God;
>   to comfort all who mourn;
> to provide for those who mourn in Zion—
>   to give them a garland instead of ashes,
> the oil of gladness instead of mourning,
>   the mantle of praise instead of a faint spirit.
>   Isaiah 61:1–2

THE ENDURING LEGACY OF GREECE

The military success of Alexander the Great brought with it the triumph of *Hellenism*, the Greek way of life. Alexander died in Babylon in 323 B.C., but the Mediterranean world continued to feel the influence of Greek religion and philosophy, art and architecture, politics and culture. Even the Romans did little more than serve up their own flavor of Hellenism. The Greek language became the language of commerce and diplomacy and eventually the common language of the Mediterranean world for five hundred years. The importance of this for Christianity can hardly be overstated, since the production of the New Testament in Greek gave almost everyone

Strikingly handsome and with the physique of an athlete, Alexander was a consummate leader who, at the age of twenty-three, conquered Greece's formidable enemy, Persia. Tutored as a youth by the philosopher Aristotle, Alexander was a complex personality trained in Greek poetry, ethics, geography, and medicine as well as military strategy.

Above: *Alexander the Great conquered most of the then-known world and gave a new direction to history. Convinced that the eastern limit of the world lay not far beyond the Indus River, he spent three years campaigning in India. A scene from that campaign is preserved in this ancient manuscript.*
Below: *Weakened by wounds and his long march back from India with his army, Alexander succumbed to fever in Babylon on June 13, 323 B.C.*

access to events and ideas that might otherwise have been limited to people who spoke Aramaic or Hebrew. Furthermore, the character of the Greek language influenced Christianity, making it possible to explain difficult ideas in the precise terms of this highly developed language.

Soon after Alexander began his conquest, he marched down the Mediterranean coast, driving the weak Persian forces out of the area. The Jews offered no resistance as the Greek army entered Judea. Jerusalem surrendered voluntarily, and there is no record that Alexander himself entered the area, which had little meaning in his grand plan of conquest. In just a few years, his armies defeated and took over the entire Persian Empire.

Alexander never made it home, dying in Babylon at the age of thirty-two, and his generals divided up his vast territories among themselves. For one hundred years, the Jews enjoyed peace and success under Alexander's gen-

eral Ptolemy and his successors, and their population grew through the establishment of *diaspora* communities (groups of Jews who lived outside of Palestine) throughout the Mediterranean world. One important accomplishment during this time was the translation of the Old Testament into Greek by Jews living in Egypt. Called the *Septuagint,* it became the Bible of the early Christians until the New Testament was added.

In the early second century B.C., successors of Alexander's general Seleucus wrested control of Jewish territory from the Ptolemies, and there began a turbulent period under harsh new taskmasters. Many Jews found that Hellenism posed a direct challenge to their faith, especially when commercial and social activities required acknowledgment of pagan deities. Greek monarchs from Alexander onward accepted worship as divine beings, and they were understood to join the pantheon of gods after death. Devout Jews believed in only one God, and they were forbidden to give divine honors to any mortal.

The clash of religions came to a head when Antiochus IV seized the throne in 175 B.C. The Seleucid kingdom was reeling from internal conflict and external threats. In order to increase his power and wealth, Antiochus determined to take Egypt from the Ptolemies. And in an effort to unify the people in his vast domains, Antiochus decided to enforce the cult of Olympian Zeus. All his subjects were ordered to worship him as Zeus. He took the surname Epiphanes, which means "appearance (of the god)."

Unsuccessful in his bid for Egypt, Antiochus returned north through Judea and decided to ensure his control of the populace by outlawing Judaism and replacing it with his own brand of Hellenism. On pain of death, sabbath observance and temple sacrifices to God were banned,

The Greek practice of bestowing divine honors upon their kings originated with Alexander the Great. Later monarchs, including Antiochus IV, here pictured on a second-century B.C. coin, believed they shared the divine nature of Alexander. The monotheistic Jews considered this practice to be profoundly offensive.

la louenge de dieu tout
puissant ne createur
et redempteur qui par
sa saincte misericorde
voult en ce mortel monde
naistre homme de mere vierge et souffrir
mort et passion par les mains des
iuifs pour nous tous rachetter denfer

au quel par le pechie du premier homme
nous fusmes soubzmis et obligiez
Et pour auoir entendement par
langage francois de lhistoire de la
destruction des iuifs et de la cite de
iherlm ensemble de toute la vie dieeulx
iuifs ce que plusieurs appellent la
vengence de la mort et passion de nre

and the people were required to worship Zeus—and therefore Antiochus.
Pigs, unclean animals to the Jews,
were sacrificed on the altar in
Jerusalem and throughout the area.
The Jews were enraged, and the stage
was set for a religious war that would
have far-ranging historical consequences.

Many Jews, refusing to compromise their faith, fled to the wilderness or died as martyrs. Others
rallied behind an elderly village
priest named Mattathias, who, when
ordered to take part in a sacrifice to
Zeus, instead drew a sword and
killed the emissary of Antiochus and
a Jewish collaborator. Fleeing to the
desert with his five grown sons, Mat-

tathias began to gather resistance forces. He soon died of
old age, but his son Judas proved a brilliant commander,
and his nickname, *makkaba* ("hammer"), gave the movement its name, the Maccabean Revolt.

Against great odds, Jewish freedom fighters under
Judas moved quickly to consolidate control over Judea. In
164 B.C., on the twenty-fifth of the month of Chislev
(roughly December), the Jews were able to purify the temple of the pagan sacrifices, a holiday celebrated today as
the Feast of Dedication, or Hanukkah.

While the Jews won some impressive victories on the
battlefield and recaptured the temple, the war was far from
over. The Seleucids continued to send forces, eventually
defeating the small army of Judas and killing him in battle. The mantle of leadership went to his brother Jonathan,

*Facing page: In this illustration
from a fifteenth-century French
manuscript, pious Jews rally to
Mattathias, spurred by the
murder of priests and the blas-
phemous sacrifice of swine in the
temple. Drawing swords and led
by the Maccabee brothers, they
wage war against Antiochus IV.
Above: "Behold, our enemies
are crushed. Let us go up to
cleanse the sanctuary and
dedicate it," a victorious Judas
Maccabeus was quoted as saying
after routing the Seleucids. In
this sixteenth-century French
manuscript, Judas distributes
captured booty in front of the
pagan shrine to Zeus Olympus.
This Roman shrine defiled the
Jewish temple and was one of the
reasons the Maccabean revolt
began.*

who, through clever diplomacy and timely alliances, secured more territory for the Jews. In exchange for backing a rival claimant to the Seleucid throne who ultimately prevailed, Jonathan took the Jewish high priesthood as a political appointment, thereby outraging orthodox Jews who would only accept a high priest chosen traditionally by lot from certain families. His political gambles finally caught up with him, however, when another hostile Seleucid general captured him by treachery and put him to death.

There was yet another brother to lead the struggle against the Seleucids, and this one, Simon, proved most successful. In a series of political and diplomatic moves, Simon achieved independence for the Jewish people. At the same time, he offended the pious by adopting the characteristics of a Greek monarch. Like his brother, Simon took the office of high priest.

Having a military leader from the wrong family in the high priesthood was an impetus for the formation of a new Jewish sect, the Essenes. This group promoted separation from the temple activities and religious purity

This Hebrew manuscript of the Book of Isaiah was found near Qumran. It is the earliest known copy of any complete book of the Bible. The scroll, written on vellum parchment and dated to the second century B.C., was discovered in 1947 by a Bedouin shepherd boy pursuing a lost goat among the caves along the shores of the Dead Sea.

as the appropriate responses to the moral laxity and Hellenism of their leaders. Members of the sect lived in strict disciplinary communities throughout the region, like Qumran on the shores of the Dead Sea. Here a group of Essenes in the first century A.D. hid copies of the Scriptures and their own writings in caves that were not unearthed until the late 1940s. The Dead Sea Scrolls became the most important archaeological find of the twentieth century, shedding light on the religious life and thought of the Jews at the time of Jesus.

The Essenes lived austerely, avoiding luxury and pleasure, severely disciplining rule-breakers, dressing in white garments, rising before dawn for prayer, eating in silence, and taking ritual baths for purity. Study of biblical law was their primary activity, and they spent much time copying biblical manuscripts and their own religious writings onto large scrolls. In this way, they believed, they were preparing for God to break into history and by his miraculous power restore the Jews (led by the Essenes, of course) to world dominance. Under the leadership of two messiahs, one a priest and the other a military commander, they believed they would prevail in battle, thereby expelling the evil foreigners and their collaborators, the religious establishment of Jerusalem. The temple and people would once again be pure.

Essene life and hopes held little appeal for the majority of Judeans. They were enjoying prosperity under the

Excavations at the Essene settlement at Qumran revealed a sophisticated system for providing water in the arid, desolate environment of the Dead Sea. Also uncovered were numerous public buildings, including a pottery room with communal kilns for baking pottery, a scriptorium for copying religious texts, and a refectory (dining area) containing hundreds of carefully stacked cups and bowls.

Jewish leadership of the Hasmonean kingdom, named after an ancestor of Mattathias. The days of violence were far from over, however. In 134 B.C., Simon and two of his sons were assassinated near Jericho. Simon's surviving son, Hyrcanus, took over, and along with his successors, embarked on an ambitious expansion of Judea's borders.

One noteworthy achievement of Hyrcanus was the annexation of the region south of Judea called Idumea, forcing the people there to convert to Judaism. This might have been an obscure historical footnote were it not for a single Idumean born a century later who became known as Herod the Great. His heritage as an ethnic and religious outsider, from the perspective of tradition-minded Jews, would contribute to the mutual hatred between Herod and the people he ruled.

Herod the Great is portrayed seated on his throne in all his royal splendor in this Byzantine mosaic. Herod was granted the title "King of the Jews" by the Romans, who installed him in Judea to maintain order after the collapse of the Hasmonean kingdom through internal strife. The iron-fisted rule of the half-Jew Herod was resented by all but the most pro-Roman factions of Judean society.

Religious discord in the Hasmonean kingdom grew between factions that would become dominant by the time of Jesus. The aristocratic priestly party known as the Sadducees were in conflict with the Pharisees, who believed in strictly following the law. Unlike the Essenes, the Pharisees did not withdraw from society but chose to pursue reform through education, political pressure, and, at times, armed conflict.

This would happen during the reign of Alexander Janneus, who ruled between 103 and 76 B.C. Janneus was the first Hasmonean to assume the title of king, which the

Pharisees believed could only be claimed by a direct descendant of David. Janneus also earned the wrath of the Pharisees for his Hellenization of Judea's civil administration. Judea erupted in a civil war, which, according to the first-century A.D. Jewish historian Josephus, cost more than fifty thousand lives. Janneus prevailed, however, and by the time he died, the Hasmonean kingdom had reached its greatest limits, achieving a size and prosperity unknown since the days of Solomon.

But the nation was deeply divided, as the powerful but opposing parties of the Sadducees and Pharisees remained locked in bitter conflict. This conflict would find partial rest during the ten-year reign of Salome Alexandra, who succeeded her husband as the first female Jewish monarch and made concessions to the conservative Pharisees. While the Jews were sorting out their internal problems, however, another great power was emerging to end their near-century of independence. The days of the nation of Judea were numbered.

ROMAN CONQUEST

Upon the death of Salome Alexandra in 67 B.C., Judea erupted in a civil war pitting her two sons against one another. Hyrcanus held the title of high priest and was the rightful heir, but his ambitious younger brother, Aristobulus, seized the throne with the support of foreign allies. Rome viewed the instability in Judea as an opportunity to gain territory, which would be a buffer on the border of its expanding empire. Control of the eastern Mediterranean could strengthen Rome against Parthia, her enemy in the East.

Hyrcanus and Aristobulus both appealed for support to the Roman general Pompey, whose army was poised

Roman army standards, such as this artistic re-creation of the Legion X standard, were flags or banners used to identify individual legions. The army marched into battle with its standards, which also included a representation of the eagle, the emblem of Rome, as well as the image of the emperor.

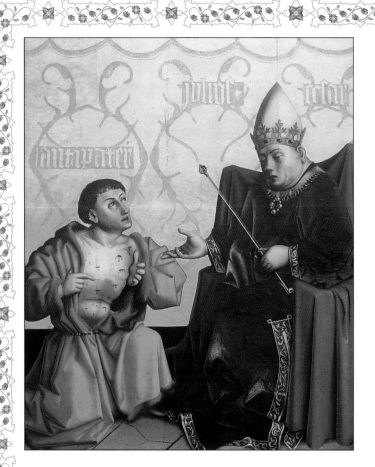

Josephus records that Antipater, father of Herod the Great, "proved himself the most intrepid of fighters, and wounded again and again he bore on almost every part of his body the marks of his valor." Here Antipater appears before Julius Caesar, who awarded him with citizenship and other honors for his bravery on behalf of Rome.

in the north. Instead of helping either, Pompey marched his troops south into Palestine. After a brief but bloody fight, Aristobulus was defeated and Hyrcanus was installed as puppet ruler and high priest. Hyrcanus' success in gaining Rome's patronage was partly due to Antipater, his shrewd Idumean advisor, whose son Herod would soon figure prominently in Jewish history.

The date of 63 B.C. would mark the beginning of seven centuries of Roman rule. The entire eastern Mediterranean area became the province of Syria, with the Jewish population concentrated in territories such as Judea and Galilee. Judea continued to be wracked by division and intrigue, and when Rome itself was weakened by civil war following the death of Julius Caesar in 44 B.C., the Parthians took advantage and invaded. In an attempt to ensure Jewish allegiance, Parthia placed a member of the Hasmonean family on the throne as their servant. Herod, the governor of Galilee, escaped to Rome, where in honor of his father Antipater's faithful allegiance to Rome, he was proclaimed "King of the Jews." But Herod was a king without a country—Judea was still in the hands of his political enemies. Three years later, when Rome gained the strength to supply financial and military backing, Herod returned. Ousting the Parthians, Herod installed himself in Jerusalem and took the title of king.

Herod found the city in shambles, and he set about rebuilding the walls and repairing the temple. But in spite of the prestige gained by these and other ambitious building projects, Herod never won acceptance from the Jews. His heavy taxation and fierce repression of real or suspected opponents, including the murder of many in his own family, made the people fear and despise him. His Idumean ancestry deprived him of status as a pure ethnic Jew, and he could never claim descent from the royal line of David.

Herod's strength was political intrigue, and he rode the shifting winds of Roman power struggles to his own advantage. His most dramatic move was to back the general Octavian—later known as Augustus—in his battle against Mark Anthony in 31 B.C. Anthony and his cohort, Cleopatra, wanted to set up a rival empire in Herod's backyard, Egypt. Herod survived only by choosing the right alliance at the critical moment. In exchange for his support, the new emperor permitted Herod to keep his territory and the title "King of the Jews."

Herod continued his building projects, which included a remarkable port on a coast with no natural harbor. Rolling boulders into the water nearly a third of a mile out to sea, Herod constructed a massive breakwater to shelter ships, and he created a complete Roman-style city that he named Caesarea in honor of the emperor. Caesarea was important not only as a port but also as the headquarters of the Roman army. Out of sensitivity to the Jews, they stationed only a small force in Jerusalem in a fortress overlooking the temple area.

Herod's most famous project was rebuilding the temple in the heart of Jerusalem. The massive structure of the temple mount covers a quarter of the area of the ancient city. Even today visitors to Jerusalem can see the enor-

Gaius Octavius Augustus, the first emperor of Rome, ruled from 27 B.C. to A.D. 14. During his long reign, the Roman world enjoyed a splendid era of civil peace and prosperity. Augustus installed Herod as king of Judea, part of the imperial province of Syria, to create a buffer state against Parthia, Rome's enemy to the east.

The invention by Roman engineers of hydraulic (waterproof) concrete that hardened underwater made possible the construction of the massive breakwater at Caesarea, originally stretching fifteen hundred feet out into the sea. The more modest remains visible in this aerial photo date to the time of the Crusades.

mous blocks of one of the most impressive structures of ancient times. Some blocks used in the massive retaining wall weigh as much as fifty tons or more.

On top of the temple mount, Herod built the temple that Jesus knew. Solomon's original temple was destroyed by the Babylonians and rebuilt on a modest scale when the Jews returned from the Exile. Despite its run-down condition, the Jews at first did not trust Herod to dismantle this holy and beloved building. Only after Herod promised to have all the materials prepared in advance for the new temple did they agree to have the old structure dismantled. He also had one thousand priests trained as masons to build the inner temple, which only priests were allowed to enter.

Herod began construction in 20 B.C., but the massive project was not completed until A.D. 64, although the main part of the construction was finished by Jesus' day. Tragically, just six years after its completion, the temple was destroyed by the Romans following a siege against Jewish freedom fighters in Jerusalem. But before then, the building was a tribute to Herod and the pride of the Jews.

Herod died in old age, suffering an agonizingly slow death from disease, which may have contributed to the paranoia and brutality of his last years. His three surviving sons strove for control over his domain. Augustus divided the kingdom into three parts, with Judea, Samaria, and Idumea going to the eldest, Archelaus. Hated like his father, Archelaus was banished to Gaul after nine years of complaints from the Jews. Rather than allowing the Jews to rule themselves, the Romans began to administer the territory directly through their own officials.

Another of Herod's sons, Antipas, is simply called Herod in the gospels. Herod Antipas also had a reputation for cruelty, an example of which was his execution

These coins date from the rule of Archelaus (4 B.C.–A.D. 6). In accord with the prohibition against graven images found in the second of the Ten Commandments, Jewish coins did not bear the image of any ruler but used typical Judean symbols such as clusters of grapes, wreaths, cornucopias, or the seven-branched lampstand of the temple.

of John the Baptist. Because he controlled Galilee, the Roman procurator Pontius Pilate sent Jesus to Antipas for interrogation prior to his crucifixion. A few years later, Antipas fell out of favor with Caesar and was exiled.

Roman Administration of the Provinces: In the time of Augustus, the ruling emperor when Jesus was born, the Roman Empire had a population of more than seventy million. Augustus was an administrative genius, but the real power of the emperor resided in the loyalty of the army. The presence of Roman armies throughout the vast empire required that Augustus and his successors carefully monitor the loyalty of generals who rose in power and popularity through conquest of new territories. Generals such as Mark Anthony and Pompey were necessary friends and also potential threats.

Roman forces occupying the far-flung provinces of the empire usually consisted of legions, each numbering six thousand men. Each of ten cohorts was commanded by a tribune, and a centurion commanded each group of one hundred soldiers. Several centurions are mentioned in the gospels and the Book of Acts. Curiously, each is mentioned in a positive light. Jesus healed the servant of a centurion in Capernaum, and when he saw the soldier's faith he declared, "Truly I tell you, in no one in Israel have I found such faith" (Matthew 8:10). Three of the gospels mention a centurion at the foot of the cross who, impressed by what he saw and heard, concluded that Jesus was both innocent and divine. In the Book of Acts, the first Gentile convert to the Christian faith was the "god-fearing" centurion Cornelius. Later, another centurion, named Julius, treated Paul kindly when he was charged with accompanying Paul to Rome.

Rule by Procurators: After Herod's son Archelaus was deposed, Rome was concerned about the internal security of Judea, a vital territory controlling important trade routes and forming a land bridge to Egypt and the rest of Africa. To keep the potentially rebellious population in check, Rome governed Judea through a series of governors, known as *procurators*. The fifth of these was Pontius Pilate, who administered the territory from A.D. 26 to 36.

Pilate had many clashes with the Jews, and he often employed force to crush protests. It is somewhat surprising, given his antipathy for the Jews, that Pilate would have agreed with their demand to put Jesus to death. But Pilate may have been in trouble at the time with the paranoid emperor Tiberius. Just around the time of Jesus' crucifixion, Tiberius executed his chief lieutenant, Sejanus, on the charge of treason. Pilate, who had been appointed

This ancient inscription found in Jerusalem commemorates the Legion X Fretensis. The legions, composed of Rome's best soldiers, numbered between forty-five hundred and six thousand soldiers. They were composed of men skilled as spear throwers, commandos, and cavalry. When not engaged in warfare, Roman legions were often employed in various construction projects.

Jorg Breu portrays a sinister Pontius Pilate washing his hands in this distinctly European depiction of the trial of Christ. History confirms that Pilate was intent upon the brutal subjugation of the Jewish people. His procuratorship consisted of one provocation of Jewish sensibilities after another until he was finally removed from office in A.D. 36.

by Sejanus, must have been acting very carefully at this time to show his loyalty to the emperor.

Although the gospels make it clear that he did not think Jesus guilty of any serious crime, he buckled under the pressure of Jewish religious leaders who shouted their loyalty to Caesar and accused Jesus of sedition against Rome. This may have been Pilate's vulnerable spot, and an otherwise violent and reactionary ruler gave in to the demand to have Jesus crucified.

Pilate ruled for several more years, until another crisis brought his rule to an end. This time he cruelly attacked a group of Samaritan worshipers who had gathered on Mount Gerizim, supposing them to be planning a revolt. The Samaritans complained to Pilate's immediate superior, Vitellius, governor of the province of Syria. Pilate was ordered to give an account in Rome, which led to his removal as procurator. Few mourned his leaving, and fewer still could have guessed that his name would live on in infamy.

THE PEOPLE AND THEIR RELIGION

❖ ❖ ❖

ROM THE CALL OF ABRAHAM, to the Ten Commandments, to the teachings of Jesus, the Bible records how God has guided his people and shaped their religion. In return, his pilgrim people strived to show their love and thanksgiving to their God. The Israelites built great temples in Jerusalem, improvised with synagogues while they were in exile and under Roman rule, and instructed their children in the Torah and other holy books and traditions.

The first followers and critics of Jesus were Jewish, yet they came with a variety of political agendas that made for some dramatic moments recorded in Scripture. What role did party politics play in shaping Jesus' teachings? How did the average Jewish person worship at the dawn of the Christian era? Why did all religious establishments, in one form or another, come into conflict with Jesus of Nazareth? The answers to these questions will help us better understand the people and their religion, not only in Jesus' day, but in our era, too.

THE TEMPLE

In Jesus' day, the temple at Jerusalem was thought to be where God lived. It was known as Herod's Temple, named after the Roman vassal king Herod the Great (37–4 B.C.). Herod's Temple was built on the site of, and patterned after, Solomon's Temple (which was built beginning in 966 B.C.). Solomon's Temple had been destroyed in 586 B.C. by Babylon's King Nebuchadnezzar.

Above: *This depiction of Moses holding aloft the Ten Commandments is by Rembrandt. These two tablets of the law epitomized God's self-revelation to a people called to be holy, as God is holy. Facing page: Jesus, regarded by some followers as a second Moses, is depicted here in James J. Tissot's "Jesus Preaching on a Boat." Preaching classes with Jesus were always in session. As he walked along the Galilean lakeshore, by a farmer's vineyard, or into the Jerusalem temple, Jesus hooked his audience with images drawn from all walks of life.*

THREE TEMPLES, ONE SITE

Also built on this site (in 516–515 B.C.) was Zerubbabel's Temple, which is also called the second temple. This second temple was considered inferior to the first house (Ezra 3:12), but it lasted many years longer than Solomon's. Herod rebuilt the temple, beginning in 19 B.C., in order to appease his Jewish subjects. This was to be an elegant, ornate, dazzling, cream-colored reproduction of the original. Herod did not live long enough to see that dream project fulfilled. Yet his successors did, only to see it destroyed a few short years later, in the Jewish–Roman War of A.D. 66–70. Today, the Islamic Dome of the Rock stands on or near where the temple once stood.

Herod's temple building itself occupied a space that was four hundred ninety yards by three hundred twenty-five yards. The sanctuary was fifteen stories high. The temple, trimmed in gold at vast expense, was a source of pride by which people made solemn oaths (Matthew 23:16). Solomon's porch and the temple courtyards provided an open classroom for Jesus to teach in. This was also where scribes debated one another and where merchants and moneychangers did business. The temple's southeast corner had a parapet on top—the so-called "pinnacle of the

Above: *Jesus was tempted by Satan to jump from the highest point of the temple as a test of God's faithfulness and as an attention-getting device to gather a popular following. The highest point was the southeast corner of the temple colonnade, which had a tall parapet wall on top, and from which there was a dramatic a one-hundred-foot drop-off to the Kidron Valley below.* Right: *The golden Dome of the Rock, a Muslim shrine dating from the eighth century, dominates the temple mount in the Old City of Jerusalem. Some scholars believe the shrine is built on or near the site of the ancient temple.*

temple." The temple's pinnacle, to which Jesus would have been brought by Satan (see Matthew 4:5–7), overlooked the city and valley below.

JESUS AND THE TEMPLE

The temple complex was in its forty-sixth year of construction at the time Jesus began his public ministry. Jesus related to this temple in various ways that marked his total ministry. First, Jesus respected the temple as zealously as any pious Jew of his day. To him, it was the "house of God" and "my Father's house" (Matthew 12:4; John 2:16).

Second, while every pious Jew expected the temple to endure several more centuries, Jesus wept as he envisioned its total destruction within "this generation" (Matthew 24:1–2; Mark 13:1–2; Luke 21:5–6). Indeed, forty years later (A.D. 70), Roman legions led by Titus and his father Vespasian invaded Jerusalem to quell a Jewish insurrection. They reduced the temple to rubble.

These first-century coins carry images of Caesar Vespasian. Vespasian was called from the siege of Jerusalem to rule Rome (A.D. 69–79). This left his son Titus in charge of the Roman legions, who finished sacking Jerusalem and destroying the temple in A.D. 70. Rome itself was in a state of disrepair following Nero's rule, and Emperor Vespasian had to raise taxes from the Roman provinces to fund public works projects such as the famous Colosseum.

Third, Jesus made an important self-disclosure and comparison regarding the temple. He taught that he was "greater than" the temple, and he compared the temple to his body, which Jesus claimed would be destroyed and raised up within "three days"! This claim was used against him when witnesses ridiculed what he said and charged him with blasphemy (Matthew 12:6; 26:60–61).

Greater still, according to Jesus and his followers, was the Church, understood metaphorically as the new living temple or "spiritual house," of which Christ was said to be the "chief cornerstone." They believed that God no longer manifested his presence in a building made by human hands, but chose to dwell by his Spirit in a special way among his people.

The gospels record that Jesus and his disciples "went to Capernaum; and when the sabbath came, he entered the synagogue and taught." This excavated synagogue at Capernaum was built of white limestone and dates to the fourth century A.D. It is built over the foundations of a public structure dating to the first century. This earlier structure was in all probability the synagogue built by the Roman centurion and visited by Jesus.

The temple in Jesus' day was also a metaphor for heaven, where "its temple is the Lord God" himself (see Hebrews 9:24). Using temple imagery for heaven, or for the ideal gathering of God's people in worship, was not a distinctly Christian idea, but also occurred in Jewish thought (see Ezekiel 40—48).

SYNAGOGUE

The destruction of Herod's temple forced the Jews once again to fall back on the synagogue approach to Judaism, an approach born during the Exile, in the wake of the first temple's destruction. Jews exiled in Babylon centuries before had needed to recapture their cultural and religious identity, which had been centered in the temple that was destroyed in 586 B.C. But building another temple in Babylon was out of the question. So the captives began meeting in local gatherings or assemblies on the sabbath, everywhere they lived, throughout Persia and the Roman Empire. These scattered congregations came to be known as synagogues.

GIFT OF EXILE

The Jews' desire to study God's Word and learn in community, following their return from captivity in Babylon, gave birth to the era of the "Great Synagogue." This synagogue, first organized by Ezra (465–424 B.C.), consisted of a council of one hundred twenty scribes and lasted one hundred fifty years, until the beginning of the Greek period. This council, which handled theological and political matters, was a precursor to the seventy-member Sanhedrin active at the time of Christ.

In effect, the Babylonian Exile proved to be a blessing in disguise. It produced a new place for Torah studies that could be moved, was adaptable to other cultures, and was lay-oriented in its teaching—much more so than the temple had ever been.

The formal organization of a synagogue required only ten members, with lay leaders instead of priests. Priests were not needed, as the animal sacrifices associated with priestly temple worship could not be practiced in the synagogues. At the end of the Babylonian Exile, the Jewish lay leaders brought this synagogue model with them to

"Mourning Jews in Babylon," by German artist Eduard Bendemann, depicts God's people during the Captivity. Captivity for these Jews meant bondage and deportation from Jerusalem to a foreign land for a period of seventy years. The Exile was seen as a shameful and humiliating punishment by God because of the disobedience of the people.

147

Judah. There it competed, in some sense, with the restoration of temple worship (which was led exclusively by priests). Those Jews who were scattered throughout the ancient world had little or no access to the temple rebuilt at Jerusalem, so they continued to worship in synagogues.

Instead of killing Judaism by destroying the temple, the Babylonians actually helped strengthen Judaism by forcing Jews to adopt new ways of instructing their people in the laws of Moses. Synagogues also served as centers for organizing their community life, administering justice, and teaching their children to read and write.

ORGANIZATION AND OFFICES

By the time of Jesus, these synagogues had become institutionalized, with a formally appointed leadership. There were about five officers—some paid, some volunteer.

A board of elders was made up of devout men who made policy decisions. A ruler of the synagogue, who was appointed by the elder board, acted as the chief executive. He arranged all the worship services and served as facilities coordinator: Jairus, Crispus, and Sosthenes are three examples named in the Bible (see Mark 5:22; Acts 18:8,17).

To ancient Jews, all education was religious education. The role of teaching fell to parents, but after the Exile the first "houses of instruction," or synagogues, in Israel were begun. Elementary schools were organized as a public service in the century before Christ, and they became universally mandated a century later. Only boys were eligible to attend, and they began as early as age five. Synagogue studies continue to this day.

The second functionary was the *hazzan,* or attendant of the synagogue. He was keeper of the sacred scrolls and superintendent for the building. This servant kept the synagogue clean, kept enough oil in the lamps, and taught synagogue classes. Later, this term came to be applied to "ministers of the Gospel." In later Jewish circles, this term applied to the "cantor" (or singer) of prayers.

The third officer functioning in the synagogue was the lay liturgist. This temporary position was filled week-to-week by a homegrown or visiting rabbi ("teacher" or "master"). The rabbi read two Scripture selections: one from the Law (the *Sedrayim*), which rotated on a one-year cycle; and one from the Prophets (the *Haphtorah*), which rotated on a three-year cycle.

Both readings were followed by an interpreter or translator. This fourth functional officer translated the Hebrew text into the Aramaic language of the people, after prefacing his remarks to the effect, "which being interpreted is." The rabbi's commentary on the text was supposed to be extemporaneous (without notes) and was usually memorized. At the Nazareth synagogue, when Jesus read from Isaiah 61 (in Hebrew) and commented on it (presumably in Aramaic), he played either the third or fourth role, as did Paul in many synagogues of his day.

Other less formal, more fluid officers have been identified. *Almoners* ("collectors" or prototype "deacons") were in charge of collecting the tithes and alms for the poor, who often camped on the synagogue premises. The *herald of the shema* led the opening prayer from the great *shema* text ("Hear, O Israel: The Lord is our God, the Lord alone," from Deuteronomy 6:4).

Many addressed Jesus simply as rabbi, a term of respect accorded to teachers of the law. This term conveyed a personal sense of "my teacher," but today it is more of a title applied to someone with professional training and ordained to lead a Jewish congregation. The Pharisees loved to be called rabbi because of its connotation ("great"), but Jesus forbade his disciples to use the term for themselves (Matthew 23:7–8).

This ancient synagogue was excavated at Masada, a remote mountain fortress in the Judean desert. Before the synagogue came to be associated with a place or building, it was first a designation for people of the Jewish faith gathered together and acting as a body. The word "church" serves the same dual purpose today: as a designation for a group of God's people first, and secondarily for the physical building.

Eventually, the rabbis became their own religious order, replacing the priests, but at no time did the rabbinic office become a priestly or ordained office. Any learned layman could become rabbi of a synagogue if he became sufficiently schooled in Hebrew, the Torah, the Talmud, and Jewish customs.

SYNAGOGUE IMPACT ON CHRISTIANITY

Ironically, the presence of these lay-led synagogues in almost every city of the Roman Empire also helped Christianity to advance as rapidly as it did. For it was in the synagogues that Jesus, the Apostle Paul, and the other early Christian missionaries preached the gospel.

By the time of Jesus, the synagogue had replaced the temple as the primary place of weekly worship for Jews living outside Jerusalem. However, it is likely that one or more synagogues met in the temple complex itself. (The Greek term *synagogee*, like the New Testament term for church, *ekkleesia,* originally referred to people, not a place.) Because the earliest followers of Jesus were also Jews, synagogue worship also influenced the pattern of early Christian worship.

At both Jewish and Christian assemblies, the shema and the related blessings were recited by the people, but the "herald of the shema" was paralleled by the "herald of the Gospel" (see 1 Timothy 2:7; 2 Timothy 1:11). Public bidding prayer by the liturgist was followed by the people chanting prayers and singing hymns from the Psalter. (Jews and Christians originally used the same hymnbook.) After the closing benediction by a priest (if one was on hand), "Amen" was echoed by the people of God (in both Jewish and Christian worship).

Considerable latitude and lively debate about the interpretation and authority of the Old Testament characterized the lives of both Jews and early Christians. Commentaries written by the early Church Fathers grew out of the church schools and libraries, much as the Talmud grew out of the synagogue schools and libraries.

LOCATION AND ARCHITECTURE

In the centuries before Jesus, the synagogue (as people) met outdoors. The synagogue (as a place) was of simple construction and was located on a hill or prominence of land. By the first century A.D., synagogues were located in the center of the town square and often resembled massively ornate basilicas or miniature temples (with a porch, columns, and elaborately carved stone edifices or guardian animals). The Torah, the ark of the covenant, and other

This stone-carved representation of the ark of the covenant was excavated at a synagogue in Capernaum. The ark itself was made of acacia wood and overlaid with gold. It was a portable coffin-size chest on wheels that rarely moved from the Holy of Holies, where the high priest entered once a year to make atonement. Inside the ark were the two tablets of the law conveying God's covenant, Aaron's rod, and a pot of manna.

These Hasidic boys in Jerusalem are reminiscent of ancient Hasideans or Hasidim, the pious Jews who participated in the Maccabean revolt against Syria in the second century B.C. Their otherworldly agenda was not so much political or nationalistic; they wanted freedom to worship God according to the Torah. The modern Hasidim constitute a Jewish sect, founded by Baal Shem Tov (1700–1760) in eastern Europe and popularized by the philosopher Martin Buber (1878–1965).

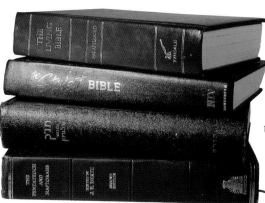

Today's student can read many translations and versions of the Old and New Testaments. But the first Christians had only the Hebrew Scriptures. As their worship focused on Jesus Christ, accounts of his life and ministry were added. As eyewitnesses to Jesus Christ began to die off, the four gospels were written. By A.D. 100, letters from Paul and other apostles were collected into codices.

synagogue furniture were also elaborately decorated at this time. All synagogues (people) faced the ark and Jerusalem. Otherwise, synagogues had no uniform design, but rather an eclectic blend of the (Greek or Roman) culture around them.

The modern synagogue varies little from its first-century counterpart in its three major functions: house of worship, school for study, and social center for community life. However, unlike today's wall of separation between church and state, in the first century it was impossible to separate religion from education and government. But as synagogues took on these important functions seven days a week, a system of professional educators and administrators evolved from the groups of lay leaders that ran the synagogues.

HOLY BOOKS

The word *canon* (meaning a "rule" or "rod" used for measuring), as it applies to Holy Scripture, refers to the collection of books that Jewish leaders and the Church have determined are divine and authoritative. Through their various historic councils, early commentaries, and centuries of popular usage, certain books were eventually declared the only ones with ultimate and universal authority—fit for use by all people, in all places, and of all times, in their worship of God and in the teaching of faith.

CANON OF THE OLD TESTAMENT

Just when and how certain inspirational texts made the canon list for the Old Testament, while others were excluded, is a subject of considerable debate. The debate over the Old Testament canon is clouded by two unavoidable factors: Any extrabiblical corroborative testimony has long since perished; and the Old Testament books themselves are incomplete in their claims to authorship or dating.

Yet the centuries-long process of recognizing certain books as authoritative and others as not was driven by an ironic circumstance: The faithful of Israel blatantly opposed the prophets to their faces, even "killed them" (see Luke 11:47–51; Hebrews 11:32–37). But later, the descendants of these same Jews built a shrine to the prophets and enshrined their writings as Holy Writ.

By the time of Jesus, the Old Testament canon—at least the Law and the Prophets, if not also the *Hagiographa* (or "Sacred Writings")—had been adopted as complete, immutable, and authoritative. Here is a listing of the three major groups of Jewish holy books, as they later came to be canonized:

Law (5 books): Genesis, Exodus, Leviticus, Numbers, and Deuteronomy.

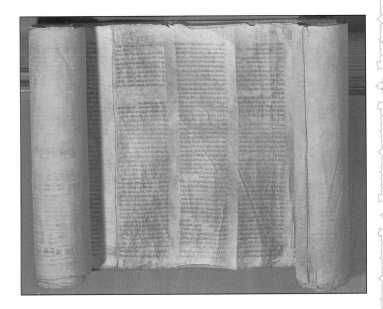

In ancient days, the art of making books was very different than the high-speed printing and mass-market publishing industry of today. Back then, scribes used a quill pen and ink on parchment or vellum scrolls (made from animal skins) to make single copies of Scripture. Pictured here is a copy of the first five books of the Bible, known as the Pentateuch or Torah.

Prophets (7 books): Joshua, Judges, 1 and 2 Samuel with 1 and 2 Kings (as one book), Isaiah, Jeremiah and Lamentations (as one book), Ezekiel, and the Minor Prophets (as one book—Hosea, Joel, Amos, Obadiah, Jonah, Micah, Nahum, Habakkuk, Zephaniah, Haggai, Zechariah, and Malachi).

Hagiographa (10 books): Psalms, Proverbs, Job, Song of Songs, Ruth, Ecclesiastes, Esther, Daniel, Ezra and Nehemiah (as one book), and 1 and 2 Chronicles (as one book).

Jesus said, "Do not think that I have come to abolish the law or the prophets.... not one stroke of a letter, will pass from the law until all is accomplished" (Matthew 5:17–18). Since Jesus quoted extensively from the Old Testament but left no instruction about the need for forming a new collection of authoritative writings, the Old Testament was retained by the early Church as its Bible, but with a slightly different order and grouping.

On the Law and the Prophets, ancient Jews and early Christians were in total agreement. Although each group of believers used other holy books for devotional purposes (much as today), early Christians revered the same twenty-two-book canon long held by Jews as their only authoritative guide to faith and practice. (Because of grouping and naming, the Old Testament canon of the early Church contained twenty-seven books, while today's has thirty-nine books.)

From the outset, however, first-century Jews and Christians understood and used the Old Testament so differently that they may as well have been reading from two different Bibles. These different uses stem from the belief by Christians that the Old Testament prophecies found their fulfillment in Jesus as the Messiah.

Above: *The prophet Daniel, pictured here holding the scroll of his prophecy, was taken captive by Nebuchadnezzar, king of Babylon, in 605 B.C. He was trained in the arts, letters, and wisdom in the Babylonian capital and rose to high rank among the Babylonian men of wisdom. Facing page: Michelangelo's "Ezekiel" depicts another major prophet revered by Jews and Christians alike. The visions received by these two men of God, and the accounts of their courageous lives of faith, comprised part of that body of literature known as the Law and the Prophets.*

THE SEPTUAGINT

There is another sense in which two different Bibles were circulating at the time of Jesus. The Bible quoted by Jesus and used for preaching by his disciples was the Greek or Alexandrian version of the Hebrew Bible, known as the *Septuagint,* the Latin word for seventy (LXX). This Bible was so named because seventy Greek-speaking Hebrew elders were brought to Alexandria, Egypt, for the historic translation project, completed in the second century B.C.

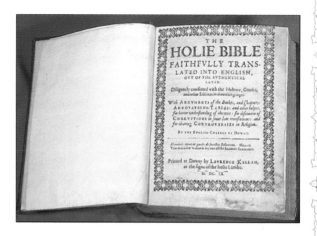

However, because it lent itself so easily to Christian interpretation, the Septuagint lost favor with the Jewish people, who then produced other Greek versions to suit their purposes.

EXTRACANONICAL "HOLY BOOKS"

In that historic translation process, the Septuagint included some other holy books not found in today's Hebrew Bible but current at the time of Jesus. These extra books were later called by Protestants the *Apocrypha* (meaning "hidden"). This term came to imply noncanonical, even heretical, because of the books' esoteric content.

Against the judgment of early Jews and later Protestants, these same extra books adopted from the Septuagint were validated and called *deuterocanonical* by Roman Catholics. This term means, simply and without judgment, "later added to the canon."

Added to the confusing mix was the so-called *Pseudepigrapha.* This was a large body of Jewish writings (with some Christian additions), written about 200 B.C. to A.D. 100, but ascribed to famous Old Testament personalities such as Adam and Eve, Abraham, Baruch, and Enoch. The imaginative and colorful Pseudepigrapha never made it

Facing page: Jesus, shown in this fresco, said he came not to abolish the Law and the Prophets, but to fulfill them. He was referring to the Hebrew Scriptures. Above: The first Roman Catholic Bible in English, called the Douai Version, was published in France a year before the King James Version of 1611 came out in England. Five revisions later, an acceptable version replaced the original Douai and became the official Roman Catholic version.

into the canon of holy books recognized by either Jews or Christians.

MIDRASH

Rabbinic *Midrash* (exposition or commentary) on the Mosaic Law and Old Testament historical narratives was also considered to be holy, having an authority derived from the biblical text. The Midrash was not a body of literature, but a distinctive kind of writing. By these extrabiblical "rules" or "traditions," Ezra and the other scribes returning from the Babylonian Exile attempted to give general principles of the Torah to provide guidance for their new situation. For several generations this midrashic material (or *midrashim*) was preserved by word of mouth.

From the days of Ezra the Scribe until the days of Christ, scribes were busy copying and commenting on Scripture. With a quill pen or stylus in one hand and the Bible text in the other, scribes wrote in either the haggadah *style (nonlegal, devotional narrative, which instructed like good sermon notes) or the* hallakah *style (detailed case law, or rules applying the Torah to specific situations).*

Haggadah and Hallakah: There were two literary genres of Midrash in Jesus' day: the Midrash *haggadah* and the Midrash *hallakah*. The haggadah is a teaching, nonlegal discussion meant to edify and drive home a moral point with the force of the teacher's personality and following. The hallakah concerned itself mostly with legal decisions, or detailed case law, applying the Torah to every possible aspect of Jewish life—religious and civil, private and public, local and national, economic and political.

Soferin and Zugoth: The midrashic form of teaching is thought to have started with the Great Synagogue in the days of Ezra. It then peaked with an era of popularity known as the *soferin* ("bibliophiles"), which lasted until about 270 B.C. The midrashic genre lost its popularity after narrowing itself to two major schools or paired traditions, called the *zugoth*, ending with the last pair—Rabbis Shammai and Hillel (10–5 B.C.).

This first-century B.C. inscription, written in Greek and found in Jerusalem, mentions a synagogue that could be one of the earliest known synagogues in Israel.

A century or two after Jesus, these two kinds of Midrash came to be written down and took on an independent life and authority of their own. But Jesus denounced these human traditions, in their oral form, whenever they obscured or negated the clear teaching of God's laws (for example, on what makes a person "clean" or "unclean," see Mark 7:1–13).

Mishnah

Mishnah is the "fence around the law," the written version of the oral tradition of the Pharisees first recorded in the third century A.D. After the destruction of the temple in A.D. 70, the following wars, and the further dispersion of Jews outside Palestine, the Mishnah grew out of a concern that Jewish traditions would be lost if not written down. Writing Mishnah and collecting these legal discussions became the life work of certain rabbis two and three centuries after Jesus.

This hedge around the sacred canon of Holy Writ may have begun, in oral form, as early as the Great Synagogue of Ezra's day. At that stage in the development of Jewish holy books, the Mishnah's alleged purpose was to make sure that Israel would never again lapse into ignorance and idolatry, which led to captivity in Babylon.

TALMUD

This collection of Mishnah and midrashic commentary was later called the *Talmud*. This material might well be seen as a series of concentric circles: the Scriptures surrounded by the "fence" of the Mishnah, and that surrounded by the all-encompassing circle of the Talmud. The Talmud was kept "open" for centuries until it was closed around A.D. 495, when a definitive Talmud took final shape.

Today the Talmud exists in nearly fifty detailed legal volumes of intellectual treasure. Without the Talmud, we would not have the first-hand knowledge of the Jewish culture and customs that help us understand the everyday life and times of Jesus.

SOURCE DOCUMENTS AND BOOKMAKING

No discussion of Jewish holy books would be complete without discussing the evolution of record-keeping, source documents, and bookmaking itself.

Above: *The Talmud exists today much as it did fifteen hundred years ago. Jews who master the Talmud aspire to a calling held in high esteem.* Right: *Books are not the only source of information about this period. Many letters and legal documents were recorded on fragments of clay pottery called* ostraca.

More than four hundred references to "writing" in various forms can be found in the Bible. Clay tablets, or metal seals with crude inscriptions, trace the origins of this craft back to prehistoric times. Other ancient and timeless materials to write on included stone, clay, wax, bricks, metal, even the inner side of papyrus bark. The latter is called *biblios*, from which we get the word "bible," or "book."

Paginated and bound books as we know them today, however, did

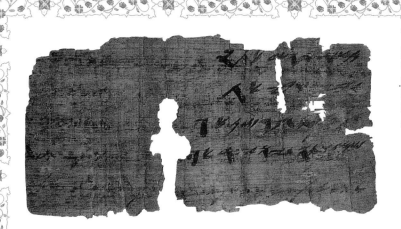

This letter in Hebrew, written on perishable papyrus, dates from the seventh century B.C. It was found in a cave in Wadi Mura-bat, near the Dead Sea. The dry, hot desert conditions kept it from completely deteriorating.

not exist in the first century. Instead, people wrote on scrolls made of papyrus, leather, or parchment. Papyrus manuscripts were so perishable that copywriters were kept busy full-time transcribing the records each year onto new papyrus. Needless to say, if it were not for faithful copywriters, we would have no Bible. The most faithful copyist named in Scripture was Baruch, who rewrote a scroll-length portion of Jeremiah after King Jehoiakim cut up Jeremiah's first-draft papyrus manuscript and threw it, piece by piece, into the fire (see Jeremiah 36).

Scrolls were rolled up on two sticks and were usually about ten to twelve inches wide and up to thirty-five feet long. Such a scroll could fit one book of the Pentateuch or the Book of Luke or Book of Acts. More than that would require two scrolls. Just one side of a papyrus was used—with rare exceptions. The writing in many books was in Hebrew, laid out in columns that are read from right to left.

This is the seal of Baruch, secretary to the prophet Jeremiah. Seals offered protection for property, indicated ownership, authenticated documents, and made a king's edict irrevocable.

We now take it for granted that we have a few versions of the Bible around the house, but finding a Bible was a big discovery just centuries before Jesus. The "Book of the Law" (probably Deuteronomy) was found "in the house of the Lord" by Hilkiah the high priest (2 Kings 22:8). This discovery led to repentance and nationwide revival under Judah's King Josiah.

Above: *Scrolls were made of papyrus, leather, or parchment sheets joined together in long rolls and taken up on wooden rollers or spindles at one end or the other. These rolls, each the equivalent of a modern book, measured ten to twelve inches tall and up to thirty-five feet long.* Below: *The scriptorium at Qumran was where many papyrus scripts and temple scrolls (such as the one above) were found still stored in pottery jars.*

The nature of this unique discovery implies the existence of temple archives, catacombs, even a temple library, but also something about how perishable these early manuscripts were. Several biblical accounts were compiled from primary source documents long since lost. For example, "Now the acts of King David, from first to last, are written in the records of the seer Samuel, and in the records of the prophet Nathan, and in the records of the seer Gad" (1 Chronicles 29:29; compare that to 2 Chronicles 9:29; 12:15). The records of Nathan and Gad have not survived.

Jesus would not have owned his own Bible. The Bible that existed in Jesus' day consisted of a collection of ancient scrolls of parchment or sheets of papyrus. Though few copies existed at any one time or place, these Scriptures were available to visiting speakers in the temple.

The Codex Purpureus, containing the Gospel of Mark, was found at Patmos, an island just off the coast of Asia Minor. Covered and bound books, called codices, were first used to preserve original New Testament manuscripts from as early as the third century A.D. Several early codices, some containing manuscripts of the whole Bible, have survived to this day.

Centuries later, even when Torah studies were flourishing, there were still only a few papyrus manuscripts in each temple or synagogue library. Copies were produced in *scriptoriums*—so called because that is where a team of scribes and copywriters gathered to painstakingly transcribe and preserve the Scriptures. (Some of these were found among the Dead Sea Scrolls at Qumran.) To satisfy the need for Christian Scriptures, the production of bound books, called codices, began. Several ancient *codices*, which became predominant over the scroll by the third century A.D., have survived to this day.

This ink pot was excavated from the scriptorium at Qumran. Working day and night in shifts, the Essenes faithfully copied their sacred texts. Portions of every book of the Hebrew Bible except Esther, as well as many Essene religious documents, have been found at Qumran.

RELIGIOUS GROUPS IN JESUS' DAY

Was Jesus political? Or did he espouse a nonpolitical, otherworldly utopia? What did Jesus think of nationalism? Of political fanaticism? Was Jesus interested in what we might call citizenship or democracy? Was Jesus a reactionary, a revolutionary, a liberal, a conservative, or something else? The following are the six major groups in the religious-political arena of Jesus' day.

PHARISEES—THE LEGAL EXPERTS

Origins: The Pharisees derived from a group of the faithful called the *Hasidim* (as did the Essenes). The Hasidim (or "pious men") took loyalty oaths to their

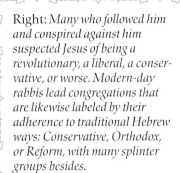

Right: *Many who followed him and conspired against him suspected Jesus of being a revolutionary, a liberal, a conservative, or worse. Modern-day rabbis lead congregations that are likewise labeled by their adherence to traditional Hebrew ways: Conservative, Orthodox, or Reform, with many splinter groups besides.*

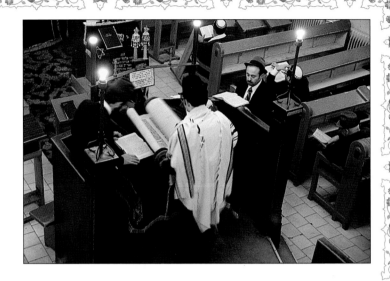

Facing page: *The middle-class Pharisees ("separated ones") may have felt inferior to the elitist Sadducees, but they felt far superior to publicans or "sinners," from whom they "separated" themselves.*

covenant relationship with God, setting an example of resistance to the Seleucid dynasty of Syria, which had desecrated the temple in 167 B.C. The Hasidim were purely religious, and the Pharisees claim a direct connection. The political wing of the resistance movement was the Maccabeans, who advocated guerrilla warfare against the Seleucids.

The etymology of Pharisaism suggests "to separate," but it is not clear, historically, which group the first Pharisees were separating from. Perhaps the Pharisees earned their name by separating from all worldly Gentiles, or from the predominant Greco-Roman society, or from common Jews who were indifferent to the law, or from the Hasmonean dynasty (descended from the Maccabean rebels). The best answer may be all of the above.

Comparisons to Other Groups: The Pharisees were "doctors" of the law, concerned about every jot and tittle, compared to scribes, who were "laymen." But compared to the wealthy, elitist Sadducees, the Pharisees were common middle-class tradesmen. The Pharisees, like the Herodians, favored local political autonomy and the status quo. They refused to eat with Gentiles or any non-Pharisees, for fear of being contaminated by "unclean" food.

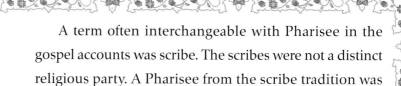

A term often interchangeable with Pharisee in the gospel accounts was scribe. The scribes were not a distinct religious party. A Pharisee from the scribe tradition was called a "sage" when he educated children, a "rabbi" when became a scholar of the law, and a "lawyer" if he had a role in law, government, or the Sanhedrin.

The Pharisees collected and preserved the oral law, until it was finally written down (after A.D. 200) in the Mishnah and Talmud. By reputation, they were legalistic, literal-minded, and fanatical in their orthodoxy—of which Paul, the apostle and tentmaker, was once a prime example (Acts 26:5). Their political clout in Palestine far exceeded their few numbers, which was estimated by Josephus to be about six thousand at the time of Jesus.

Beliefs: The Pharisees believed in resurrection, the immortality of the soul, and life after death. The Pharisees believed that angels intervened in human affairs. And they understood the coming kingdom as a literal fulfillment of the promise to David for a king to reign over Israel forever. They were rigorously strict about keeping the sabbath, marriage, and oaths, but in other interpretations of the law they were liberal compared to the literal-minded Sadducees.

"Listen to the sound of my cry, my King and my God, for to you I pray," implores the psalmist, identified as David. Throughout his many trials, whether attacks of his enemies or those of his own causing, King David never failed to call upon God for help in his hour of need. Simon Marmion captures a contemplative David in a detail from the medieval devotional Book of Hours.

On the question of "God's sovereignty" versus "humanity's free will," the Pharisees held a moderate view, halfway between the extreme views of the Essenes and the Sadducees. The Pharisees kept themselves aloof from inferiors and "sinners" who, by definition, did not keep the law. They maintained ritual purity and the laws of tithing.

The Pharisees held that the entire Old Testament (the Law, the Prophets, and the Writings) was inspired and authoritative, as was the oral tradition of the elders—which contrasts with the Sadducees, who believed only in the written Law (Torah).

The Pharisees were the object of Jesus' warnings about hypocrisy for failing to live up to their beliefs while requiring adherence by others. Others, notably Nicodemus, became followers of Jesus.

SADDUCEES—GUARDIANS OF THE TORAH

Origins: The Sadducees may have derived from Zadok, high priest when King David reigned. Or this priestly group may have derived their name from the Hebrew word *sadduk*, which means "righteous." However, the group was unpopular with the masses, they had to make deals with the Pharisees, and they might have lost their distinct identity had it not been for a bloody episode during the reign of John Hyrcanus' son, Alexander Janneus (103–76 B.C.). For showing contempt for their tradition during the Feast of Tabernacles one year, the Pharisees waged a six-year civil war (94–88

B.C.) against the Hasmonean king and his supporters (the Sadducees). Janneus quelled the insurrection, but only after killing thousands of Pharisees and their supporters. The remaining Pharisees never forgave the Sadducees.

Comparisons to Other Groups: The Sadducees represented aristocrats, priests, merchants, the urban elite, and conservative business interests in Jerusalem and

Above: *The Pharisee Nicodemus was "a ruler of the Jews"; that is, he was member of the Sanhedrin, the Jewish ruling council. Nicodemus visited Jesus under cover of darkness because he feared the Sadducean members of the Sanhedrin would discover his visits. Nicodemus greeted Jesus with the respectful title "rabbi."* Left: *This Torah scroll is encased in an elaborate container. The Pharisees believed in the entire Old Testament, which included the Law, the Prophets, and the Writings, but the Sadducees believed only in the Torah—the Law.*

Verdier captures the boldness of the Apostle Paul fearlessly proclaiming the gospel throughout the Roman world. Caesarea was the port of debarkation for Paul's missionary journeys; later it would be the site of his hearing before the Roman procurator Festus, which resulted in Paul's being sent to Rome for trial and eventual martyrdom.

other cities in Judea. As members and high priests of the Sanhedrin, the Sadducees were hostile to Jesus, Paul, and their followers—perhaps even more so than the Pharisees.

Beliefs: The Sadducees denied the resurrection of the body, immortality of the soul, life after death, everlasting punishment, the existence of angels, and a literal kingdom. All such doctrines and oral traditions were deemed foreign imports to the Torah (the five books of Moses). To a Sadducee, the Pentateuch was the one supreme authority and a sufficient guide to the Jewish way of life.

Sadducees loved debate, almost as a sport, and a group of them once tried to trap Jesus with a "what if" question about resurrection (see Matthew 22:23–33; Mark 12:18–27; Luke 20:27–40). Paul, knowing the Sadducees flatly denied the doctrine of a future life, once used this to cause dissension with their rivals, the Pharisees (Acts 23:6–10).

The Sadducees insisted on free will and individual responsibility to make wise choices by the law. This view was adopted from the Epicurean philosophers and stood opposite the Essenes (who believed in predestination) and the Pharisees (who took a moderating view).

ESSENES—THE RADICAL "COMMUNISTS"

Origins: Once members of the Hasidim (as were the Pharisees), this third major religious group, unlike the Pharisees and Sadducees, separated from the Greco-Roman world and withdrew to communities such as Qumran (home of the now-famous Dead Sea Scrolls).

Until the scrolls were discovered, what we knew of the group came from secondary (and divergent) sources—Philo the Alexandrian Jew (20 B.C.–A.D. 52); Josephus the Jewish historian (A.D. 37–98); Pliny the Elder, a Roman historian (also of the first century A.D.); and Hippolytus the Christian (A.D. 170–230). Found among the Dead Sea Scrolls, the "Rules of Behavior," "Manual of Discipline," and "Zadokite Fragment" tell us about the organization, lifestyle, and worship patterns of the Qumran sect. This sect thrived from the midsecond century B.C. to the Jewish–Roman War of A.D. 66–70.

Political and Social Role: Essenes were separatists who organized themselves into a communal, pacifist society (holding all property in common). They could be compared to a utopian socialist party or a modern Amish sect. Essenes were known for celibacy, opposing slavery, caring for their own sick and elderly, avoiding military service, and trading only within their own sect. Despite their low numbers at the time of Jesus (estimated at four thousand by Josephus), they are credited with having indirect influence over early Christian thought. For example, some

At thirteen hundred feet below sea level and saturated with mineral salts, the Dead Sea is the lowest inhabited and one of the most unusual geological regions on Earth. In ancient times, asphalt was collected from the surface and used for caulking boats. This cave was used by the Essene community that inhabited the shores of the Dead Sea.

Above: *John the Baptist lived in the wilderness of Judea, where he ate locusts and wild honey and wore camel's hair and a leather girdle, the dress of a prophet. Because of his radical lifestyle, his priestly background, his preaching of repentance to Israel, and his practice of baptism, many of his disciples mistakenly concluded that he was the messiah.* Right: *This depiction of Simon the Zealot, by Peter Paul Rubens, shows another man zealous for God and his truth.*

think John the Baptist was an Essene. The Essenes rejected the priesthood at Jerusalem, but maintained friendly terms with the Herodians until their pullout from Jerusalem following the death of the last Herod.

Beliefs: Essenes believed in the immortality of the soul, in angels, and in an elaborate eschatology (belief about the end of the world). They were looking for up to three different messiahs in the end-times who would judge the nations and establish justice. The Essenes were dualistic, believing that they were the true children of light and most others were children of darkness.

The Essenes paid even more attention to ceremonial purity than the Pharisees, and they carefully guarded the sabbath—all with rigorous self-discipline. Noted for simplicity in meals and in their dress, Essenes believed that the possession of riches was hateful, so they freely shared what they had with others.

ZEALOTS—THE FREEDOM FIGHTERS

Origins: The first Zealot of note was Judas the Galilean. He tried to get his fellow Jews to resist the census of Quirinius (not the first census noted in Luke 2:2, but the second one, in A.D. 6) and to resist paying taxes to Rome (Acts 5:37). He gave Galilee the reputation of the seedbed of revolutionaries. Another one was "Simon the Zealot" (see Luke 6:15; Acts 1:13). Before formation of the Zealots' formal protest movement there was the Maccabean revolt against Syria's Seleucid dynasty. In their zeal for the God of Israel, Mattathias and Judas Maccabeus courageously defended the pu-

The Galilean territory was not only fertile soil for growing crops but also fertile ground for breeding political revolutionaries.

rity of the temple and secured religious freedom for the Jews by 163 B.C.

Political and Social Role: Zealots were ardent nationalists who awaited the opportunity to revolt against Rome. That meant becoming tax resisters and not paying Roman taxes or the temple tax. That also meant opposing the Herodians and Sadducees, who tried to maintain the political system. Some blame misguided Zealots for the conquest of Judea by Rome in the Jewish–Roman War of A.D. 66–70. According to Josephus, the Zealots degenerated into mere *sicarii*—dagger-men, or assassins (like present-day terrorist hit squads).

Galilee was largely Gentile (non-Jewish) territory—fertile ground for political revolutionaries, such as Judas the Galilean (6 B.C., see Acts 5:37). Hence, at the time of Jesus, "Galilean" came to mean the political party of the Zealots, or "freedom-fighters." Jesus was a Galilean, as were his inner circle of disciples. That Galilean association contributed to the perception that Jesus and his followers were either up to no good, or that they would help overthrow Rome's iron rule.

Beliefs: The Zealots were close in thought to the Pharisees; they affirmed the entire Jewish law and wanted to see the nation once again living under that law. But this militaristic group disagreed with their counterparts on political tactics and outlook toward their Roman captors. Whereas most Pharisees thought God would intervene on their behalf to liberate them from Rome only if they first did proper penitence and acquiesced to foreign domination, the Zealots believed that Rome had to be overthrown forcefully. The Zealots believed that God would personally intervene by sending them a political messiah. The Zealots were intolerant of Christians and Essenes who tended toward pacifism. In their unflagging zeal and refusal to call Caesar Lord, many Zealots were martyred along with the early Christians.

The Sanhedrin—the Ruling Council

Origins: According to Mishnah tradition, the first Sanhedrin dates back to the seventy elders of Israel that gathered with Moses (see Numbers 11:16), but it fell into disuse and was reorganized by Ezra (Nehemiah 8—10). According to Josephus, these were the historic precursors to the Sanhedrin; no group by that name was convened until the New Testament period.

James Tissot paints Jesus in front of the Sanhedrin, the Jewish ruling council. Rome gave the Sanhedrin authority to pass sentence, but they could not condemn anyone to death. So Pontius Pilate, Rome's appointed ruler, had to condemn Jesus to death.

Outstanding members of the Sanhedrin included Gamaliel (Acts 5:34–39), Joseph of Arimathea (John 19:38), Nicodemus (John 3:1–10; 7:45–51; 19:39), and possibly Saul-turned-Paul.

This religious council, which was pivotal in the trial of Jesus, included Pharisees (scholars) and scribes (lay members), but was dominated by the aristocratic Sadducees (elders and chief priests). Called simply rulers (sixty-four times in the New Testament), this highest governing authority in Palestine also ruled over Jews throughout the Roman Empire. Its Senate-like authority was both religious and political in nature, as the Law of Moses was both civil and sacred or ceremonial. Most important, Rome did not give the Sanhedrin the power to pass a sentence of capital punishment.

PRIESTS AND LEVITES

Origins: The priesthood is an Old Testament institution dating back to the days of Moses and Aaron. Israel's priesthood came from the tribe of Levi (from which Moses and Aaron descended). No one could work their way into this esteemed position; you were born into it. Some priests, those descended from Aaron (sometimes called Aaronites), could administer the sacrifices at the altar, as in the days of Moses. Other priests from the tribe of Levi, those simply called "Levites," were assigned lesser sanctuary duties along with some oversight and teaching responsibilities. Only a high priest could offer the annual ritual sacrifices and enter the Holy of Holies of the tabernacle or temple to intercede between the people and God.

In the Law of Moses, the tribe of Levi was chosen to assist the family of Aaron in fulfilling the priestly duties of offering sacrifices in the tabernacle. The Levites were appointed because they were the only tribe that stood with Moses against the people who worshiped the golden calf. The Levites were in charge of the temple; they prepared the grain offerings, purified all the holy instruments used in the temple, and assisted the priests with burnt offerings on the sabbath and feast days.

(It should be noted that critical scholars see "priest" and "Levite" as interchangeable terms in the Pentateuch.)

Political and Social Role: By the time of Jesus, some priests held positions of political power; most exercised that power in opposition to Jesus, especially the chief priests on the Sanhedrin. Some Levites pulled "guard duty" at the temple (John 7:32,45–46) and were the police force of the Sanhedrin who tried in vain to arrest Jesus. (They also guarded Jesus' tomb, and they later accompanied Saul to Damascus.) But most priests remained ordinary temple workers, such as Zechariah, who embraced Jesus as the promised Messiah (Luke 1:5).

Following the servant-worker pattern of the levitical priesthood, the Church had also understood itself as a "kingdom of priests" (see 1 Peter 2:5,9). Likewise, the Church had vested its ordained clergy with some priestly authority, but regarded Christ as its only high priest and mediator of a new covenant (see the Book of Hebrews).

FOLLOWERS OF JOHN THE BAPTIST

John, a descendant from the priestly family of Aaron, was also thought to be tied in with the radical desert-dwelling Essene community. John fearlessly challenged the status quo. His radical opposition to Herod Antipas—especially Herod's marriage to Herodias (Herod's sister-in-law) while Herod Philip I (the brother/husband) was still alive—cost John his life (Mark 6:14–29).

Herod Antipas and many followers of John believed he was the messiah. While most followers of John were turned to Jesus, some stayed with him and formed their own sect. Today, the Mandeans, a small religious sect, claim descent from the followers of John the Baptist.

SAMARITANS

In the New Testament this term identified the Israelite sect that lived in the former northern kingdom of Israel

Levites were laymen who served all around the temple, often doing temple service or guard duty, sometimes exercising oversight and teaching responsibilities. Some unfortunate Levites fell asleep while guarding the tomb where Jesus was buried. In James J. Tissot's painting of the women at the tomb after the Resurrection, the Levites are on the ground.

(Samaria) after it was invaded by Assyria in 722 B.C. The Samaritans who remained in Palestine intermarried with the pagan colonists brought in by Assyria, and they adopted some of the pagan idolatrous religious views. The Samaritans opposed the monotheistic Jews from the southern kingdom who had returned to resettle Judea and rebuild Jerusalem and its temple.

The half-breed Samaritans, with their mixed marriages and eclectic faith, were hateful to the Jews who remained loyal to Yahweh. The fierce Jewish–Samaritan hatred only worsened over the next five hundred and fifty years and was made worse by John Hyrcanus, who, in 128 B.C., destroyed the temple that the Samaritans had built at Mount Gerizim. That temple had been built in direct opposition to the temple at Jerusalem (John 4:20–21).

A modern-day Samaritan celebrates Passover atop Mount Gerizim, the holy mountain of the Samaritans.

Politically, if the Samaritans had any allies at all among Jerusalem Jews it was the Sadducees, with whom they shared a strict emphasis on the Pentateuch.

Against all taboos, Jesus was willing to go through Samaria and talk to the woman at the well. She decided to follow Jesus as the Messiah and tell everyone she knew. Many more Samaritans converted. Their story, along with the disciples' retelling of Jesus' controversial parables of the good Samaritan (Luke 10:30–37) and the one grateful Samaritan leper (Luke 17:11–19), helped to break through the long-standing ethnic and religious barriers between Jews and Samaritans. That, in turn, led even more in Samaria to accept Christ as the Messiah (see Acts 8:5–25).

Interestingly, a few hundred present-day Samaritans still live in religious communities near Mount Gerizim.

THE PEOPLE AND THE LAND

❖ ❖ ❖

PALESTINE HAS BEEN FOUGHT OVER by many hostile foreign emperors, "friendly" trading partners, and splintered religious groups. Even today, three major world religions—Judaism, Christianity, and Islam—vie for holy sites in Jerusalem.

Studying the land of Palestine is a helpful aid to understanding the New Testament world. This idea is not new, nor is it unique to the twentieth century. Scholars just a century removed from Jesus were studying first-century Palestine.

Many study-abroad and tourist groups who go to Israel come away with a renewed appreciation for what it means to walk where Jesus walked. Of course, the miracles cannot be duplicated for show-and-tell classes. Some things will always remain unique to the first century.

But enough remains the same and enough artifacts have been dug up to show how people in this land actu-

Right: *Jesus often taught by the seashore, which James Tissot depicts in this picture. Along the Galilean lakeshore, it is still possible to get a sense of the world in which Jesus lived.* Facing page: *Jerusalem was the holy citadel in Jesus' day and the most important city of the New Testament world. Jerusalem, which means "possession of peace," has been the site of many disputes, which continue even today. This view of the modern city shows the gold-topped Dome of the Rock mosque, as seen from the Mount of Olives.*

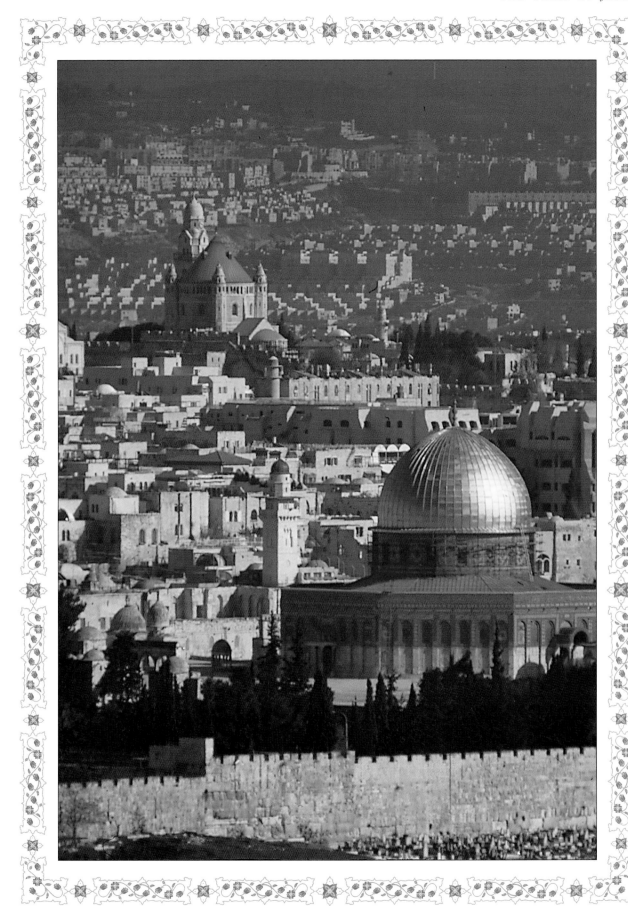

ally lived. Their everyday concerns were mundane, more down to Earth than looking for miracles: building homes suitable to their climate and geography, making a decent living off the land, getting around the city to sell their goods in the marketplace, and finding something to eat.

The New Testament era was populated with ordinary people, doing ordinary things, who happened to live at a unique period in history.

PEOPLE AT HOME

In biblical times, the home was the hub of people's lives. Birth, marriage, and death all took place there, and it was often the center of social activity, a workplace, and somewhere to eat and sleep, as well. Several generations might live under the same roof. Housing varied only somewhat from place to place and period to period, but between the rich and the poor classes of the same period, there was a wide gap in home values.

FIVE TYPES OF HOUSES

Housing trends varied between different periods of biblical history, although

"The Birth of Christ" by Abraham Bloomaert shows this unique event with overtones of the everyday life of the first-century Jews, which centered around the home. Also, Bloomaert paints Jesus' birth in a cavelike shed, which is probably where Jesus was born, rather than in a barn.

many models were handed down and copied from one generation to the next. Five basic types survived throughout the centuries.

Caves: Many people lived in caves, perhaps in soft limestone cliffs, during the biblical period of history. Cave dwellings needed very little maintenance, and they provided good shelter from the elements—they were warm in the winter and cool in the summer. Animals were frequently herded into caves. Jesus may have been born in just such an animal shelter or cave dwelling when there was "no room for him at the inn."

Tents: In the time of the Patriarchs (two thousand years before Christ), the tent was the most common form of housing. Tent-dwellings survived well into the New Testament period, too.

These portable, practical homes were easily taken down, bundled up, and moved to a new site, allowing shepherds and other workers to move from place to place. A farmer might live in a tent during the growing season to be near his crops but otherwise would live in the city. Tent-making was a trade learned by Paul of Tarsus, who made his living as a tentmaker while preaching the gospel (see Acts 18:1–3).

Many people still live in tents in Israel today, including this family near Bethlehem. This Bedouin woman is giving her small daughter a drink of well water.

One-Room Courtyard Houses: When the Israelites first conquered the Canaanites, they took over their towns and homes, and they copied their style of building. The typical house in Palestine during the time of the Patriarchs was one room (no bigger than an average bathroom or kitchen today), built off the side of a courtyard. Surprisingly, these cramped quarters provided shelter for entire families. Terraces of these small one-room homes have been excavated; such houses date from the Patriarchal period to the New Testament period.

Four-Room, Flat-Roof Houses: Not surprisingly, as Jewish families grew in size and stature and became more settled in cities, they also began building larger houses. The four-room house became the standard pattern of homes for centuries, well into the New Testament period. The design was simple: The courtyard was entered from the street. On one side there were one or two rooms for storage; on the other side, a cattle barn. At the end was a large room for living and sleeping. The roof was flat and strong—good for many activities, such as weaving and washing; drying goods (figs, dates, and flax), retreating for prayer (see Acts 10:9), relaying public announcements as a town crier (see Matthew 10:27), or entertaining over-night guests who camped in booths set up there.

Mud-Brick Houses: Down in the Jordan Valley, because of its rich mud, homes were built of bricks. The first mud bricks were made by hand and were oval-shaped, but with the advent of wooden molds, the mud bricks became rectangular in shape. Mud bricks, when baked, were white or pale red in color. The roof had a long cross beam, which was covered with brush and mud or clay. Often the roof line was domelike, giving the home a beehive appearance.

Homes of the Rich

Besides the four-room, flat-roof house typical of Jesus' day, there were some dwellings built just for the rich, with features that the poor could not afford. When Jesus ate his last supper with his closest followers, it was in a large "upper room," likely in one of Jerusalem's wealthier

With its mud-brick dwellings and shepherds watching their sheep, this village scene from the Syrian village of Hama near Aleppo has changed little since ancient times. Abraham drove his flocks of sheep and goats before him through northern Syria on his way to Canaan.

homes. Likewise, a furnished upstairs guest room was made available for Elisha's use by the woman at Shunem (see 2 Kings 4:8–11).

Palestinian homes of the rich were built in the Roman style, with two rectangular courtyards each surrounded by rooms. These larger homes often had a double thickness of stone, and the corners and doorways were made of squared stones.

A locked door opened onto a porch furnished with seats or benches. A short flight of stairs led to the rooms and the open court. This courtyard area, paved with tile or rock, was the center of the Jewish home and was where its social life was carried on; even weddings took place there. Sometimes homeowners built the courtyard around a fountain, well, or garden.

This painting by Gerbrand van der Eeckhout depicts Elisha and the Shunammite woman. She furnished a special room for Elisha to use when he traveled through her region. Elisha later raised her only son from the dead.

Many upper rooms had balconies or galleries that faced this central area. A stone stairway led from the court to the roof. The upper rooms were often quite large and nicely furnished. Paul preached his last sermon in this type of balcony area, from which a sleepy Eutychus fell to the street below (Acts 20:7–12).

The most lavish area in the house was the master's quarters, located on the lower level, facing the entrance, with a reception area. Some homes had equally nice rooms built over the porch or gateway of the house, called the *alliyah*. This was used for guests or storage; it was also a place to rest or pray.

In ancient houses, windows were small rectangular holes facing the street (or inside, facing the open court-yard). A front porch, which not every house had, was care-

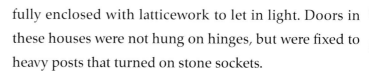

fully enclosed with latticework to let in light. Doors in these houses were not hung on hinges, but were fixed to heavy posts that turned on stone sockets.

In wealthy homes, the hard mud floors might be paved with stone slabs and covered with plush carpets. By the time of Christ, wealthy people were adding bathrooms, with tubs set into the tiled floors.

A variety of building materials were readily available to the wealthy in Palestine. Rich landowners could easily obtain stone, brick, and the best timber for their homes. They used hewn stone and marble, cedar paneling, and gold, silver, and ivory for ornamental work for their "winter homes" and "summer homes" (see Amos 3:15). The latter were built partly underground, paved with marble, and constructed to bring in the cool currents of air. They were refreshing and delightful sanctuaries during the hot summer months.

Household Furnishings

If someone from Jesus' day were to visit a modern home, the guest would be amazed at the number and variety of furnishings. This is a typical inventory of household furnishings in biblical times:

Mats and Rugs: In the average home, straw mats were used as a floor covering or for seating. In poor homes, the animal skin or straw mat would also be used for eating and sleeping on the floor. The wealthy homeowner, on the other hand, would have beautiful rugs, skins to recline on, and cushions of rich fabric.

Stools, Tables, Benches, and Chairs: While the rich Shunammite woman furnished the prophet Elisha's room with a bed, a table, a stool, and a candlestick (see 2 Kings 4:10–13), ordinary New Testament homes had no such luxurious furnishings. Their only table was a circular piece

These models of a low-rising table and eating utensils were made from terra cotta (glazed or unglazed fired clay). This table setting is similar to what Jesus and the people of his day would have used. Note the absence of chairs. Commoners sat on the floor to eat their meals, while the upper class reclined on couches while eating.

In this depiction of the Last Supper by James Tissot, he paints the scene more realistically than most painters. Jesus and his disciples most likely would have reclined on a Roman triclinium (a three-sided couch) rather than sit on separate chairs or a long bench.

of leather placed on the floor mat. Their only furniture was a three-sided couch much like the Roman triclinium. This couch extended around three sides of a rectangular table, and it was used for reclining during meals. Very likely, Jesus and his disciples observed the Jewish Passover feast, the Last Supper, while reclining on a triclinium.

Beds: At night, the poor rolled out thick, coarse mattresses to sleep on and covered themselves with goat-hair quilts. Goatskin pillows were stuffed with feathers, wool, or some other soft material.

Lamps: Lamplight was important because homes were very dark. Olive oil, pitch, animal fat, or wax were used, and torchlike wicks were made of cotton or flax. The poor made their lamps of clay; the rich, of bronze and other metals. The typical Palestinian lamp at the time of Jesus was plain, round, and pinched on two sides to form a spout (for the wick) and a handle (for holding), leaving a hole for filling with oil. The lamps in Jesus' parable of the wise and foolish bridesmaids (see Matthew 25:1–13) were likely the torches used in Greek and Roman wedding ceremonies.

Pots, Pans, and Storage Bins: Most household utensils were earthenware or terra cotta. Later in biblical times, wealthy homes had kitchenware made of metal. Pots for carrying and storing water were distinct from cooking pots, for which there were six different biblical terms. Jars for storing flour and olive oil were of a special type. Every house had stone or clay storage bins for animal fodder, as well as for food for the family. Every family also had bowls and cups for serving food and drink. Soldiers and travelers drank out of a "pilgrim flask." When Jesus washed the disciples' feet (John 13:5), he probably used a *krater*, a large two- or four-handled container used since the days of Solomon.

FOOD AND EATING HABITS

Jesus encouraged his hearers not to worry about food or clothing. Despite the ready availability of basic staples (except in times of famine), as well as the miraculous feedings Jesus was known to have done, these were basic concerns of ordinary people.

BASIC STAPLES

This man harvests olives by hand from an orchard, reminiscent of the way that people harvested their crops in biblical times. Not just olives, but figs, grapes, pomegranates, and apples—all of which were considered luxury items—were also harvested by hand.

Cereal grains (wheat, barley, millet, and spelt) were ground into flour and made into bread. Leaven (to make the bread rise) was used to make round, flat loaves. The unleavened bread of biblical times was much like today's pita bread. Vegetables (cucumbers, melons, garlic, onions, beans, and lentils) were staples in the Hebrew diet, but drought and pests such as locusts took their toll. Fruit (grapes, raisins, figs, pomegranate, and apples) was a luxury.

Sheep and goats were raised for meat by wealthy Jews, as were pigs by the Gentiles. Oxen and the "fatted calf" were shared only on special occasions. Several types of fowl (but no scavenger birds, which were unclean according to Jewish law) and some wildlife also provided meat for the table. But fish (only those with fins and scales—no shellfish, which were also unclean) was the main dish preferred by Jesus and his first followers, many of whom were fishermen by trade.

Meal Preparation

Meal preparation was woman's work. Women (the wife or a maidservant) were generally the cooks at home (see Matthew 24:41), while men were the chefs and bakers in the royal houses and marketplace (Genesis 40:16).

In the typical Israelite home, there was no breakfast. A snack might be eaten on the way to work; fig cakes were especially practical for taking on a journey. The midday meal was usually bread, olives, and, rarely, fruit; this was called "dinner." The sack lunch from which Jesus fed the five thousand men, plus women and children, consisted of five barley loaves (food of the poor) and two fish (probably dried pieces of fish).

In the evening, the family sat on the floor (the rich reclined on couches) to eat supper after the day's work was done. Appetizers consisted of raw vegetables, locusts, crickets, or grasshoppers. A main meal of vegetable stew was served from a common pot, along with bread for dipping. In the Roman period, a divided oven was invented, with the fire separate from the cooking area. Before that, fire for cooking was made on the earth floor or sometimes in an earthenware pot. Most people ate with their fingers, although a spoon was used for soup or stew. For dessert, wealthier people enjoyed pastries or fruit.

Milk came from the family goat and juice from fresh-squeezed grapes. Since grapes grew well in the Mediterranean climate but had to be fermented in order to keep without refrigeration, wine was naturally the most common drink of Jesus' day. Intoxication, however, was always condemned.

This bedouin woman in the Negev Desert makes flat loaves of bread much the same way that women did in biblical times. Typically, dough made of wheat or barley grain was kneaded in a bowl, made into circular cakes, and baked over an open fire. Every stage of bread making—from grinding the grain to baking—was done, daily, by women at home.

Butter was seldom used because it would not keep, but cheese and yogurt were common. Flat loaves of bread and milk were always part of the meal, but meat and milk dishes were not to be cooked or eaten together. Instead, meat was boiled in water, and the broth was eaten the same day. Pork was never eaten by Jews because it was considered unclean.

CLOTHING AND COSMETICS

Jesus taught his followers not to give any extra thought to what they had to eat. He also said not to worry about what they wore. "If God so clothes the grass of the field, which is alive today and tomorrow is thrown into the oven, will he not much more clothe you—you of little faith?" (Matthew 6:30).

FABRICS FOR MAKING CLOTHES

Ever since the Garden of Eden, fabric for clothing has been important. An embarrassed Adam and Eve used fig leaves to cover their nakedness, then God clothed them in animal skins (see Genesis 3:7,21–23). Later, a variety of fabrics was used to make clothes.

Adam and Eve first sewed together leaves to cover themselves after being expelled from the Garden of Eden. Afterward, God made them clothes from animal skins. During biblical times, in addition to leather, a variety of fabrics was used to make clothing. Linen was made from the flax plant, wool was made from the shearing of sheep, sackcloth was made from goat hair, and the rich imported silk from China.

Linen: Woven from yarn made from the flax plant, linen was an important fabric for the Israelites and Egyptians. Women did this work at home, but so did a whole guild of linen workers at Beth-ashbea in Judea (see 1 Chronicles 4:21). After harvest, flax was dried in the sun, then soaked in water for several days to loosen the fibers. The fibers were then separated, beaten with a wooden mallet, and finally combed. It could then be made into coarse, thick, fine, or delicate fabric. Easily bleached, it came to symbolize "whiteness" and was used for priestly garments. Angels and saints in heaven are said to wear fine linens (see Ezekiel 9:2; Revelation 19:8,14).

Wool: Most clothes in biblical times were made from wool because it was more readily available than linen or cotton (but wool was never mixed with linen; see Deuteronomy 22:11). After the sheep were sheared, the wool was washed, bleached, and beaten by the "fuller" using a purifying soap. The natural oils had to be removed from the fibers before the wool could be dyed, spun, and woven.

Silk: Since the days of Alexander the Great (he ruled from 336 to 323 B.C.), this Chinese import was available in Asia Minor, but Solomon may have traded for it centuries earlier. Silk was highly valued, no doubt because of its rich texture and vivid colors.

Sackcloth: The dark color and coarse, itchy texture of goat-hair material made it ideal as a ritual sign of distress, danger, grief, crisis, personal repentance, or national emergency. It was sometimes worn as a loincloth or as an undergarment (see 2 Kings 6:30). Sackcloth gets its name because of its primary use: The material was used to make grain sacks.

Manufacture and Care for Clothes

Preparing fabrics and making clothes were done by women. Most clothes were sewn by hand from two or three pieces of woven cloth; however, some robes were seamless. A number of steps were involved in making any garment:

Distaff Spinning: Women attached wool or flax to a rod or stick called a distaff, then used a spindle to twist the fibers into thread.

Weaving: After raw materials were spun into thread, the thread was used to make cloth. The warp (lengthwise thread) was attached to a wooden beam on the loom, and the weaver stood while working. Various types of woven

In ancient days, Jewish women did distaff spinning much as this Bedouin woman is doing. The women attached wool or flax to the distaff (rod or stick) and then used a spindle (a take-up reel) to twist the fibers into threads.

fabrics were made this way, including woolen garments, linen, and the embroidered clothing of priests.

Embroidering: The Jews were noted for their fine needlework, but it was different from the embroidery we know today. Cloth was woven with a variety of colors, then a design of gold thread was sewn onto it.

Dyeing: Purple dye was extracted from the murex shellfish native to the Phoenician coast. Purple goods were highly valued and used mostly by the elite in Jesus' day.

Tanning: The tanner's trade was not for Jews or women, so Gentile males did most of it, including Simon the tanner (see Acts 9:43). This line of work involved flaying dead animals and drying the animal skins to make garments. Lime, the juice of particular plants, and the leaves or bark of certain trees were all used to tan the skins.

Cleaning and Bleaching: Washing the garments often included stamping on them and beating them with a stick in a tub of water. Niter, soap, and chalk were used for cleaning by a fuller, who did his business outside town. "Fuller's Field," set up to process wool east of Jerusalem, smelled foul (see 2 Kings 2:18; Isaiah 7:3). On the Mount of Transfiguration, Jesus' garments appeared "as no launderer on earth could whiten them" (Mark 9:3).

What People Wore

Only Roman citizens could wear the Roman toga. The Greek tunic was often sleeveless. The Israelite dress was not influenced by surrounding countries, but by climate. Fashions tended to remain the same from one generation to the next. Although some of the clothing for men and women looked similar, women were forbidden to wear

In Tissot's painting of Mary Magdalene, we see typical clothing worn by women in the New Testament era. Dyes or coloring were added to certain cloths that were then woven together to form an outer garment. A woman's outer garment was longer than a man's; the front, when tucked over the girdle, made an apron. Her sandals, made of leather straps and wood or leather soles, were worn only outdoors.

anything that belonged to a man, and men were forbidden to wear a woman's garment (see Deuteronomy 22:5).

The poor, who had little clothing, used their outer garment as a covering at night. The rich, on the other hand, had extensive and colorful collections of apparel. The following side-by-side comparison samples the typical wardrobe worn by men and women.

	MEN'S WEAR	WOMEN'S WEAR
Inner garment	Close-fitting and made of wool, cotton, or linen. Worn by both sexes.	Described as a coat, robe, or tunic.
Girdle	A belt or band was used to secure the inner or outer garment.	Used to secure the outer garment.
Outer garment	A coat, robe, or mantle made of linen or goat hair. Very thin, fine garments were worn over colorful tunics as robes of honor.	Longer than a man's, the front, when tucked over the girdle, made an apron. Tied tassels on corners of garment were reminders of God's commandments.
Accessories	A purse and scrip were used to carry necessities.	A veil was worn to show modesty and to indicate an unmarried state.
Sandals	A sole of wood or leather fastened with straps of leather. Worn by both sexes, but never indoors.	For both sexes, when putting on shoes, the right sandal was always put on and taken off before the left.
Mourning garments	Made of goat-hair material and worn next to the skin in times of deep sorrow.	Ashes were placed on the head when wearing sackcloth.
Winter clothing	Cattle skins were worn by the poor.	Fur robes or skins were worn by both sexes.
Jewelry	Rings were worn as a seal or token of personal authority.	Wore bracelets, earrings, nose rings, necklaces, gold anklets (Isaiah 3:16–23).
Cosmetics & perfume	An alabaster jar full of perfume made of pure nard from India (worth a year's wages) was poured on Jesus (Mark 14:3).	Henna was used as a cosmetic stain; frankincense, myrrh, aloes, and spikenard were sources of perfume.
Hair care	Head of hair and beards adorned men; lots of attention to hair care, which was usually long in Old Testament times. As a sign of mourning, men shaved off their beards.	Women's hair was an object of lust, so it had to be covered. Upperclass Greeks bared their heads and wore hair ornaments.
Ornaments	Pharisees wore phylacteries, little boxes of Scripture verses, on forehead and arm.	Both sexes wore headdresses, but only occasionally.

FAMILY ROLES

In the Hebrew culture of Jesus' day, making meals and clothes were not the only family jobs that were divided by gender or age. Grandparents, parents, children, relatives, and even servants often formed a unique social unit that was defined along patriarchal lines. In the extended family setting, the grandfather had complete authority, and when he died, his eldest son took over by right of gender and birth. Jesus was most affirming of families—especially honoring parents, welcoming children, and holding marriages together.

HUSBAND/FATHER

As absolute head of the household, the husband was responsible for its well-being. He was expected to provide adequately for his family, and when necessary, defend his family's rights before the judges. The father taught his son the law; the Talmud specified that the father was also to circumcise his son, buy him back from God if he were the firstborn, find him a wife, and teach him a trade.

If the husband died leaving his wife childless, she was expected to continue living with her husband's family and to marry one of her husband's brothers or a near relative (a levirate marriage). If this was not an option, the widowed wife was free to marry outside the clan (a cluster of extended families, with hundreds of males in its ranks, all with a common ancestor). The widow could even return to her family of origin. An elderly widow might be cared for by one of her sons. If she had become wealthy, she could choose to live alone.

Though men worked in the fields, women did help during the hectic days of harvest. Pictured here are two men and a woman working alongside each other harvesting wheat in the hills of Judea in much the same way as people did in biblical times. They cut the stalks of wheat with a sickle and then bundled them. Later the grain was tossed and winnowed to separate the wheat from the chaff.

WIFE/MOTHER

A wife's primary goal was to bear children, then take care of them, nursing each child until age two or three. Besides child care, the mother prepared meals and made clothing for the family. Sometimes the wife's role extended to the marketplace, but always with the family's welfare in mind (see Proverbs 31). When necessary, she helped her husband in the fields, planting or harvesting the crops.

A mother helped to train the children in their early years, and as they grew she turned more attention to her daughters, training them to become productive wives and mothers. Children were taught to respect their mother even though she had low status in the Hebrew society, having few rights of her own.

By comparison, Egyptian women of biblical times could be heads of household, and Babylonian women could acquire or inherit property and enter into contracts in their own name. Even though Israelite society was patriarchal, family life was not always oppressive to women. Only a general climate of respect for women could have produced capable leaders that included Miriam, Deborah, Huldah, and Athaliah.

Tissot's "Athaliah and Joash" reminds us that some Hebrew women ascended to leadership roles. Athaliah succeeded in killing off all rival claimants to her throne except her one-year-old son, who was taken into protective custody. When the boy was presented as rightful king six years later, the murderous Athaliah challenged this "treason"; she was executed anyway.

CHILD CARE AND CHILDLESSNESS

In the Greco-Roman worldview of Jesus' day, childhood was considered an insignificant phase of life. Unwanted babies were routinely aborted, abandoned by the roadside, or left in garbage dumps. Those who were rescued from that fate were often sold into slavery, prostitution, or the gladiator games. More girls than boys were abandoned in the surrounding pagan cultures, as they represented another mouth to feed; boys represented a potential contributing asset.

Contrast that pagan view of children with the Jewish view of children as a gift from God. A big family was a sign of God's special blessing (Psalm 127:3–5). A childless family was perceived as having displeased God in some way, and "barren" women were regarded with disfavor, even ridicule (see 1 Samuel 1:1–11). A childless husband sometimes married a second woman, divorced his wife, or conceived children with a slave.

A childless widow was often required to enter into a levirate marriage with a brother of her dead husband. The hope was to conceive male children to carry forward the man's family name. Three generations removed from such an arrangement, David was born (see Ruth 4:1–22). In succession, Jesus was a "son of" (descended from) King David.

However well these practices resolved the issue of childlessness, they created other social problems (see Genesis 16; 38). Levirate marriage laws about "marriage at the resurrection" were also the source of theological debate and entrapment for Jesus (Matthew 22:22–33).

Jean Charles Cazin's painting of Hagar and Ishmael portrays the anguish of a slave woman (Hagar) scorned by her master's husband (Abraham), even though she did nothing wrong in conceiving a child (Ishmael) in accord with the laws of the land. A childless husband could take a new wife or conceive children with a slave to perpetuate the man's family. Ishmael is considered to be the father of today's Arab nations.

Sons and Daughters

For Israelite children, play, work, and education were all closely tied to the home. Children had to help in the fields, workshop, or kitchen as soon as they could manage the simplest task.

In this male-dominated culture, boys carried on the family name, continued the work of the land, supported elderly parents, and even ensured a proper burial for their parents. Hence, Hebrew society valued sons as "holy to the Lord." The more sons the better, but the firstborn son held a particular place of honor and responsibility in the family. After the father's death, the firstborn son received a double portion of the family inheritance, and he became the next head of the family. An important part of Jewish family life, then and now, was the blessing of the children by their parents at the sabbath meal.

In "Isaac Blessing Jacob," by Girolamo da Treviso, we see a prime example of the parent blessing the child and passing along the double portion of the family inheritance that usually went to the firstborn son. In this case, the scheming Jacob, with the help of his mother, Rebecca, got the blessing instead of Esau (pictured in the distant fields) by pretending to be Esau.

To dishonor one's parents was considered such a serious offense that Moses ordered the punishment of death for any person who cursed or struck a father or mother (see Exodus 21:15). Although there is no record of this punishment actually being carried out, the Bible does describe many instances in which children disrespected their parents (Matthew 15:4–9). Jesus embraced all children, much to the chagrin of his disciples. And God deals with his children lovingly but firmly, as a father who regularly disciplines his sons (Hebrews 12:5–11).

In ancient Israel, Hebrew society did treat daughters more humanely than did the surrounding cultures. Though even in Israel daughters were not as important as sons. Firstborn daughters were given a special place of honor and duty, and if the family was without sons, daughters could inherit their father's possessions (see Numbers 27:1–11). With mastery of domestic skills learned early on, a twelve-year-old daughter-homemaker was allowed to get married. Until her marriage, a daughter was under the legal jurisdiction of her father. He made all important decisions for her, including whom she should marry.

Extended Family

This included everyone who shared the same dwelling place under the protection of the head of the family. This might mean grandparents, a husband's wives, sons and their wives, widowed daughters, the children of these various relationships, servants, and even visitors. In Old Testament times, the extended family was headed by the oldest male in the household, who might be a grandfather or great-grandfather and who seemed to hold the power of life and death over its members.

By New Testament times, when the clans of Israel settled in permanent homes, the normal family unit became smaller—father, mother, and children. The New Testament church also functioned as an extended family, especially for widows. A childless widow of the New Testament could turn to the church for help and support (see 1 Timothy 5:2–16).

Jewish Social Life

To the Jewish families of this era, home was not only where you slept, ate, and worked or went to school. Home was where people played and socialized. Though most Palestinians had to work hard just to get by, they did have time for social activities—even for games, sports, music, and dancing. (The wealthy had slaves and servants to do the hard labor, so they had more time for leisure activities, such as games.)

From archaeological evidence, we know that Hebrew children played much like children do today—with dolls, ball games, and board and dice games. They kept pets,

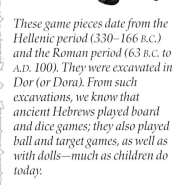

These game pieces date from the Hellenic period (330–166 B.C.) and the Roman period (63 B.C. to A.D. 100). They were excavated in Dor (or Dora). From such excavations, we know that ancient Hebrews played board and dice games; they also played ball and target games, as well as with dolls—much as children do today.

such as birds. Children also played target games (what we might call "bows and arrows" and "slings and stones"). Children of all ages enjoyed music and dance, indoors and out, in synagogues and at the marketplace, and at weddings and funerals. Music and dancing were often tied in with religious life.

FAMILY LIFE PASSAGES

Each family member had a clearly defined role in the home and in the community. Every stage of life—from birth to death— was marked by appropriate ceremonies to affirm social position and place.

BIRTH AND CIRCUMCISION

At a child's birth, salt was rubbed into its skin to make it firm, and the infant was wrapped tightly with cloth to make the limbs grow straight. The name of the infant was carefully chosen by the father to reflect something about the child's character. When a boy was eight days old he was

circumcised by his father or a rabbi. After that had happened, in order to be considered "clean" again, the mother had to sacrifice a pigeon and then a lamb.

One month after circumcision, parents brought their firstborn son to the temple to offer more sacrifices in order to "redeem" (buy back) their son. This Jewish tradition dates from the Exodus, when Israelite freedom cost the Egyptians the lives of their sons (see Exodus 13:11–16; Numbers 3:39–51). The family of Jesus followed each of these Jewish customs (Luke 2:21–24).

Sebastien Bourdon's "Presentation at the Temple" portrays one of the rites of passage that all Jewish boys participated in. Jewish families circumcised boys at eight days old, had a naming ceremony for the child, and, for the firstborn, "bought back" the child from God with the appropriate sacrifice (two doves for a family as poor as Jesus' parents) at the presentation at the temple.

BAR MITZVAH

An important rite of passage for Jewish males then, as now, was the bar mitzvah (here celebrated at the Western Wall). At his bar mitzvah, Jesus would have read aloud from the Torah, as this thirteen-year-old boy is doing.

Parents taught children their first lessons and prayers, and the entire family attended worship on the sabbath and festival days. Time was not rushed in the Jewish home. Children were encouraged to ask questions and find out about their history and religion. When he was a boy, Jesus probably went to a synagogue school, where he learned the Torah.

This modern-day couple get married under the huppah, or canopy. Those who married in Jesus' day would have enjoyed a two-stage wedding, culminated by a weeklong ceremony at which the betrothed couple would have received the blessing from the rabbi.

Schooling for boys started when they were about six. Girls, however, were not formally educated. The rabbi of the local synagogue gave moral and religious instruction based on the Torah, and the boys learned largely by repetition.

At thirteen, the boy became a man in a special rite of passage called the bar mitzvah ("son of the law"). After coming of age, the boy was regarded as a responsible member of Israel in the home, the community, and the synagogue.

WEDDINGS

Thirteen was also the age when some "adults" started getting married. Women were not given any formal education or public employment; they had no bar mitzvah or a future job to look forward to. The rite of passage that marked a girl's coming of age was an elaborate wedding.

Arranged by Parents: Because of the extreme importance attached to parental blessings and cursings, contracting a marriage without consent of both father and mother was rare in biblical times. Jewish marriages of young adults were arranged by parents, mostly within the same clan, often to a first cousin, and sometimes even with a half-sister or brother, as with Abraham and Sarah (see Genesis 20:12).

Later, in the priestly code of unlawful sexual relations (Leviticus 18), marriage with any close relative was barred. Marriage to foreigners was officially prohibited, too.

A Two-Stage Wedding: From the days of Moses to the time of Joseph and Mary, Jewish weddings came in two stages: the betrothal (called the *kiddushin*) and the actual week-long wedding ceremony of bringing home the bride (called the *huppah,* meaning "canopy"). At the binding ceremony of betrothal, gifts were exchanged between the couple or their families.

These Bedouins in the Negev Desert practice an ancient wedding tradition. All the men, including the groom, sit in two rows facing each other to celebrate, while the bride and the women celebrate on their own in another tent.

On the day of the wedding, in the evening, the bridegroom and his party walked to the bride's home, where she was waiting in her wedding dress and wearing a veil, which she only took off in the bridal chamber. The wedding party then proceeded back to the home of the husband's family. (In surrounding Near Eastern culture it was the other way around: The groom customarily embraced the bride's family as his own.)

King for a Week: After receiving the blessing from her father before the actual ceremony, the bride and groom

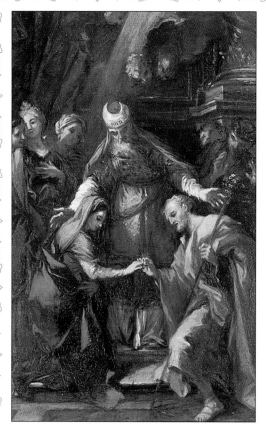

"The Marriage of the Virgin," by Giuseppe Passeri, shows the hopes and dreams of all young Jewish couples. At the wedding ceremony, the father's blessing is received. After the wedding, the attendants serenade the couple and escort them to the bridegroom's home.

were serenaded and escorted by their wedding attendants through the village to the bridegroom's home, where he was "king" during a week-long celebration. Friends went in torchlight procession to the couple's new home for the wedding celebration and feast, at which oxen and fatted calves were prepared, and special "wedding clothes" were required.

The Bride Price: The bride-to-be had to be paid for, not because she was property but because she was considered a working asset. The "bride-price" (called the *mohar*) was paid to the girl's father. In return, the young woman's father gave the couple a dowry, which also provided for her in the event she were to be widowed.

A virgin who had been seduced or raped fetched fifty shekels—no doubt inflated for punitive damages (Deuteronomy 22:28–29). It follows that virgins received less, while widows and divorcees were half price to the groom. By the law of the kiddushin, the bride was bought (betrothed) either by money or its equivalent, such as clothes or valuable animals.

Betrothal was legally binding, as if the couple were already married. That made sex with any other person adultery, which was punishable by death. Joseph and Mary were engaged when she was pregnant with Jesus, yet Matthew speaks of them as already "husband" (1:19) and "wife" (1:24), leaving divorce the only honorable way out of an engagement.

Wedding Dates: During the period of the second temple, Jewish weddings most often took place on Wednesdays (for virgins) or Thursdays (for widows and divorcees).

That extra day left the couple enough time to enjoy each other intimately before being interrupted by sabbath obligations (which began Friday evening).

FUNERALS

A death in the household is always a tragedy, and for the ancient Hebrews, elaborate mourning rituals followed such an event. As in the case of Jesus' death and burial, the body was prepared for a quick burial because of the hot climate. It was washed and clothed, then wrapped in special grave cloths, with a linen napkin bound around the head. The body was then put on a wooden stretcher (a bier) and carried to the place of burial. Family and friends—and sometimes hired professional mourners—made a great public display of sorrow. Weeping, wailing, tearing clothing, wearing ashes, and fasting were all part of the seven-day mourning ceremonies. Some of the most dramatic events in Jesus' public ministry were when he raised the dead to life and changed everyone's mourning to dancing (see Mark 5:21–24,35–43).

Ordinary Israelites buried their dead in common graves or caves. Some caves were large enough for all members of the family. Wealthy families could afford to have tombs hewn out of rock and sealed with a boulder.

James Tissot shows mourners rejoicing at the city gate outside the village of Nain, where Jesus has just healed the widow's only son. As reported by Luke, what had begun as a funeral procession ended with the celebration of a miraculous healing. Jewish families, if they were small, often hired people to come along with the funeral procession to mourn with the family.

Graves were painted white to draw attention to them. They were not to be touched, as any contact with the dead made a person "unclean." However, the skeletal remains of loved ones were sometimes removed from graves and stored in stone chests called ossuaries.

Marriage, Divorce, and Singleness

The institution of Jewish marriage—coupled with a rigorous spiritual upbringing for the children—was the means by which God's people were preserved and multiplied. Since it centered around the mother-child bond, marriage was held in high esteem as the unifying force throughout biblical history.

But as ancient as the marriage ritual is, so is divorce. Divorce laws in Roman society favored the man, who usually won custody of the children in a divorce. Divorce laws in Palestine were similar. However, the Torah and its oral traditions limited the right of the husband to exercise that option in several significant ways.

Grounds for Divorce

Dissolution of the marriage by divorce was granted to the husband-petitioner if any of the following behaviors by the wife were present: adultery, moral indecency, change of religion, refusal of conjugal rights for one year, refusal to follow the husband's move to another domicile, adding insult to injury, or certain incurable diseases that blocked sexual relations.

If any of the following prohibitive conditions were present, the husband could not divorce the wife: seducing or ravishing the wife before the marriage; the wife's insanity, alcoholism, or disability (of a deaf-mute) after the marriage; captivity (in which case his duty was to buy her back); or if the wife was still a minor.

This large cave appears to have been the final resting place for several family members. The skeletal remains were sometimes removed from graves and placed in white stone (or ceramic) chests called ossuaries, pictured here.

Alternately, dissolution of the marriage by legal divorce was granted to the wife-petitioner if any of the following behaviors by the husband were present: false accusation of premarital sex, refusal of conjugal rights, impotence, a vow of abstinence, physical blemishes, nonsupport, unlawful imprisonment, wife-beating, or committing a crime that compelled him to flee the country.

The net result of these complementary rights obliged the divorcing couple to meet with a rabbi for mediation, at which point some rabbis tried to make it difficult, complex, and expensive. Before Jesus, the strict school of Rabbi Shammai argued that divorce could be allowed only on grounds of unfaithfulness, whereas the liberal school of Hillel argued that even "burnt toast" or "someone more attractive" could be grounds for divorce (see Matthew 19:3–9).

POLYGAMY OVER MONOGAMY?

From the beginning, men were discouraged from having more than one wife, although this was clearly allowed. Some patriarchs (Abraham, Jacob), priests and judges (Elkanah, Gideon), and kings (David, Solomon, Ahab) took advantage of this allowance and had as many wives as they could afford. For economic and political reasons, Solomon had seven hundred wives (see 1 Kings 11:3). But for less politically connected and less wealthy individuals, polygamous arrangements created jealous partners, sibling favoritism, and domestic violence—as Solomon, Elkanah, Saul, and David found out.

The need for polygamy was cultural, historical, and situational. Having more than one wife was good for childbearing purposes, for extending the man's family line, and for increasing his status and wealth. Polygamy also bene-

Solomon lies lazily in the company of some of his reputed one thousand wives and concubines in James Tissot's "Solomon and His Harem." In ancient times, kings often married foreign women to cement treaties with other nations, ranking Solomon as one of the most politically connected rulers in history.

fited widows in a wartime economy. Widows had few options for supporting themselves if they stayed unmarried.

By the time of Jesus, most Israelite marriages were monogamous, affirming God's ideal from creation. The early Church banned polygamists from leadership roles (see 1 Timothy 3:2) and urged its female members to care directly for widows.

ABSTINENCE OVER MARRIAGE?

Jesus blessed and sanctioned marriage and took a moderating view between mercy and justice. He affirmed that marriage was for life and that divorce should barely be tolerated and justly regulated. Jesus ducked the Shammai-Hillel rabbinic debate over particular grounds for divorce. Instead, he appealed to the creation mandate—God's original and universal grounds for marriage (see Genesis 1:21–24).

THE LAND OF PALESTINE

VILLAGES AND TOWNS

Walled towns developed in the Old Testament period as nomadic tribes or clans began to settle down. The clan chief became "king" of his own territory. With no central government, kings of different towns had conflicts. Under

The walled city of Masada, high atop a mountain along the western shore of the Dead Sea, was an ideal locale for a rebellious group of Jews to hold out during the first revolt against Rome. But Rome's Tenth Legion finally breached the wall with a giant rampart and captured Masada in A.D. 73. Inside the fortress, they found nine hundred men, women, and children dead in a group suicide. The Jews chose death over submission to Roman rule.

King Solomon, the government became centralized at Jerusalem. Besides being the government center, Jerusalem also became the religious capital, thanks to the magnificent temple built there.

The difference between "villages" and "towns" in biblical times was their fortification. Villages were settlements without walls. Towns were walled settlements built on a hilltop and near a good water supply. Towns were usually built in fertile areas or at a strategic junction (for example, a mountain pass) along trade routes. Unprotected villages often surrounded fortified towns. An Old Testament town was generally small (between six to ten acres). Within its walls were about one hundred fifty to two hundred fifty houses and possibly one thousand crowded residents.

CITIES

The great cities of New Testament times were different than early fortified towns. With the rise of Greece and Rome, towns and cities were planned carefully. In some locales, particularly Samaria and Caesarea, streets were made wider and paved, piped water was brought in from aqueducts, shops and public baths were built in central locations, and drainage for waste water and sewage was put in place. Life in the cities improved, especially for the wealthy.

The Roman city of Caesarea was modern and efficient for its day. The aqueducts provided drainage for waste water, and the system was actually flushed daily by the incoming tide.

JERUSALEM: THE HOLY CITADEL

Jerusalem was the most important city during the New Testament era; it was the city of hope and promise for the Jewish people. There the temple stood, signifying the presence of God. This city is also where God was to free the Jews from oppression and to make of them a great nation. Jerusalem was to be where other nations would come to pay tribute to Israel. Jerusalem was also important to Jesus; he respected the temple as zealously as any pious Jew of his day. He traveled there for festivals with his family when he was growing up, and later he went there with his disciples.

In Jesus' day, the city's population was probably about one hundred thousand, but it would have swelled to a million during festivals when people flocked to the city.

The Damascus Gate was one of seven well-trafficked locations in Old Jerusalem, where city merchants and village artisans could set up shop and be guaranteed a crowd of customers. Today, shopkeepers still keep stores in this busy place.

By comparison, first-century Palestine, which included Jerusalem, was home to as many as three million people.

The city was important to different people for different reasons. For devout Jews, the temple was the reason Jerusalem was significant. It was the center of Jewish worship; though, by Jesus' time, the majority of Palestinian Jews worshiped in scattered synagogues.

Commerce was also a reason for Jerusalem's importance. There were seven different markets at the city gates, and many village artisans served its population.

Jerusalem had a hub-and-spokes relationship to surrounding cities. The neighboring villages and cities depended upon Jerusalem commercially, politically, and, in the event of an armed conflict, militarily.

JESUS AND HIS EVERYDAY WORLD

Many think of Jesus as a country preacher or rural shepherd, but Jesus' ministry outside Jerusalem was not as rural or as provincial as we might suppose. Jesus was just as comfortable in cities as in the country.

Jesus appealed to groups commonly found in urban areas. Jesus conversed with soldiers, Pharisees, scribes, Sadducees, Gentiles, prostitutes, beggars, and the poor—all of whom were found in more urban settings. Everywhere he went, Jesus preached to large crowds of people, often using work-world images consistent with the marketplace economy of the day.

WORK-WORLD PARABLES

In simpler times, when towns were few and far between, the Israelites were primarily shepherds, wandering around tending flocks, or farmers who eked out a meager living from the land. Beyond that, there were a few village artisans. But as towns became cities, new trades and small industries began to emerge from them.

The nature of trade and industry in Jesus' day is evident in his teachings. In Matthew 13, for example, Jesus used no less than eight different images from the first-century world of work. His stories connected with people working in agriculture (sowing, harvesting, growing), in the food industry (baking, fishing), in real estate (land purchasing, home ownership), and in retailing (sale of pearls).

Though excluded from inner courts of the temple, women of the city met Jesus in their homes. Jacopo Tintoretto's "Christ in the House of Mary and Martha" depicts two of the better known women who followed Jesus faithfully. The gospels name several women among his loyal followers. From what we know of first-century Jewish culture, the presence of women no doubt gave offense to many Jews.

FARMERS

Pastoral life has changed very little over the centuries. Terms in the Bible that refer to the farmer include, depending on the translation, plowman, husbandman, vinedresser, gardener, and tiller. Farmers grew olive and fig trees, almonds, apples, dates, grapes, mulberries, and pomegranates.

Their work was done mostly by hand with the aid of simple machinery: a wooden plow pulled by an ox, a wooden sickle to cut the stalks of grain, and a pronged fork to winnow the kernels of grain from the chaff. Crops were planted after the autumn rains had softened the ground, then they were harvested in the spring. Prosperous farmers hired day laborers for this work.

The promised land was full of promise for farmers, but it had to be tamed. The biggest problems for farmers were lack of water, locusts, wild animals, and invading armies, not to mention finding tillable soil among all the rocky ground. The farmer understood all too well the parable of the sower (Mark 4:2–20).

SHEPHERDS

Sheep and goats were raised for their wool. Goats were used for milk and both animals for meat. The shepherd tended sheep and goats, sometimes as a mixed herd, other times separately. The faithful shepherd had to find pastures, water, and shelter to protect the herd at night. He had to watch for and fend off wild animals, plus thieves and robbers, some of which lay in ambush in the Jordan Valley; others invaded the sheep pen at night. Any lost sheep had to be found before nightfall; injured animals were carried on one's back. Good shepherds were so diligent and faithful in their exercise of these duties that this profession became a metaphor for the spiritual direction and pastoral leadership offered by Christian teachers. Jesus himself was described as the Good Shepherd (John 10:1–16).

FISHERMEN OF GALILEE

On the Sea of Galilee, where sharp climatic changes whipped up storms without warning—as Jesus' disciples knew all too well—the fishing industry thrived. Little wonder that Jesus' teaching images occasionally shifted from shepherding (the dominant Old Testament metaphor) to

A farmer separates wheat kernels from chaff by tossing the cut grain into the air so that currents of air cause the lighter husks to separate and blow away. In this process of winnowing wheat, the heavier kernels fall to the ground, to be scooped up and then ground into flour.

fishing (the dominant New Testament metaphor). Nine Galilean cities dotted the shoreline in support of this industry.

At Bethsaida (meaning "fish town") almost everyone worked in the fishing industry. Simon Peter, Andrew, Philip, and brothers James and John all lived there.

Tarichaea (meaning "the place of salt fish") was where people packed fresh salt fish for shipping to Jerusalem and exporting to Rome. Salt was used as a preservative because there was no refrigeration and no other way of preserving the "fresh catch of the day."

Three kinds of nets were used—the *sagene* (or "drag net," used for trawling), the *amphiblestron* (or "cast net"), and the *diktuon* (or "gill net," which would catch certain medium-size fish).

A fisherman's work did not end with the day's catch. He also mended and washed the nets, cleaned the fish, maintained the boats and supplies, trained and supervised the crews, negotiated with merchants, and worked with the shipping industry.

In "The Calling of Peter and Andrew," James Tissot paints two of the inner circle of disciples whom Jesus called to leave their nets as fishermen to "fish for people." Peter and Andrew typify many who put aside careers and family concerns to put Jesus at the center of their life and livelihood.

THE GALILEE BOAT

In 1986, the remains of a fishing boat were discovered along the shores of the Sea of Galilee in a mud bar that had been exposed by receding waters. Upon examining the vessel, archaeologists dated it between 100 B.C. and A.D. 100; it was the first ancient ship found in the Sea of Galilee.

The boat is almost certainly the same type with which Jesus and his fishermen disciples would have been familiar. The boat is twenty-six feet long and seven feet wide, and it is built in the mortise-and-tenon style with wooden joints, which is characteristic of this period. The boat was repaired on several occasions, indicating it had a long life.

The boat was likely decked, with storage areas below. It was in the hold created by such a deck that Jesus likely rested as in the story, told by Mark, of a storm on the Sea of Galilee: "A great windstorm arose, and the waves beat into the boat, so that the boat was already being swamped. But he was in the stern, asleep on the cushion; and they woke him up and said to him, 'Teacher, do you not care that we are perishing?' He woke up and rebuked the wind, and said to the sea, 'Peace! Be still!' Then the wind ceased, and there was a dead calm" (Mark 4:37–39).

Ancient sources indicate that ships of this size had a crew of five, including four rowers and a helmsman. Josephus refers to ships of this size holding a total of fifteen people. Jesus and his twelve disciples would have fit comfortably into such a boat. While there is no evidence connecting the Sea of Galilee boat with Jesus, he or his disciples may well have seen it or even ridden in it. Capernaum, his adopted hometown, was only a few miles north along the shore where the boat was found.

One of the casualties of an ancient storm on the Sea of Galilee was this fishing boat, found in 1986 in a mud flat when the level of the sea dropped dramatically as the result of a long drought. Also at that time, several previously unknown ancient harbors around the sea were discovered along the exposed shoreline, confirming the Sea of Galilee as the site of a thriving fishing industry in the time of Jesus.

TRANSPORTING GOODS AND SERVICES

The ways of transporting goods and services in ancient times were not like those in today's "global village," where worldwide access is instant and overnight delivery is assured. Travel and transport in Jesus' day were slow and difficult. Most folk walked from one place to the next. They often walked late in the day to avoid the hot sun.

Pack animals were used to carry baggage. Average citizens, and most in-town deliveries, used the donkey. Camels were most often employed in international trade,

A white ass, which is indigenous to the Negev Desert, carries water for a Bedouin girl returning to camp. Pack animals are as important to many isolated areas in Israel today as they were in Jesus' day.

but some horses were used in the first century. A solitary camel, free of excess baggage, could travel up to seventy miles a day! Caravans were protection against marauders; traders traveled together—donkeys, camels, goods, and men—along three main trade routes. Donkey caravans covered about twenty miles per day; fully loaded camel caravans, between eighteen and twenty miles.

Carts drawn by donkeys were used on farms. In New Testament times, when roads were much better, a variety of chariots were popular. The rich traveled in horse-drawn or man-drawn carts on the narrow city streets.

The Romans built and maintained an excellent system of roads connecting all their provinces. (Hence the idiom, "All roads lead to Rome.") The King's Highway connected Saudi Arabia and Damascus through the mountains. The Way of the Sea (this is the so-called Via Maris of a later period) connected Canaan and Egypt. Some sections of these ancient paved roads remain in fine condition today. Yet out-of-the-way journeys had to be made on the old, unpaved roads worn out by many centuries of use by cattle herdsmen, camel caravans, and military troops.

Village Artisans

While the agrarian Hebrews may well have feared the sea, they felt comfortable working the land and finding work at home. Cottage industries of village artisans flourished, as people pooled energies and resources to create primitive manufacturing "plants." Linen workers, potters, bakers, perfume makers, goldsmiths, and silversmiths each had their own work district or worker's guild in their respective cities. Only the tanner did his work outside city limits, as his work product was "unclean" (offensive and smelly) to Jews, even though tanning was necessary for making tents and sandals.

Potters: The potter's work was a significant specialized trade in Israelite society. Because of the constant demand for their wares, the potter's work was a dawn-till-dusk operation, with little time off from the steady routine of making and selling. The potter made bowls, jars, and other utensils from clay, which were fashioned as they rotated on a wheel. Once a vessel was shaped and had dried, it was dipped in a solution to seal the pores, and designs were applied. Then it was baked in an oven or

These kitchen utensils are several examples of the potter's craft. A potter used his foot on a lower wheel to kick or power a rotating turntable or upper wheel, where he formed a jar or pot or plate from a well-kneaded lump of clay. Clay vessels meant to hold liquids were hardened by fire in a kiln. The earliest potter's wheel and kiln date from 3000 B.C.

kiln, with gradual incremental temperature changes, over several days, to avoid cracking and breaking.

By the time of Jesus, potter's guilds had been around for a thousand years. Potters lived in settlements in the lower part of Jerusalem (near the Potsherd Gate), and in the neighborhood of Hebron and other locations where clay was in abundant supply. In one potter's shop uncovered by archaeologists, there was space for preparing the clay, an area for storing both clay and fuel for the kiln, a drying area, and a storage area for pots needing further treatment. A stone mortar, pottery templates, and objects for cutting clay were also among the tools found.

Metalworkers: In the ancient world, metal was hard to obtain and the smelting process difficult to control. Without any extensive ore deposits, Israel had to import. Ships brought silver, iron, tin, lead, and copper—all in exchange for Israel's wares. The process of purifying silver or gold in the refiner's furnace was a lengthy one. Melted in a small crucible that stood on hot charcoal, molten gold or silver was sometimes poured into a mold to form a fine ornament.

In later periods, the metal industry flourished and found a ready market. Skilled metalworkers banded together in guilds and made a variety of tools and weapons, including axes, sickles, ox-goads, knives, spearheads, javelins, and swords.

Metalworkers were known by several different terms in the Old Testament, depending on the translation: artificer, artisan, blacksmith, bronze worker, craftsman, engraver, forger, founder, metalsmith, refiner, and smelter. From the New Testament, we know two by name: "Alexander the coppersmith" (2 Timothy 4:14) and "Demetrius, a silversmith" at Ephesus (Acts 19:24–28).

These iron nails, excavated from Judea and Jerusalem, date from the Roman period (66 B.C. to A.D. 100). Excavators have unearthed metal tools used by many professions: saws, chisels, awls, and hammers used by carpenters and stone masons; hoes, plows, sickles, and goads used by farmers; and hooks and anchors used by fishermen.

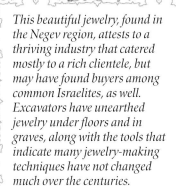

This beautiful jewelry, found in the Negev region, attests to a thriving industry that catered mostly to a rich clientele, but may have found buyers among common Israelites, as well. Excavators have unearthed jewelry under floors and in graves, along with the tools that indicate many jewelry-making techniques have not changed much over the centuries.

Jewelers: Even though most industries were centered around the necessities of life, the Israelites enjoyed trinkets, ornaments, and other indulgences. The jewelry business, catering mostly to the rich, crafted objects made of fine gold, silver, ivory, and precious stones. Fine gold wire, thread, and bells were made and embroidered into priestly garments.

The Bible mentions several precious stones, including rubies, sapphires, topaz, emeralds, jasper, and amethyst. With techniques that are still in use today, precious stones were set in gold and silver, examples of which have been discovered hidden under floors and in graves. And, just like today, those who could not afford expensive jewelry made substitutions with less expensive items. Substitute ornaments were made from baked clay, bone, limestone, wood, and leather. Homemade beads were often made from inexpensive stones, bones, and clay, and they were likely fashioned by peasant women instead of by professional jewelers.

CITY MERCHANTS

Today's big factories, modern ways of manufacturing, and fast-paced international trade are far removed from the cottage industries, local workshops, and limited ways of transporting goods in ancient times.

Commercial Trade: Marketplaces for local trade developed around the gates of cities. Seven different markets were renowned at the Jerusalem city gates. Animals were butchered and sold at the Sheep Gate, pottery at the Potsherd Gate, fish at the Fish Gate, and metalwork and jewelry at the Golden Gate. Merchants from out of town also set up stalls at these civic centers. However, goods were expensive, and taxes were high. Merchants had two sets of weights: one for use when they were buying and the other for when they were selling merchandise. Sometimes they used the weights dishonestly and cheated their customers, so Jewish rabbis enforced strict business rules and ethics that regulated bartering and banking.

Bartering: In earlier times, trade was done by "bartering," a common business practice whereby one item or service was exchanged for another. A carpenter would help a fisherman build his house in exchange for fresh and salted fish; a shepherd might trade wool for a farmer's grain. Bartering is still often practiced in biblical lands today. A part of each modern city, similar to the biblical gates, is designated as the place where merchants, farmers, potters, and the like can meet to exchange goods and services.

Banking: As the economy developed, gold and silver were introduced, and, eventually, money. Although not actually coins, a shekel or talent was a weight of gold or silver. Trading involved shekels and talents, which had to be weighed and measured.

Left: *A gate of Jerusalem is pictured here. The Golden Gate in Jerusalem was so named because of the many jewelry merchants who set up shop there.* Above: *These bronze scales, which date from the late Roman period, were used to weigh items bought or sold.*

Above: *James Tissot's painting is of a statue of King Nebuchadnezzar, who took Judah's King Jehoiachin captive to Babylon, along with "all the treasures of the house of the Lord, and the treasures of the king's house; he cut in pieces all the vessels of gold in the temple" (2 Kings 24:13). Most of the treasury of Judah was in the gold that was part of the temple.* Right: *The ostracon pictured here was found in Lachish, and it dates from the sixth century B.C. The writing is ancient Hebrew, but the prophet named in the business deal remains unclear in this pottery fragment.*

The first banks were temples and palaces, which safeguarded much wealth, while others hid their treasures and valuables. Nebuchadnezzar's heist of gold from the great temple was like robbing a bank. There is no mention of banking in the Old Testament, because lending to other Jews for profit was forbidden (Deuteronomy 23:19–20). Jews were permitted to make loans to foreigners, though. Some Jews still ended up in debt to creditors; fortunately the law anticipated that with a merciful provision for debtors (Deuteronomy 15:1–6).

In New Testament times, however, a regular banking system of money changers handled currencies of various countries. Under Roman law, bankers could put a debtor in prison. But Jesus urged his followers to lend without interest and give without expecting return of principal (Luke 6:35), except when they were investing talents in the Lord's work (Matthew 25:14–30), when a fivefold and twofold return were commended.

IOUs and Legal Documents: A great deal of business was conducted without a written bill of sale, not even an IOU. Large transactions were documented in specific ways. Jeremiah's purchase of land was transacted with money, a sealed deed of purchase, and an open copy, all before several witnesses (Jeremiah 32:1–15). Legal and business proceedings took place at the city gate, a public and busy spot where people could be called on to witness the signing of documents or attest to word-of-mouth business deals and the exchange of money (Ruth 4:1–12).

Pottery bits or chards, known as *ostraca*, were the equivalent of today's scrap paper or cash receipts. Business transactions, dates, and names of people were often listed on them. Contracts were drawn up on such "paper" for supplying commodities, statements of building rights, securing loans, and settlements of claims. Excavations have uncovered examples of these, plus many personal wax seals, throughout Palestine. These seals were affixed to documents, packages, and handles of food jars to authenticate ownership; this was yet another form of commercial documentation.

THE BUILDING TRADES

A variety of trades were involved in the housing business: foresters, carvers, masons, woodworkers, carpenters, plasters, bricklayers, and day laborers.

Stonemasons: Judging from the large number of Bible references to building projects requiring fine work in stone (2 Samuel 5:11; 2 Kings 22:6; 1 Chronicles 22:2; 2 Chronicles 24:12), this occupation was vital to the housing industry of early Israel. Public buildings and large homes of the wealthy were built using ashlar masonry, requiring skilled stonemasons to carefully cut blocks of limestone and fit them together—without mortar. The best example of ashlar masonry is the Western Wall in Jerusalem. This and other building projects would have used local limestone quarried throughout the hill country by groups of stonecutters. Ancient quarries have been found near Jerusalem, in Megiddo, Samaria, and Hazor.

Woodworkers: This trade included not just the shaping of wood, but also of metal or stone. Their products included furniture, farm implements, and buildings.

The two-thousand-year-old Western Wall—the holiest site in Jerusalem and the only still-standing remnant of the second temple—remains the best example of ashlar masonry. Ashlar masonry required skilled stonemasons to carefully cut and fit blocks of limestone rocks. Today, prayers scrawled by Orthodox Jewish pilgrims are wedged into the cracks of the stone blocks.

Some estimate that Jesus probably spent eighty to ninety percent of his life in the family business of carpentry. Justin Martyr (A.D. 100–165) testifies to this secular career of Jesus. In his *Dialogue With Trypho,* he describes Jesus as "working as a carpenter when among men, making plows and yokes, by which he taught the symbols of righteousness and an active life."

Archaeologists have unearthed many woodworking implements used in biblical times—from saws and hammers to various chisels, awls, and wood planes. The Bible not only describes how carpenters selected wood in Israel—some olive groves and cypress, cedar, and sycamore trees remained, perhaps even acacia, oak, and ash—it also provides details concerning actual carpentry: "The carpenter measures with a line and marks an outline with a marker; he roughs it out with chisels and marks it with compasses" (Isaiah 44:13, NIV). That might well describe Joseph and Jesus—except that the carpenter in Isaiah's day was fashioning a wooden idol.

While little is known from Scripture about Jesus' childhood, he probably learned carpentry as a child in Joseph's carpenter shop. Pictured here are some of the tools that they would have been most familiar with: the saw and awl (in Jesus' hands), and the adze (in Joseph's hand). The adze was used to shape or "plane" wood.

THE MEDICAL PROFESSION

Medical practice, for the Hebrews, was based on the health and hygiene laws given in the Pentateuch. (In that regard, the term "doctor" in some Bible translations refers not to the medical profession but to experts on the Mosaic law.) Washing and bathing, including cleansing after childbirth and for leprosy, were done for religious and health reasons. The Bethesda Pool in northeast Jerusalem, believed to possess healing properties, was an especially popular bathing spot and therapeutic spa.

Excavations have revealed collections of surgical instruments and evidence that certain surgical operations were

performed. The role of "perfume maker" (today's pharmacist) was as important as that of the doctor. He prepared oils, ointments, and potions for the sick, spices for embalming, incense and oils for the temple, and cosmetics for everyday use.

These glass containers, dating from the Roman period, were used for cosmetics, such as ointment, perfume, and eye paint. Only the rich could afford to enhance their personal appearance with such cosmetics. All the more startling that an alabaster jar of expensive perfume (pure nard), costing a year's wages, was used to anoint Jesus at Bethany.

Unlike surrounding tribes who mixed medical practice with superstition, magic, and sorcery, the Jews trusted God for good health and believed that sickness indicated spiritual disobedience or lack of faith. Along with their religious responsibilities, local priests were expected to fulfill medical duties.

THE LEGAL PROFESSION

In Israel, civil law and religious law were practically inseparable. Priests, Levites, and elders worked toward the same goals and shared the administration of justice. The city gate was where grievances were aired, local quarrels settled, and cases tried. During New Testament times, the supreme court was the Sanhedrin, which consisted of seventy rulers who met in the temple. The authorities in Rome allowed them to pass any sentence under Jewish law except the death penalty.

WOMEN: AT WORK IN THE HOME

Most women had low status, few rights, and did much of the hard work. Every day, beginning at sunrise, a rural woman collected water in heavy pots from the local spring or well and fetched the firewood (grasses and brush) to fuel the oven for the day's baking. Making bread first required the woman to push a heavy millstone to grind the grain into flour. Then she added some water and a left-

This reconstructed weaver's loom was used by women to make cloth. The lengthwise threads, which had clay weights hanging on the ends to keep them taut, are called the warp. The cross thread, called the woof, was attached to a shuttle, which was woven between the weighted warp.

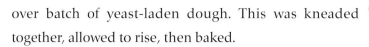

over batch of yeast-laden dough. This was kneaded together, allowed to rise, then baked.

While baking the bread, the mother might make cheese or yogurt from milk. At some point, she made kitchen pots and cooking utensils in the home pottery shop. During the harvest season, women sometimes worked in the fields—picking fruit, crushing the grapes and olives in the presses, winnowing the grain.

Also on her "to do" list were spinning wool, weaving fabric, and cleaning or mending other clothes. Her long workday ended with the evening meal, when the whole family gathered.

A woman's work was not confined to putting food on the table or clothes on the family's back. The mother also passed along her practical home-making skills, mentoring daughters in what she had learned from her own mother.

CLIMATE AND GEOGRAPHY

TREES IN PALESTINE

Looking across the war-torn, treeless land-scape of modern-day Lebanon and northern Israel, it's hard to imagine a time when this region was once covered with massive cedar trees that were used in huge housing projects. Yet it's true: King Solomon imported cedars of Lebanon to build the temple and all its elaborate wood furnishings (1 Kings 5:10; 7:2). Likewise, Zerubbabel used the "king's forest" of lumber reserves in constructing the second temple and related housing projects, as did Nebuchadnezzar in his Babylonian palaces.

Sadly, all these forests had long since disappeared by the time of Jesus. By the first century (and for the next two thousand years), there were no forests to support the housing industry. The average home in Palestine was, and still is, made of stone.

This modern Bedouin woman is making cheese from goat's milk, much as people did in ancient times. The Israelites were promised a "land flowing with milk and honey" (Exodus 3:8). The milk came from camels, sheep, and goats. Without refrigeration, milk quickly goes sour, so ancient Hebrews would pour the milk into a goatskin bag and churn it into butter, yogurt, curds, or cheese, which kept much longer in the hot Palestine climate.

Environmentalists contend that the forests of Lebanon were decimated, even "violated," by overzealous kings with their indiscriminate over cutting. The prophets Isaiah and Ezekiel offer another perspective: The ruin of the land was a judgment from God for the sins of the people. They hint that ecological disaster came upon Palestine, destroying its cedar forests, fir trees, and verdant valleys (see Isaiah 2:12–13; 10:19; 24:5–13; Ezekiel 31:1–14).

FORMER RAINS AND LATTER RAINS

These two terms refer to the precipitation that comes in the fall months ("former rains") and spring months ("latter rains"). Rain is plentiful and cold in the winter months (October to January) and rare in the summer months (May to September). Rain during the two growing seasons is crucial for crops to germinate and mature before being wiped out or dried up.

Drought and the resultant famine are conditions frequently mentioned in the Bible and associated with God's judgment. Latitude and height of the land naturally determine who gets how much water. Rain decreases from west (on the Mediterranean coast) to east (the Transjordan) because the mountains interfere with rain-bearing clouds. Rain also decreases from north (Mount Carmel and the Upper Jordan River Valley) to south (the Dead Sea, and the Negev and Arabah deserts). What is more, an east wind not only dries up everything, but it also brings such scorching heat that people lose even their will to live (Jonah 4:8).

Water for daily use (meal preparation, washing), never mind agricultural uses, was not readily available to Jerusalem residents. The finding, carrying, and saving of water was a daily struggle and perennial problem, not just

Isaiah, painted by James J. Tissot, prophesied that Israel's green valleys, fir trees, and cedar forests would one day come to ruin, and that this ecological disaster would be God's judgment on an idolatrous nation.

in times of drought. This prompted some enterprising families and kings to be most creative. King Hezekiah, for one, built a tunnel that brought water into Jerusalem's Pool of Siloam from a spring located five hundred yards outside the city.

Roman rulers later constructed amazing aqueduct systems that conducted water into the city from as far away as twenty-five miles, plus the cisterns to hold the water. Under the temple district in Old Jerusalem, archaeologists have found thirty-seven cisterns (with an average capacity of seven hundred cubic feet), one of which held two million gallons! But even when channeled by aqueduct or pipeline and stored in huge cisterns, this water was not always very sanitary or safe.

Well water, dug out of the limestone rock and siphoned from the underground streams below, was best. Many primitive city wells lasted for several centuries and became the local watering holes. Some still-useful wells have been discovered to have a depth of one hundred forty feet. The well in Samaria, reportedly dug by Jacob (John 4:6), is still there today. When Jesus offered "living

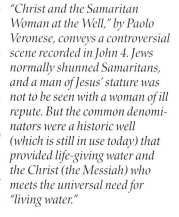

"Christ and the Samaritan Woman at the Well," by Paolo Veronese, conveys a controversial scene recorded in John 4. Jews normally shunned Samaritans, and a man of Jesus' stature was not to be seen with a woman of ill repute. But the common denominators were a historic well (which is still in use today) that provided life-giving water and the Christ (the Messiah) who meets the universal need for "living water."

Another watering hole of some biblical significance, and one that survives to this day, is the En-gedi ("spring of the goat") oasis by the Dead Sea. David sought refuge here from King Saul. The En-gedi oasis was also called Hazezon Tamar, which means "place of palms." It is one of the few hospitable places in this area of deep rocky ravines, intense heat, and little vegetation or water.

water" to the woman at that well, her first response was joy at being relieved of this daily struggle for life-giving water (John 4:11,15). She understood the "former" and "latter" rains, but had missed the "eternal." Then Jesus explained living water in reference to himself.

The Biblical Wilderness

Mary, the mother of Jesus, took a journey into the Judean hill country to see her cousin Elizabeth (Luke 1:39–40). This was no blessed event—at least not until she got to Elizabeth's. To appreciate the difficulty and danger associated with such a trip, it helps to see the landscape. The Judean mountains have their beauty—desert yellows, Dead Sea blues, violet-red mountains, and some green fruit trees. And the land had one good north-south road linking its principal cities—Jerusalem to the north, and Bethlehem, Beth-zur, and Hebron to the south.

But east of the Judean hill country was mostly impassable desert, stretching ten to fifteen miles toward the Dead Sea from its highest point (three thousand feet, near Hebron). This vast wasteland is broken up only by imposing cliffs and canyons, plus a few forts and oases (including En-gedi). This wilderness area was fit only for rebels, hermits, or fugitives like David.

SUMMARY

KNOWING WHAT THE WORLD of Jesus was like gives us some insights into the person Jesus was. He cannot be seen completely separate from the world in which he lived.

Jesus lived in a time of great turmoil, in a country that was constantly under siege. The history of God's people is also the history of Jesus. He was a descendant of the greatest ruler of Israel, King David. His history was bound to the history of the nation.

Religion was an important aspect of his life; Jesus and his family followed all the religious rules and traditions of his day. His family presented him at the temple in Jerusalem at eight days old, and they went to Jerusalem for

Galilee is much the same as in Jesus' day. Scenes like this of blue water, green hills, and rocky shores have remained virtually unchanged for over two thousand years.

Tissot's painting of Jesus reading the Torah in his hometown synagogue of Nazareth shows one of the important events in Jesus' life. That synagogue must have been special to him—after all, that is where he grew up and where he was taught the Torah. Rejection by this group of people must have been discouraging to Jesus.

holy days. Like other devout Jews of his day, Jesus defended the sanctity of the temple. But Jesus also saw problems with the religious establishment. In fact, it was the religious authorities who eventually conspired to put him to death.

There were no modern conveniences in Jesus' day—he walked the hilly, hot, dry lands of Palestine to preach and teach. Growing up, he probably lived in a one-room, tiny house with no running water. Work was backbreaking and time-consuming.

The times in which Jesus lived show us the humanity of Jesus. Despite his godliness, he undoubtedly struggled with the everyday problems of a Palestinian peasant.

THE TEACHINGS OF JESUS

❖ ❖ ❖

ESUS WASN'T JUST A TEACHER—many people followed him as a healer, a revolutionary, a Savior—but he taught brilliantly. He threw open the windows of God's kingdom and let everyone look inside. Through his parables and promises, witticisms and criticisms, bold claims and quiet assurances, he entertained and inspired, challenging people to understand God in a new way. Listen with new ears to this ancient sage.

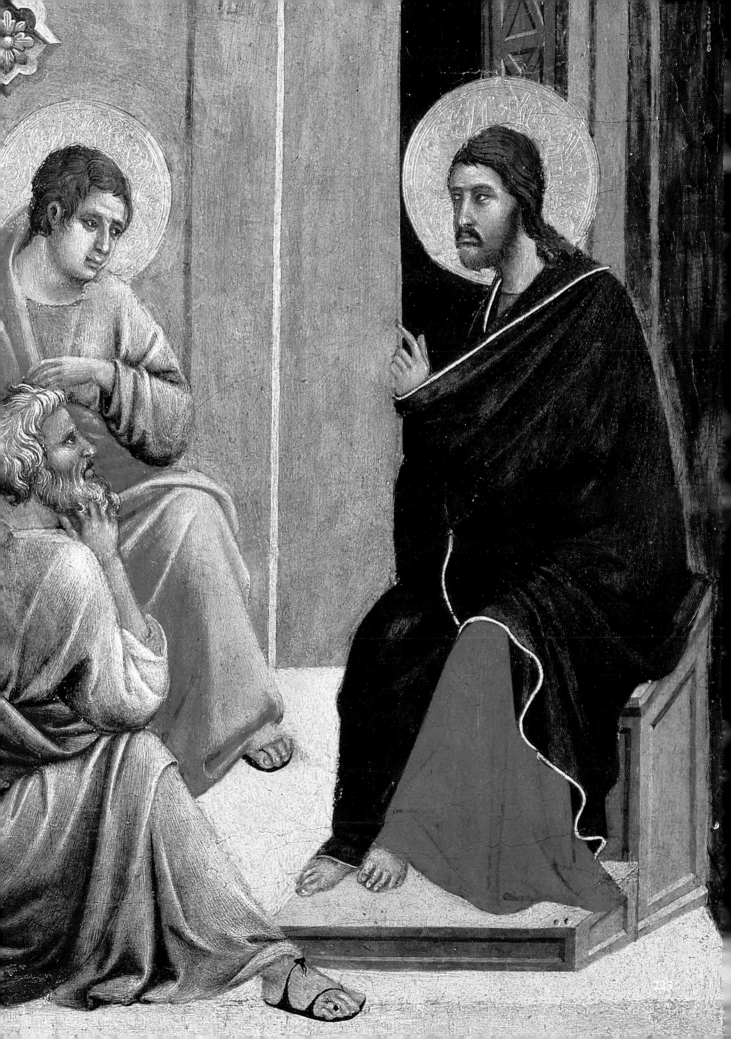

A NEW STYLE OF TEACHING

❖ ❖ ❖

AUTHORITY

W HEN JESUS TAUGHT, he turned heads, he raised eyebrows. His hearers were "astounded," Matthew tells us. Why? Because of his booming voice or smooth delivery? No. Because "he taught them as one having authority, and not as their scribes" (Matthew 7:28–29).

Above: *The Church of the Beatitudes rests on a hillside overlooking the Sea of Galilee, near the traditional site of Jesus' Sermon on the Mount.* Facing page: *In a Danish painting from the early 1800s, a red-robed Jesus delivers the Sermon on the Mount. Matthew says that Jesus "went up the mountain; and ... sat down" before beginning to teach (Matthew 5:1). In Jewish tradition, rabbis sat as they taught.*

From the start, authority was a hallmark of the teachings of Jesus. His Sermon on the Mount (Matthew 5—7) radiated with it. "You have heard that it was said, 'You shall love your neighbor....' But I say to you, Love your enemies." Six times in one chapter he placed his own teaching next to the accepted wisdom of his day. In each case he developed the previous command—not necessarily contradicting it, but always strengthening the command in some way.

"Do not murder" became "Do not mistreat."

"Do not commit adultery" became "Do not lust."

"Divorce legally" became "Stay married."

"Do not swear falsely" became "Always tell the truth."

"Retaliate fairly" became "Don't retaliate."

"Love your neighbors" became "Love everyone, including your enemies."

It was customary for rabbis to quote other rabbis, who in turn were often quoting other rabbis. There has also

been a rich tradition of Jewish wisdom rooted in the Torah, God's law. This had blossomed outward through many generations. The revered books of Judaism include not only the Torah, but the Midrash and the Talmud—essentially commentaries on the Torah and commentaries on those commentaries.

But Jesus dared to cut out the people in the middle. He didn't cite sources for his teaching. As far as he was concerned, it was true because it was true. No footnotes were necessary.

"Do not think that I have come to abolish the law or the prophets," he announced. "I have come not to abolish but to fulfill" (Matthew 5:17). Indeed, we can see the Sermon on the Mount as a new kind of law, one that seems to get to the heart of what God originally told Moses.

Some thought it arrogance, of course, to suggest that he *could* abolish the law and the prophets. But this was typical of Jesus' self-awareness. He saw himself as more than just a prophet; he set himself above and beyond the prophets. He was their fulfillment.

Jesus' self-concept undergirds his entire teaching ministry. Even as a child he told his parents, "I must be in my Father's house" (Luke 2:49), when he was found in the Jerusalem temple. His teaching was intimately entwined with his identity and his mission. He was not just showing the way to God, talking about the truth, or sharing the secrets of life. As he told his disciple Thomas, "I *am* the way, the truth, and the life."

HIS AUTHORITY TO HEAL

Jesus' sense of authority came through in the way he healed people and cast out demons. There were other wonderworkers and exorcists in ancient times, but these people would generally invoke the name of some higher

Above: *The Jewish love for Scripture is seen in the ornate housing given to this Torah. When Jesus taught in his hometown synagogue, he probably handled a scroll much like this one as he read from Isaiah and announced that the ancient prophecies were being fulfilled (Luke 4:16–21). Facing page: Jesus showed his spiritual authority by casting out demons. This ornate French illustration depicts such an exorcism (Matthew 15:22–28). Notice the escaping demon above the girl's head.*

power: "In the name of the Almighty Lord, I command you …." But Jesus used no such invocation. When a leper said, "If you choose, you can make me clean," Jesus said simply, "I do choose. Be made clean!" (Matthew 8:2–3). No elaborate formula, no fancy rituals, just a few words and the man was healed.

A short time later, Jesus came across two men possessed by demons. The demons begged him to cast them into a nearby herd of swine. Jesus just said, "Go," and the pigs rushed downhill into a watery grave (Matthew 8:28–34). No lengthy summoning of supernatural force; just a word or two from Jesus had incredible power.

One day early in his ministry, Jesus' teaching was interrupted. A paralyzed man was being lowered by friends through a hole in the roof. Moved by the faith of this man and his friends, Jesus said, "Son, your sins are forgiven."

This was a problem for some of the religious experts in the crowd. Only God could forgive sins. As they saw it, Jesus was speaking blasphemy.

A paralyzed man is lowered through the roof in front of Jesus (Mark 2:1–12). Many houses in ancient Israel had flat roofs that could be reached from an outside stairway, allowing this man and his friends access to Jesus when the house was too crowded.

But Jesus anticipated this problem and asked, "Which is easier, to say to the paralytic, 'Your sins are forgiven,' or to say, 'Stand up and take your mat and walk'?"

Which *is* easier? Well, it's easier to *say* sins are forgiven, though that's probably harder to *do*. Since it's a spiritual transaction, no one can prove whether it really happens or not. Not so with a healing. Everyone could quickly see whether Jesus had the power to heal the man.

Jesus went on: "But so that you may know that the Son of Man [Jesus' term for himself] has authority on Earth to

In a fifteenth-century work from the Sistine Chapel, we see the Sermon on the Mount. Notice the second story at the right. In Matthew's account, after Jesus finished the sermon, he healed a leper.

THE SERMON ON THE MOUNT

It has been called the Constitution of Christianity, the first collection of Jesus' teachings that you find as you read through the gospels. Many common phrases and proverbs come from these three chapters (Matthew 5—7): The Beatitudes (including *Blessed are the meek*); *salt of the earth; light of the world; turn the other cheek; love your enemies; don't let your left hand know what your right hand is doing;* the Lord's Prayer; *no one can serve two masters; consider the lilies; seek first the kingdom of God; do not judge; don't throw your pearls before swine; seek and you will find; wolves in sheep's clothing; the house built on sand.*

Was this in fact the first teaching Jesus did? Not necessarily. Matthew may have placed this sermon early because it serves as a splendid introduction to Jesus' teaching. It's also possible that Matthew collected portions of various sermons and grouped them here.

Luke has much of the same material (6:20–49), but in his account Jesus is teaching in a "level place" (6:17), not on a mountain. It's possible that Jesus gave the same basic talk on different occasions, but some scholars suggest that Matthew put Jesus on a mountain for a different reason.

Of the four gospel writers, Matthew seems the most steeped in Jewish tradition. He quotes Old Testament Scripture frequently, and he includes five major sermons of Jesus, possibly matching the five books of Moses. By putting the first sermon on a mountain, is he alluding to Moses' trip up Mount Sinai? Is he suggesting that this new "law" of Jesus should be understood on a par with the law given at Sinai?

forgive sins . . . ." He then turned to the paralyzed man and told him to walk. The man did, and the people were "amazed" (Mark 2:1–12).

This story shows that Jesus' healings were not just demonstrations of power, but of authority. He saw his spiritual authority wrapped up with his power to heal. That's why he didn't need to invoke God's power when he cast out demons or healed someone of a disease. He already had the authority to make that happen.

CRITIQUING THE COMMANDMENTS

His self-understanding gave Jesus the courage to criticize the common religious teachings of his day. In the Sermon on the Mount, he cut away the layers of religious teachings as if he were peeling the skin off an onion. Certain commands came right from the Torah—no murder, no adultery—and Jesus affirmed these. But in each case he found a godly principle of behavior that went far beyond the specific command. You might congratulate yourself on

Against the backdrop of the temple, Jesus fields questions from the Pharisees as he stands among his puzzled disciples. He dared to challenge the accepted wisdom of religious tradition, especially when it embellished Scripture.

avoiding the extreme sins of murder and adultery, but if your anger or lust are making you want to commit these sins, your attitude is not pleasing to God.

Some of these teachings seem similar to those of the strict religionists of his day. In their effort to avoid breaking God's law by accident, some observant Jews built a "hedge around the law" with added restrictions. To avoid sexual temptation, for instance, a man might lower his head as a woman walked past.

But Jesus' teaching is more than just a tightening of legal restrictions. He was pulling the spotlight away from the letter of the law and focusing it on the heart of the law. Are your desires pleasing God?

Jesus' teaching about swearing oaths (Matthew 5:33–37) illustrates this point: "Again, you have heard that

At Mount Sinai, Moses presents the stone tablets bearing God's law. Notice the similarity to other artists' renderings of Jesus' Sermon on the Mount. In his gospel, Matthew showed Jesus as a new Moses, presenting a new law from another mountain.

Fra Angelico's take on the Sermon on the Mount is stark and simple, showing a desert mountain more like Sinai than the Galilee hillside where Jesus probably spoke. Here there are only the twelve disciples listening. While Matthew indicates that Jesus sat down to teach the twelve, there is the implication that many more were listening (Matthew 5:1).

it was said to those of ancient times, 'You shall not swear falsely, but carry out the vows you have made to the Lord.'" The original quote was based on the third of the Ten Commandments (against taking God's name in vain) and other Scriptures (Numbers 30:2; Deuteronomy 23:21,22). But an elaborate ethical system had developed around this commandment.

To avoid uttering God's name in vain, observant Jews would not utter the name at all (this practice is still common). Then, when they swore to tell the truth, people would use all sorts of substitutes—heaven, Earth, Jerusalem, and others. But this became a kind of game: If you were swearing by the Earth, was that less binding than if you swore by heaven? Everyone agreed that if you swore to God, you'd have to be telling the truth (or you'd have to fulfill what you were promising to do). But these substitute oaths left the door open for falsehood and hypocrisy.

Jesus' simple solution was to throw out the whole game. "Do not swear at all, either by heaven, for it is the throne of God, or by the earth, for it is his footstool, or by Jerusalem, for it is the city of the great King." Every aspect of life is connected to God in some way, so none can be safely blasphemed with a false oath. "Let your word be 'Yes, Yes' or 'No, No,'" Jesus instructed, "anything more than this comes from the evil one." To please God you need to be a truthful person, not looking for ways to deceive others and get away with it.

The teaching on divorce is similar. The Old Testament included provisions for divorce, largely as a protection for jilted wives. With a certificate of divorce, a woman could

A woman caught in the act of adultery is brought before Jesus. Should she be stoned to death, as the law requires? While Jesus did not condone adultery, he was also passionate about justice and mercy. He knew the adultery laws had been twisted to favor powerful men. Jesus calmly invites anyone "without sin" to "be the first to throw a stone at her." The accusers instead walk away (John 8:1–11).

THE LORD'S PRAYER

Pray then in this way:

Within his Sermon on the Mount, Jesus offered his disciples a pattern for prayer (Matthew 6:9–13). He placed it in stark contrast to the vaunted, attention-grabbing prayers of the "hypocrites," who prayed loudly on street corners. A Pharisee in one of Jesus' stories began his prayer, "God, I thank you that I am not like other people" (Luke 18:11). But Jesus told his disciples to start with the focus on God's goodness, not their own.

Our Father in heaven,
hallowed be your name.

As commonplace as it is today, the idea of God as Father was rather new. In the Old Testament, God is Creator, King of the Universe, the Holy One. Only once in a while is the fatherhood image evoked (Deuteronomy 32:6; Psalm 103:13; Isaiah 63:16). But Jesus regularly called God Father—seeing him not only as his own Father, but the Father of his disciples as well. Elsewhere, Jesus even used the intimate term *Abba*, which may be translated "Daddy" (Mark 14:36).

Jesus clearly sets prayer in the context of a personal relationship, but not a relationship to be taken lightly. God's name (in Hebrew thought, his essence) was still to be hallowed (held sacred).

Your kingdom come.
Your will be done,
on earth as it is in heaven.

God's kingdom was Jesus' favorite subject. Most listeners would assume first that he was talking about a political reality, that God's kingdom would supplant the Roman kingdom as the Maccabees had overthrown the Syrians. But Jesus continually made it clear that he was talking about a different kind of kingdom. Elsewhere he said, "The kingdom of God is among you" (Luke 17:21). There's a delicious ambiguity about the Greek preposition he used. Is it among you, within you, or about to come upon you? It could be any or all of the above. In Jesus' teaching, God's kingdom exists anywhere where God is king, and that could be in an individual human life, in a community of believers, or in a future political revolution.

Give us this day our daily bread.

Daily bread was a common prayer request, especially for the needy, so it's not surprising here. The term calls to mind God's provision of manna to the wandering Israelites. Each day's bread had to be eaten on that day, or it would spoil. Jesus' disciples were to trust God to provide for them each day. In fact, their lifestyle required that trust.

And forgive us our debts,
as we have also forgiven our debtors.

Jesus taught about forgiveness on several occasions, and he usually connected human forgiveness with divine forgiveness. That is, if you don't offer forgiveness to another person, it will hinder you from receiving God's forgiveness. Even in this model prayer, the expected confession of sin (see Psalms 32; 51) is tightly connected with a commitment to forgive others.

And do not bring us to the time of trial,
but rescue us from the evil one.

The common conclusion to the Lord's Prayer—"for thine is the kingdom, the power, and the glory forever"—is a later addition by the early Church, and does not appear in the earliest manuscripts of Matthew or Luke (which has a shorter version of the prayer in 11:2–4).

prove that she was free to marry again (that is, she would not be committing adultery, which was a capital offense). In Jesus' day there was quite a controversy regarding the legal grounds for divorce. The law allowed a man to divorce his wife if he found "something objectionable" about her (Deuteronomy 24:1). But what did this phrase mean? Infidelity or just too many wrinkles?

Jesus was saying, "You've missed the point! Stop hunting for legal loopholes and get into the heart of God. God wants marriages to stay together."

Among Jesus' most famous statements are "Turn the other cheek" and "Love your enemies," which are both found in the Sermon on the Mount. Again he was responding to legal details with issues of the heart. The law of retaliation stated, "An eye for an eye and a tooth for a tooth" (Matthew 5:38; see also Exodus 21:24). This was actually meant to curb overretaliation. You couldn't kill a person for knocking your tooth out. Yet for many it became a way of life—a code of justice that kept tabs on every wrong committed and promised to even the score. With Israel under occupation by a heathen Roman army, this sense of grudge-holding was prevalent.

But Jesus urged his followers to take the high road, giving and forgiving. By turning the other cheek a person refuses to keep score. When a spirit of giving permeates a person's heart, retaliation is irrelevant.

The Old Testament says clearly, "Love your neighbor" (Leviticus 19:18). Some people had assumed a parallel command: "Hate your enemy." But once again Jesus cut out the false teaching. His followers were to love neighbors and enemies alike. There's nothing special about loving those who love you, Jesus said. Everyone does that. But the true children of God do something extra, reaching out to love even those who oppose them.

Flanked by two disciples (probably Peter and John), Jesus teaches the crowds in his Sermon on the Mount. He urged the people to exceed the demands of the law by forgiving instead of taking vengeance.

Jesus reframed the discussions of his day. He didn't join the current debates; he opened a whole new dimension. The legal bickering didn't matter. He dared to say that what matters is your heart and its relationship to God.

Many of these teachings of Jesus weren't new. Others in the Jewish community had warned against anger and lust and had put forth similar teachings on divorce and oath-taking. But Jesus was not relying on the support of these teachers. He was speaking truth because it was truth. His own word was enough. And it was this sense of authority that wowed the crowd.

QUESTIONING THE AUTHORITIES

You might say it was Jesus' sense of authority that got him killed. His authoritative teaching brought him into direct conflict with the religious leadership of his culture, especially the Pharisees.

He didn't waste any time getting into trouble. His first run-ins with the religious leaders are reported in Mark 2, Luke 5, and John 2—and he took them on in the second chapter of his Sermon on the Mount (Matthew 6).

"And whenever you pray, do not be like the hypocrites; for they love to stand and pray in the synagogues and at the street corners, so that they may be seen by others" (Matthew 6:5). He was clearly talking about the Pharisees, many of whom did this sort of thing. And that's a direct insult—praying was what the Pharisees did best. If you can't follow the religious examples of your religious leaders, who can you follow?

A sixth-century mosaic illustrates one of Jesus' simplest and most striking parables—the Pharisee and the tax collector who prayed in the temple. The Pharisee proudly reviewed his own merits, while the taxman looked down and begged for mercy (Luke 18:10–14). Jesus condemned the Pharisee and praised the tax collector.

In a nineteenth-century French painting, Jesus (left) faces a question from religious leaders (on the right). This picture is based on Matthew 16:1; the Pharisees and Sadducees asked for a sign from heaven, but Jesus refused. Jesus had many other run-ins with these authorities.

True worshipers pray in their rooms, Jesus said. They give their gifts quietly. They do their fasting in private ways. If your religious observances are just for show, then that's all they are—a show. You get your applause and that should be enough for you. But if you're really interested in pleasing God, then the praise of other humans is a distraction.

Jesus' conflict with the Pharisees is a major subplot of his ministry. It enters his teaching in many overt and subtle ways. You can easily picture a group of disapproving Pharisees glaring over Jesus' shoulder whenever he healed on the sabbath day, the prescribed day of rest (Mark 3:1–6). But they also have a cameo role in Jesus' parable of the prodigal son—as the older brother who refuses to rejoice when the sinner returns home (Luke 15:25–32).

In Matthew 23, we find Jesus' most scathing attack on the Pharisees, as well as the "scribes," the experts in Jewish law. (These two may have been identical and interchangeable with "rabbis.") Yet even here, he debated his opponent with care. "Do whatever they teach you … but do not do as they do," he told the people (Matthew 23:3). Because they sat in "Moses' seat," these leaders had some God-given authority, but Jesus accused them of seriously abusing it. He attacked them for concentrating on tiny details of the law and ignoring the big picture. "For you tithe mint, dill, and cummin [that is, they carefully calculated their contribution of one-tenth of the smallest household spices], and have neglected the weightier matters of the law: justice and mercy and faith" (Matthew 23:23). They felt proud of themselves for mastering the legal code, but they laid impossibly heavy burdens on the shoulders of the common people. Jesus called them "whitewashed tombs," which look beautiful on the outside but are full of dead bones (Matthew 23:27).

Several of the gospels depict a clever cat-and-mouse game with the Pharisees that resulted in some of Jesus' most memorable phrases. The Pharisees and scribes tried to trip Jesus up with no-win questions, but Jesus elegantly evaded their traps.

"Which commandment in the law is the greatest?" they asked. This is like ask-

A tomb in Jerusalem from about the time of Jesus. Notice the large stone that would cover the entrance. At festival time, tombs like this would be whitewashed so that no one would accidentally touch them and be ceremonially defiled.

ing which of your children you love most. Someone's bound to be offended. If Jesus said, "Don't murder," then he'd be soft on adultery—and vice versa. But Jesus pulled two overarching statements from the books of Moses: Love the Lord your God with all your heart, soul, and mind, and love your neighbor as yourself. "On these two commandments hang all the law and the prophets." He triumphed over the detail-minded Pharisees by taking the broad view, the big picture, the simple thrust of God's way (see Matthew 22:34–40).

"Should we pay taxes to Caesar?" they asked. Here begins the maneuvering that eventually brought Jesus before the Roman governor Pilate. It was an explosive political situation. The Romans were occupying Judea, and the Jews hated them. The Pharisees hated the Romans too, but apparently had learned to play the Roman power card. If Jesus said, "Don't pay taxes," they'd turn him in to the Romans as a revolutionary. If he said, "Pay taxes," then he'd lose his standing with the common people of Judea.

But Jesus asked to see a coin. "Whose head is this, and whose title?" he asked. It was the head of the emperor, Tiberius Caesar, on the Roman money they used.

"Give therefore to the emperor the things that are the emperor's, and to God the things that are God's" (Matthew 22:15–22). Another great escape. Even the Pharisees were "amazed." And it's a remarkable teaching. Jesus protected his own patriotism while challenging his opponents' devotion to money.

In Jesus' day, Israel was a land under military occupation. Centurions like this one, each commanding a platoon of about one hundred soldiers, enforced Roman law.

On several other occasions Jesus warned about the power of money. "You cannot serve God and wealth," he said in the Sermon on the Mount, going on to talk of the virtues of trusting God for your everyday needs (Matthew 6:24–34). The true follower of God should have a life in which money has little power, where it doesn't matter much. And so, if Caesar stamps out the coins, he can have them. Faith in God is a much more valuable currency.

ACTING ON HIS WORDS

In the closing of the Sermon on the Mount, Jesus used a word-picture that further underscored his authority. "Everyone then who hears these words of mine and acts on them will be like a wise man who built his house on rock" (Matthew 7:24). The rock stands strong when the storms assault. On the other hand, the listener who doesn't act on Jesus' words is like the fool who builds on sand. In the rainy season the house gets washed away.

This parable puts forth a common theme of Jesus: the importance of doing the truth, not just speaking it. But notice the object of obedience here. Not the Torah, not the "law and the prophets," not the Father's will, but Jesus' own words. It was clear he saw his teaching as more than a collection of theories, thoughts on the law, or suggestions for living. He presented his words in continuity with the Hebrew Scriptures, the fulfillment of what God had already revealed to his people. And that's what gave his teaching such an astonishing sense of authority.

Facing page: *Jesus gained a following by challenging the accepted religious ideas of his day and offering the common people a chance to know God. His Sermon on the Mount and other teachings were stunning for their boldness, practicality, and simplicity.* Left: *Coins with the head of Herod Agrippa I, who ruled Judea (with Roman backing) shortly after the time of Jesus. It was common for currency to bear the image of the current ruler, which would usually be the Roman emperor or some local puppet king set up by the Romans.*

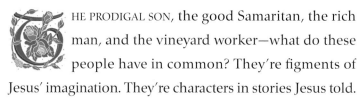

HOW JESUS TAUGHT

❖ ❖ ❖

THE STORY

THE PRODIGAL SON, the good Samaritan, the rich man, and the vineyard worker—what do these people have in common? They're figments of Jesus' imagination. They're characters in stories Jesus told.

Any successful public speaker will tell you that stories grab an audience like nothing else. You can lecture for three hours on the meaning of life and the key to happiness, but tell one story about a boy and his dog, and what do you think people will remember? The story.

Jesus knew this well, and history has proven it. The prodigal, the Samaritan—they're part of our modern consciousness, even among folks who know nothing else of Jesus' teaching.

But Jesus was doing far more than grabbing an audience. He was intentionally covering the truth beneath layers of fiction. He was shrouding some shocking ideas under a cloak of entertainment. He was teasing his hearers with big thoughts in little packages.

THE SAMARITAN

Take the good Samaritan (Luke 10:25–37). This whole story was an answer to a trick question. The law said, "Love your neighbor as yourself," but one lawyer asked Jesus, "Who is my neighbor?" Never one to give a straight answer to a crooked question, Jesus made up a story.

A traveler (presumably Jewish) was attacked, robbed, and left for dead. A priest and a Levite (a religious assistant) each passed by without helping the man. The third passerby, a Samaritan, stopped to help. Jews despised Samaritans in those days, considering them ethnic half-breeds and religious heretics. As they saw it, there was no

Above: *In stained glass, we see one of Jesus' best-known parables. A Samaritan bends to help a beaten traveler. "He went to him and bandaged his wounds.... Then he put him on his own animal, brought him to an inn, and took care of him" (Luke 10:34).* Facing page: *In Rembrandt's brilliant arrangement of light and shadow, a ragged prodigal son is embraced by his loving father (Luke 15:11–32).*

such thing as a "good" Samaritan. But in Jesus' story, it was the Samaritan who saved the life of the Jew, binding his wounds and putting him up at the local inn.

Then Jesus turned to the lawyer and asked, "Which of the three was a neighbor to the man who was robbed?"

Interestingly, the lawyer couldn't bring himself to say, "Samaritan." He answered, "The one who showed him mercy." Then Jesus urged him, "Go and do likewise."

It's typical of Jesus' parables that they raise more questions than they answer. The lawyer's question requires a simple response, something along the lines of "Your neighbor is anyone who needs your help." And many people draw that lesson from this parable.

But the fact that the helper was a Samaritan required a major mind-set change on the part of this lawyer. "The Samaritan should be the robber, not the good guy," he must have been thinking. "Samaritans are bad! A Samaritan would never help a suffering Jew."

But to go back to the original question: "Who is my neighbor?" If Jesus weren't around to shatter his preconceptions, how would the lawyer have answered this? "Well, my neighbors are people who live around me, people who share my beliefs and values. They are people like myself, and that's why I should love them as myself."

In fact, Jesus had already dealt with the idea of "Love your neighbor and hate your enemy" (Matthew 5:43). It was apparently common to draw the circle of love rather tightly around oneself. Good people were inside the circle.

Modern-day Samaritans celebrate Passover. In Jesus' day, Jews looked down on Samaritans as half-breeds and heretics. Ethnically, they were the result of the Assyrians' policy of forced relocation and race-mixing. Then, cut off from worship in the Jerusalem temple, they developed their own variation of the Jewish faith. This background made Jesus' parable of the good Samaritan especially shocking.

Bad people—like prostitutes and tax collectors and Samaritans—were left out.

If Jesus had simply said, "Show mercy to people in need," the lawyer (and others) would still find a way to exclude the "bad people" they hated. But by introducing the Samaritan as the hero of this story, Jesus challenged the whole notion of "good people" and "bad people." The Samaritan acted as a neighbor, despite his heritage. So he had to be loved as a neighbor, just as the law commanded.

PARABLES

Stories like this are known as parables, and Jesus used them often. A parable is somewhere between a metaphor and an allegory, a fiction that speaks a truth.

Jesus didn't invent parables, but he certainly refined the art. The prophet Nathan skewered King David with a simple story of a rich man who stole a poor man's beloved lamb. In reality, it was David who had stolen Bathsheba, a poor man's wife (2 Samuel 12:1–15). Isaiah sang about an "unfruitful vineyard," clearly the rebellious people of Judah (Isaiah 5:1–7). And parables appear in about 20 other Old Testament passages as well.

But Jesus told at least 40 parables of varying lengths. Some are scarcely a sentence long: The pearl of great value, for which a merchant sold his whole fortune. There. That's what the kingdom of God is like. Other parables are mini-dramas, with several scenes and supporting charac-

In parables, Jesus used common experiences to share spiritual truth. "Which of you, having a hundred sheep and losing one of them, does not leave the ninety-nine in the wilderness and go after the one that is lost until he finds it? When he has found it, he lays it on his shoulders and rejoices" (Luke 15:4–5).

ters: The landowner who leases out his fields and moves away, sending messengers to collect the rent, but the messengers are killed. That's what the kingdom of God is like.

"Like" is a key word. A parable speaks of one thing in terms of another. It teaches spiritual truth by tracing similarities to physical objects or common experiences. Jesus used the stuff of everyday life—nets, sheep, vineyards, crops, coins, banquets—to get his points across.

And he had many points to make. The chief theme of Jesus' parables was the kingdom of God. (Matthew, reflecting the Hebrew shyness about using God's name, calls it "the kingdom of heaven.") Often he began his stories with the phrase "the kingdom of God [or heaven] is like..." It's like a tiny mustard seed that grows into a huge tree (Luke 13:18); like a bit of yeast that makes the whole dough rise (Luke 13:20); like a treasure hidden in a field (Matthew 13:44); like a net that catches good and bad fish (Matthew 13:47–50). We can try to explain such word pictures with modest success: God's kingdom starts small and grows; it demands total commitment; it will eventually sort out good and evil, but not yet. And still our explanations lose something in translation. The tantalizing thing about Jesus' parables is that they invite explanation, but they also defy it. Just when you think you've got one figured out, you find a whole new angle. The kingdom that Jesus spoke of could only be painted, not pigeonholed.

Another common theme of Jesus' parables might be defined as this life and the next. A rich man tore down his

Jesus mocked the greed of the rich man who tore down his barns to build bigger ones. When God demanded his life, the man had nothing to bargain with (Luke 12:16–21). Jesus urged his followers to be "rich toward God."

barns to build bigger ones and proceeded to "eat, drink, and be merry," ignoring God. "But God said to him, 'You fool! This very night your life is being demanded of you. And the things you have prepared, whose will they be?'" (Luke 12:13–21). You can't take it with you. Poor Lazarus, who begged at the rich man's gate, gets a comfy spot in the hereafter, while the rich man lies in torment (Luke 16:19–31). This turnabout is seen again in another parable in which the Final Judgment is based on how people treated "the least of these"—that is, the poor and needy (Matthew 25:31–46). Oddly, Jesus also told his hearers to be like the dishonest manager who, fired from his job, proceeded to give deep discounts to his (former) employer's debtors. The man was using his lame-duck status in his old job to make friends who would help him in the future. Though this is a strange role model, the lesson is consistent with Jesus' instruction to invest in your heavenly future (Matthew 6:19–21).

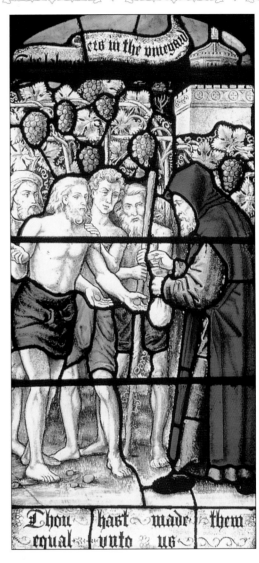

Who can blame them? After some laborers got paid a denarius for one hour's work, those who had worked all day thought they'd get more. But the master stuck with the agreed-upon fee: one denarius. In the same way, Jesus was saying that God's grace doesn't always seem fair.

Justice, mercy, and forgiveness regularly occur as parable themes. A landowner hires workers at four different times during the day and pays them all the same wage (Matthew 20:1–16). Isn't it unfair to pay one person the same for one hour as you pay another for the whole day? Not if the laborers agreed to that price. The landowner can certainly overpay some people if he wants to—and God will show mercy to sinners, no matter how much the righteous may grumble. In yet another parable (Matthew 18:23–35), a king cancels the million-dollar debt of a servant, who then goes out and demands repayment of a

Be prepared! In first-century Judea, weddings included a procession of the bridegroom and his entourage to the bride's house, where she would wait with her bridesmaids. In Jesus' story, five bridesmaids were wise enough to bring extra fuel for their lamps, while five others (shown in the background) had to go running to the store (Matthew 25:1–13). Note Peter in the center, holding the key to the kingdom.

couple of dollars from another servant. When the king hears about it, there's big trouble. Forgiven people need to forgive others.

Watchfulness is another recurring theme. In Jesus' parables, masters are always going away and leaving their servants in charge (Mark 13:34). The clever servant stays alert for the arrival of the master (Luke 12:35–40). Smart bridesmaids are prepared with extra oil for their lamps, in case the groom shows up late. Then they can light their way to the wedding reception (Matthew 25:1–13). Jesus seems to imply that God will be doing something big, and that people need to stay alert as they wait for it.

Jesus also urged his hearers to take risks. Smart servants used their master's money to play the market, while the foolish servant buried the money in the ground (Luke 19:11–27). A merchant sells all he has to buy that one fabulous pearl (Matthew 13:45–46).

THE SEED AND THE SOIL

"Why do you teach in parables?" Jesus' disciples asked him this question after he had told a rather simple story about a farmer sowing seeds (Matthew 13:10–17; see also Mark 4:10–12). The teacher replied, not with a defense of the educational value of story, but with a troubling quote from the prophet Isaiah.

"To you it has been given to know the secrets of the kingdom of heaven," Jesus told his disciples, "but to them it has not been given." He was referring to the crowds who heard his parables, adding: "The reason I speak to them in parables is that 'seeing they do not perceive, and hearing they do not listen, nor do they understand.'"

The quote is from Isaiah's commissioning as a prophet (Isaiah 6:9–10). There God seemed to say, "People won't listen to you, but go and prophesy anyway." (It may have been a bit of reverse psychology or a last attempt to get through to the people.) Yet when Jesus uses these lines, it sounds as if he's deliberately hiding his true message from people.

To some extent, this is quite clever. From the beginning of his public life, Jesus had powerful enemies. His teaching was often monitored for blasphemy, a capital crime under Jewish law. Jesus had a good sense of timing, and early in his ministry he was quite coy in his public pronouncements. He didn't want to turn up the heat too soon. And parables allowed him to say all sorts of things about God's kingdom and his own role in it without incriminating himself.

But it's also possible that Jesus was talking about the same kind of mind-set shift we saw with the good Samaritan story. The stories might shake some people's defenses, enticing them to see life in a new way. Some people

The parable of the farmer sowing seed depicts Jesus' own teaching ministry. Seed falls in different places with different results. In the same way, God's Word finds different responses in different hearts.

would "get it"—their hearts would be open to the exciting new picture of life Jesus was painting. These hearers would become followers of Jesus (among those to whom it was "given" to know God's secrets). Others wouldn't get it at all—Jesus' parables would seem like nonsense to them, or just playful diversions.

In fact, Jesus' parable of the farmer sowing seed illustrates this point (Matthew 13:1–9,18–23). The seed fell on four types of ground: 1) the footpath, where it was eaten by birds; 2) rocky ground, where it sprouted but withered; 3) among thorns, where it grew but was choked; and 4) fertile soil, where it then thrived. As Jesus explained later, the seed was God's Word, and the soils were different types of hearts. Some hear, but the word never takes root; others accept it and grow, but their understanding remains shallow, and it withers away; still others have their faith choked off by worries and temptations.

The styles in this seventeenth-century Spanish rendering come from the painter's (Bartelome Esteban Murillo) world, but the story still belongs to Jesus. The prodigal son receives his early inheritance from his father, while the older brother and a servant look on.

Only a portion of the hearers are the "good soil" that "bears fruit." These people apply Jesus' teaching.

THE PRODIGAL SON

Jesus also used parables to describe the climate of his times, almost like a political cartoonist in modern times. Once he complained that "the people of this generation" were like children who were never satisfied. Austere John the Baptist was considered demonic, while Jesus was considered a glutton. The finicky crowds were like "children sitting in the marketplace and calling to one another, 'We

played the flute for you and you did not dance; we wailed, and you did not weep.'"

One of Jesus' most cutting social commentaries is hidden in the parable of the prodigal son. Many have heard this, but most know only half the story. There are actually two sons here, and both have important roles.

The younger son asks for his inheritance early, and his father agrees. The boy goes off and wastes it in wild living. The money runs out about the time a drought hits, and the young man has to make a living feeding pigs (an especially abhorrent thought for an observant Jew). He decides to go back home, but only as a servant, since he has certainly squandered any rights to sonship.

To his surprise, the father welcomes him back with open arms and throws him a party. This angers the older

A Flemish painting tells part of the prodigal son parable. The rich boy in the background gets rejected when he runs out of money (middle) and ends up feeding pigs (foreground). While feeding the pigs, the prodigal realizes he needs to go back home.

son, who has stayed home, helping his father. He never had a party thrown for him. Oh, the injustice!

"Son, you are always with me," the father assures him, "and all that is mine is yours. But we had to celebrate and rejoice, because this brother of yours was dead and has come to life; he was lost and has been found" (Luke 15:11–32).

The prodigal son comes to his senses as he feeds the pigs. "How many of my father's hired hands have bread enough and to spare, but here I am dying of hunger! I will get up and go to my father, and I will say to him … I am no longer worthy to be called your son; treat me like one of your hired hands" (Luke 15:11–32).

When you consider that the culture of Jesus' day was sharply divided between the haves and the have-nots, religiously speaking, the story takes on new meaning. Jesus made a point of criticizing the religious establishment and welcoming those on the outside. "Tax collectors and the prostitutes are going into the kingdom of God ahead of you," he once told the religious leaders (Matthew 21:31).

These religious outcasts were clearly in the position of the prodigal son. They had willfully abandoned God's laws and squandered their lives, but now—through Jesus' teaching—they were coming back to God, their Father, who welcomed them with open arms and celebration. In fact, Jesus often characterized God's kingdom as a great party open to all sorts of unlikely guests (Luke 14:15–24).

And the older brother? He certainly stood for the religious leaders who complained when Jesus spent time with these outcasts (Matthew 9:10–11). They had always stayed close to God's law, and they resented the idea that lawbreakers could return to God so easily. They wanted no part of this party.

Did those leaders see themselves as the older brother? Perhaps. But maybe their resentment of Jesus blinded them to the truth of this political cartoon. Hearing the simple story, they may never have heard the underlying message.

HUMOR

One characteristic of Jesus' teaching style that's often overlooked is his humor. We lose some of it in translation, but some common elements of modern comedy—surprise, absurdity, recognition, social commentary—remain. On one occasion, Jesus remarked that it was hard for a rich person to enter heaven. As if someone else had asked, "How hard is it?" Jesus went on to his punch line: "It is easier for a camel to go through the eye of a needle" (Matthew 19:24).

Jesus employed this level of absurdity in several of his teachings. In his lengthy rebuke of the Pharisees, he quipped, "You strain out a gnat but swallow a camel" (Matthew 23:24). What better way to critique the absurdity of their obsession with minute details of the legal code (and their corruption in larger issues)!

Elsewhere he called the Pharisees "blind guides of the blind," evoking a tragicomic image of both leader and follower walking right into a pit (Matthew 15:14). But the leaders weren't the only victims of Jesus' comic skill.

In the Sermon on the Mount, he painted another extreme word picture. "Why do you see the speck in your neighbor's eye, but do not notice the log

Jesus could, at times, say very amusing things: How hard is it for the rich to reach heaven? Well, it's easier for a camel to get through the eye of a needle.

Even in stained glass, it's amusing. "Here," says the half-blind man, "let me get that speck out of your eye." It's just as absurd when we pass judgment on others for things that we do ourselves!

in your own eye? Or how can you say to your neighbor, 'Let me take the speck out of your eye,' while the log is in your own eye?" (Matthew 7:3–5). Once again, Jesus takes a simple aspect of life (a speck in the eye, a gnat in your soup) and pumps it up to an absurd level (a log in the eye, swallowing a camel) in order to make a point about the absurdity of hypocrisy.

Teaching about God's answers to prayer, Jesus asked the crowd, "Is there anyone among you who, if your child asks for a fish, will give a snake instead of a fish? Or if the child asks for an egg, will give a scorpion?" (Luke 11:11–12).

You can almost see this as a comedy sketch, featuring the "loving" parent who gives a child snakes and scorpions. No, it doesn't happen that way! Then Jesus nailed down his point: "If you then, who are evil, know how to give good gifts to your children, how much more will the heavenly Father give the Holy Spirit to those who ask him!" (verse 13). It was a logic Jesus used more than once. If fallible humans do this, imagine how much more our perfect God does.

The parables are packed with entertaining images: the fool building a house on sand; the tycoon tearing down his barns to build bigger ones; the foolish bridesmaids running out of oil for their lamps; one neighbor rousting another out of bed at midnight to borrow some bread; the jilted host inviting street people to his party. These may not have drawn belly-laughs from Jesus' hearers, but they would certainly elicit smiles of recognition.

Jesus' public speeches were dotted with witticisms, clever turns of phrases, fresh twists of logic. He promised his disciples they would "fish for people" (Matthew 4:19), and he warned them against the "yeast" of the Pharisees—presumably the bits they added to God's law that made it rise beyond recognition. He was a master of the rhetorical question that seemed to put everything in perspective. "If you love those who love you," he asked, "what reward do you have?" (Matthew 5:46). Even the lowly tax collectors did that much! Loving your enemies was the true challenge of God's people.

"Can any of you by worrying add a single hour to your span of life?" (Matthew 6:27). Of course not. Then why worry? Jesus went on to paint more amusing pictures—lilies of the field working hard to make their own clothes; birds planting crops and storing their harvest in barns. It doesn't happen! And why not? Because God takes care of flowers and birds. So don't worry, Jesus concluded—God will also take care of you.

Not even wealthy Solomon could dress as nicely as the flowers of the field, Jesus said, because God himself is their maker (Matthew 6:29). If God cares that much for the one-day wonders dotting the fields, won't he also provide for each of us humans?

THE WRITER'S SIDE OF THE STORY

❖ ❖ ❖

HEN WE EXAMINE THE STYLE of Jesus' teaching, we must consider our sources. How do we know what Jesus taught? We know because of the four gospels—Matthew, Mark, Luke, and John. Other than a few sentences in the New Testament epistles, everything we know about what Jesus said or did comes from these four books.

Any writer, no matter how inspired, is going to have an angle, a purpose, a way of seeing the events. And so the style of Jesus' teaching differs slightly, depending on which of our four reporters is quoting him. These differences merit a brief look.

MATTHEW: JESUS AS RABBI-KING

Plato had proposed that the ideal republic be ruled by a philosopher-king. Matthew saw Jesus as a rabbi-king, the teacher of truth who ushered in God's kingdom.

The sheer bulk of this book testifies to Matthew's emphasis on Jesus as a teacher. The longest of the four gospels, Matthew shortens most of the narrative passages of Mark, but he more than makes up for it in the lengthy passages of Jesus' teaching. Matthew gives us five major discourses of Jesus and also some shorter teachings in between those.

Remember, it's Matthew who sends Jesus up the mountain (like Moses) to deliver his new law—and Jesus "sat down" (as any rabbi would) to give it (5:1). More than the other writers, Matthew establishes Jesus' authority as a rabbi (7:29) and questions the authority of the recognized teachers of that day (23:3).

Facing page: *Matthew. According to Christian tradition, the writer of the first gospel was a tax collector-turned-apostle, also known as Levi (compare Matthew 9:9 with Mark 2:14). He left his tax booth to follow Jesus.*

When John baptized Jesus, the Spirit descended upon Jesus "like a dove." A voice from heaven was heard, affirming Jesus as the Son of God. The voice alluded to two key Old Testament passages—one about a king, the other about a servant.

But in Matthew's view, Jesus isn't just the teacher, he's the subject, too. At every turn, Matthew cites some Old Testament prophecy that Jesus is fulfilling. After Jesus' baptism, we hear the voice from heaven saying, "This is my Son, the Beloved, with whom I am well pleased" (3:17). This statement actually reflects two Old Testament verses: Isaiah 42:1, which begins several chapters about the servant who pleases God; and Psalm 2:7, part of a coronation song that says, "You are my son." According to Matthew, Jesus was the promised Messiah, the Son of God who came as a servant but would ultimately be king.

This is why Matthew starts with a genealogy, showing Jesus as a descendant of Abraham and David, both a true Jew and a royal heir. The messiah would have to come from David's line (22:42)—and Matthew underscores Jesus' royal claim with several references to him as "Son of David" (9:27; 12:23; 15:22; 20:30–31; 21:9).

So for Matthew, Jesus is both the wise rabbi and the true king waiting for the right time to establish his kingdom. Jesus speaks with truth and power.

MARK: JESUS AS WONDERWORKER

Mark is less intense. He doesn't give us a lot of Jesus' teaching, but he focuses on Jesus' actions. Skimming the first few chapters can make you dizzy. "Jesus came here, Jesus went there, immediately he did this, then he did that." But Mark does offer memorable phrases.

Challenged about socializing with sinners: "Those who are well have no need of a physician, but those who

are sick; I have come to call not the righteous but sinners" (2:17).

Challenged about breaking sabbath laws: "The sabbath was made for humankind, and not humankind for the sabbath; so the Son of Man is lord even of the sabbath" (2:27–28).

Accused of using demonic power to exorcize demons: "How can Satan cast out Satan? ... If a house is divided against itself, that house will not be able to stand" (3:23,25).

When Pharisees accused his disciples of violating their hand-washing regulations: "You abandon the commandment of God and hold to human tradition" (7:8).

To the crowd, after predicting his own death: "If any want to become my followers, let them deny themselves and take up their cross and follow me. For those who want to save their life will lose it, and those who lose their life for my sake, and for the sake of the gospel, will save it" (8:34–35).

To his disciples, who had been fighting for leadership: "Whoever wants to be first must be last of all and servant of all" (9:35).

Left: *Despite the gray beard, Mark was probably quite young during Jesus' ministry. Later he traveled with the Apostle Paul and worked with Peter. In fact, early tradition says the second gospel is actually the memoir of Peter, as told to Mark. Below: Jesus exorcizes a demon, in one of many such scenes from his ministry. His opponents accused him of being in league with the devil. In his characteristically probing way, Jesus asked, "How can Satan cast out Satan?" (Mark 3:23).*

After more of the disciples' infighting: "The Son of Man came not to be served but to serve, and to give his life a ransom for many" (10:45).

After someone suggested they should have sold the perfume lavished upon Jesus and given the money to the poor: "You always have the poor with you, and you can show kindness to them whenever you wish; but you will not always have me" (14:7).

Still, in Mark, Jesus' actions speak louder than his words. Viewing his miracles, people become amazed at his authority, but Jesus remains quiet about his true identity. About halfway through this gospel (8:27–29), Jesus has a heart-to-heart with his disciples, asking them, "Who do you say that I am?" It's Peter who replies, "You are the Messiah."

"And he sternly ordered them not to tell anyone about him. Then he began to teach them that the Son of Man must undergo great suffering, and be rejected…and be killed, and after three days rise again" (8:30–31).

Who is this "Son of Man"? It's Jesus' name for himself, used especially in Mark's Gospel. The term harks back to the Book of Daniel, in which the prophet has an apocalyptic vision of "one like a son of man, coming with the clouds of heaven" (Daniel 7:13; NRSV has "human being," but the original Aramaic literally reads "son of man"). Jesus seems to use this in a messianic sense, playing his ultimate glory against his immediate suffering.

The New Testament identifies Luke as a doctor and an associate of the Apostle Paul. The third gospel also shows a keen eye for historical detail, which might fit with a doctor's scientific mindset. Luke also wrote the Acts of the Apostles, which picks up the story after Jesus' resurrection.

LUKE: JESUS AS WANDERING PHILOSOPHER

In Luke, Jesus is often going to parties or talking about parties. The Jesus presented in the third gospel is an itinerant sage, one who will dine with anyone who wants company.

The namesake of this gospel was an associate of the Apostle Paul, a doctor, and a Gentile. So, where Matthew seemed concerned about presenting Jesus to the Jewish-Christian community, Luke painted a more European portrait. He quoted Old Testament Scripture less and explained Hebrew terms and customs his Greek readers would find puzzling.

So it's no surprise that the Jesus of the third gospel offers salvation to everyone—Jew, Samaritan, Gentile, male, female, rich, poor, Pharisee, prostitute, tax collector. Matthew, it must be noted, is not provincial, but he's more focused on the Jewish community. Luke seems to be making a point of breaking down social boundaries.

Jesus does eat in the home of a Pharisee, though a "sinful woman" slips in and anoints his feet with ointment. Jesus forgives the woman's sins and scolds the Pharisee for judging her (Luke 7:36–50).

As Jesus dined in the home of a Pharisee, a woman "who had lived a sinful life" crashed the party and caused a scene, pouring perfume on Jesus' feet and wiping them with her hair. The host was scandalized, but Jesus took the opportunity to teach about forgiveness.

263

Too short to see over the crowd, an enterprising tax agent named Zacchaeus climbed a tree. Jesus noticed him there and asked if he could come to Zacchaeus's home for dinner. The religious leaders were angry that Jesus befriended such a sinner, but the experience changed the taxman's life.

Luke makes a point of identifying the women involved in Jesus' ministry (8:2–3), and women appear frequently in the stories he presents. It's Luke who records Mary's song of praise, known as the Magnificat, in the birth narrative (1:46–55). He also tells of the exchange between Martha and Mary of Bethany—in which Mary is commended for learning from Jesus' teachings, a nontraditional activity for women in those days (10:38–42).

Samaritans are pointedly included in Luke. Only Luke tells the good Samaritan story (10:25–37) and identifies the thankful leper as another Samaritan (17:11–19). When James and John wanted to call fire down on a resistant Samaritan village, Jesus rebuked them (9:51–56).

Here Jesus cites the Old Testament examples of the widow of Zarephath and Naaman the Syrian as Gentiles who received God's grace, and he praises a Roman centurion: "Not even in Israel have I found such faith" (7:9).

We see this boundary-breaking in the dramatic story of Zacchaeus, the tiny taxman (Luke 19:1–10). Most religious people of Jesus' day would have overlooked this fellow…literally. He was so short, he had to climb a tree to get a peek at Jesus over the crowd. (You might guess that no one in the crowd wanted to let this cheating tax collector through.)

But Jesus not only noticed Zacchaeus amid the branches, he stopped and spoke with him. In fact, Jesus invited himself to dinner, giving his enemies another chance to grumble that he was "the guest of one who is a sinner." Yet in this story we see that Jesus not only socialized with "sinners"—he changed them. Zacchaeus came away from this experience crowing, "If I have defrauded anyone of anything, I will pay back four times as much." Luke sums up the story by returning to the theme of being lost: "The Son of Man came to seek out and to save the lost."

While Matthew includes parables of discovery and investment, Luke has parables about searching for the lost—the woman who sweeps her house for her lost coin, the shepherd who hunts for the lost sheep, the father who waits for his lost son (Luke 15). Matthew's Jesus challenges his fellow Jews with, "What will you do with what you've been given?" Luke's Jesus opens the doors of God's party to the disenfranchised and the lost.

The fourth gospel is attributed to John, one of Jesus' fisherman-disciples. John calls himself "the one whom Jesus loved." Tradition says he lived longer than all the other disciples, becoming a revered elder in the church at Ephesus. While the other three gospels share many stories, John usually has a different view. Many think he was writing much later than the other three and that he was trying to explain Jesus' identity rather than just reporting events.

JOHN: JESUS AS THE MEANING OF LIFE

"In the beginning was the *Logos*," says John 1:1. Usually translated "Word," this Greek term has a rich history. In the century before Christ, the Jewish philosopher Philo from Alexandria used *Logos* for the Eternal Principle, the reason behind creation, the meaning of life. John was also borrowing from intertestamental (the time between the testaments) works such as The Wisdom of Solomon, which spoke in much the same way about the wisdom of God. But the creative "Word" of God is also a Jewish concept, going back to the beginning of the Bible.

John planted the "Word of God" firmly on planet Earth. "The Word became flesh and lived among us," he wrote, "and we have seen his glory" (1:14). As John saw it, the Word was a person, his friend Jesus of Nazareth.

Most scholars agree that John wrote his gospel a decade or two after the other three. Matthew, Mark, and Luke are called the synoptic (meaning "seen together") gospels because they share many stories and seem to be working from a similar viewpoint. John is quite different. It's as if he intentionally filled in gaps left by the others. They had established

John records some priceless dialogues, such as this encounter between Jesus and a Samaritan woman. He asked her to draw him a drink from the local well, and then he offered her "living water" (John 4).

the basic events of Jesus' ministry. John addressed deeper questions: Who was Jesus? What are we to do about him?

While John records a few public speeches, he also includes several private conversations—with Nicodemus, with the woman of Samaria, with his disciples in the garden before his arrest. We glimpse a Jesus who is touchingly personal as well as shockingly cosmic. On the last day of the Festival of Booths in Jerusalem, when the water of Siloam was ritually offered, Jesus boldly announced, "Let anyone who is thirsty come to me" (7:37). But he made a similar claim one-on-one with a Samaritan woman by a well: "Those who drink of the water that I will give them will never be thirsty" (4:14).

In John, Jesus declares his identity in seven major "I am" metaphors. He called himself the "bread of life" (6:35); "the light of the world" (8:12); "the gate" through which sheep enter the fold (10:9); "the good shepherd" (10:11,14); "the resurrection and the life" (11:25); "the way, and the truth, and the life" (14:6); and "the true vine" (15:1,5).

Jesus makes his most direct claims to divinity in this fourth gospel. When he said, "Before Abraham was, I am" (8:58), he was not only transcending time and claiming priority over the father of the nation, but he was also alluding to the way God introduced himself to Moses: "I Am." It's in John that Jesus said, "The Father and I are one" (10:30), which nearly got him stoned to death for blasphemy. When a disciple asked, "Lord, show us the Father," Jesus answered, "Whoever has seen me has seen the Father" (14:8–9).

John clearly states his purpose in writing this book: "These [things] are written so that you may come to believe that Jesus is the Messiah, the Son of God, and that through believing you may have life in his name" (20:31).

In the other gospels, Jesus' claims to be God or the Messiah are infrequent or understated. But John has Jesus making bold statements about his unity with the Father. In John's view, Jesus was no mere teacher, but the powerful Word of God in human flesh, the eternal Son of God, one with God the Father.

HOW JESUS UNDERSTOOD HIMSELF

❖ ❖ ❖

OME PEOPLE ARE SURPRISED to learn that Christ was not Jesus' last name. When people needed to distinguish him from other people named Jesus (and there were others), they called him Jesus of Nazareth (Mark 10:47), or Jesus bar-Joseph—Jesus, the son of Joseph (John 6:42).

Christ (*Christos*) is the Greek translation of the Hebrew messiah (*mashiah*). Both mean "Anointed One." In the Old Testament, anointing was pouring oil on the head of a prophet, priest, or king. It signified God's empowering of that person to perform a holy task.

"Anointed One" as a title is used in the Old Testament for various kings and sometimes for all of Israel, but in a few passages it refers to a special person charged with an eternal purpose. Daniel, for instance, prophesies about a

Facing page: *Rembrandt's presentation of the risen Christ.* Right: *In Israel's history, anointing was a way of recognizing prophets, priests, and kings. Here Samuel anoints young David as king. Various Scriptures predict an "anointed one" (in Hebrew,* messiah*) who would act with God's power to save the nation and the world.*

messiah, a future ruler who would be "cut off" (Daniel 9:25–26).

Sometimes Christians get the idea that all the Jews of Jesus' time were eagerly waiting for the messiah to show up, according to the clear prophecies of the Old Testament, but somehow they had missed him. That's not quite true. Many groups of people had different expectations, based on different Old Testament prophecies and historical events.

Many prophecies referred to a king who would establish a new regime, and thus the messiah could be any leader who emerged at the front of a revolutionary band. Israel had a long history of "bandit-kings," going back to Jeroboam, David, and Gideon. The common people, hating Roman rule, may have looked for this kind of messiah, only to be disappointed when Jesus didn't follow through on his revolutionary potential.

Some religious leaders looked for a "Son of David" who would take the throne back from the family of Herod and fulfill the prophecies about David's dynasty. The scribes in Herod's court who identified Bethlehem (David's hometown) as the prophesied birthplace of the new king may have had this in mind (Matthew 2:4–6; Micah 5:2).

The Essene community of religious purists who camped out by the Dead Sea expected a priestly messiah who would lead the people back to the proper interpretation of God's law and a separate, princely messiah to lead them in battle. It's interesting that John the Baptist, whose lifestyle resembled that of the ascetic Essenes, hailed Jesus as the (sacrificial) Lamb of God, "who takes away the sin of the world" (John 1:29). This is more consistent with a priestly expectation than a kingly one. But

John the Baptist may have been associated with the Essenes, who waited for both a priestly messiah and a princely one. When he hailed Jesus as "the Lamb of God," he was certainly alluding to the priest's role of offering animal sacrifices for the sins of the people. Would this messiah be not only the sacrificer but the sacrifice itself?

even John had his doubts, later sending disciples to ask Jesus, "Are you the one who is to come, or are we to wait for another?" (Matthew 11:3). Clearly he had some sort of messianic expectation, but he seemed unsure of what to look for.

The Samaritans looked for a messiah who would be a prophet or teacher to restore their spiritual fortunes. Jesus dazzled the woman at the well in exactly these terms. When she mentioned the coming messiah, he replied, "I am he, the one who is speaking to you" (John 4:26).

That's typical of Jesus' restraint. He never quite says, "I am the Messiah," but he lets others say it. He uses ambiguous terms for himself. This may have been just good street smarts, knowing the authorities would be looking for blasphemers. But he may also have realized that "messiah" meant different things to different people. If he made that claim for himself, he would surely disappoint everyone in some way. Instead, he refused to fit into preconceived notions. He kept defining himself with various terms, using various prophecies.

Jesus often used the term Son of Man when referring to himself. This clever title meant everything and nothing, allowing Jesus to present himself as both an unassuming servant and the Lord of history. At face value, Son of Man means "human being." The prophet Ezekiel used it in this way. In fact, the term is so ordinary, it could be used almost as a personal pronoun like "I" or "me." Jesus used it in this way when he said, "Foxes have holes, and birds of the air have nests, but the Son of Man has nowhere to lay his head" (Matthew 8:20).

But Jesus was certainly aware of another strain of this title's history. Daniel had a vision in which "one like a [son

Like the Old Testament prophet Ezekiel, Jesus used the term "Son of Man." As we see in this stained-glass image, Ezekiel also used the shepherd metaphor— one of Jesus' favorites.

The prophet Daniel spoke of one who would be "like a son of man" appearing in the clouds and reigning forever. When Jesus called himself the Son of Man, he certainly had this image in mind. Thus, the same term was both humble and quite brash. (In stained glass, Daniel is associated with the beasts he saw in his visions. But both the lion and the lamb are also symbols for Christ, so this window reflects the belief that Daniel was prophesying the future glory of Jesus.)

of man] human being" arrived with the clouds and received from the Ancient One an "everlasting dominion" (Daniel 7:13–14).

Apocalyptic literature, which had a heyday in the intertestamental period (the time between the Old and New Testaments), grabbed this idea. The Book of First Enoch (the Similitudes of Enoch), written in this time, spoke of the Son of Man being "a light to the Gentiles and the hope of those who are troubled of heart," receiving worship from everyone on Earth, chosen "before the creation of the world." This book pictures the Son of Man appearing and taking "the throne of his glory." "He is born unto righteousness" and "proclaims…peace in the name of the world to come."

This was the title Jesus chose for himself, the human being who is somehow more than merely human. While he asserts his servile role—"The Son of Man came not to be served but to serve, and to give his life a ransom for many" (Matthew 20:28)—he also claims great authority. "For the Son of Man is lord of the sabbath" (Matthew 12:8).

Did people understand who the Son of Man was supposed to be? Not always. After predicting his death by saying the Son of Man would be "lifted up," Jesus got an interesting question from the crowd. "We have heard from the law that the Messiah remains forever. How can you say that the Son of Man must be lifted up? Who is this Son of Man?" (John 12:34). The crowd was making some connection between the Son of Man and the Messiah, but they were confused when Jesus was saying he'd have to die.

At one crucial point of his ministry, Jesus did an opinion poll of his disciples. "Who do people say that the Son of Man is?" he asked them. John the Baptist, Elijah, Jeremiah, some other prophet—these were the people they mentioned. Then Jesus pinned them down: "But who do you say that I am?"

Notice that Jesus was using Son of Man in his original question as equivalent to the pronoun I. By this time the disciples knew Jesus was the Son of Man—but exactly who was this Son of Man?

Peter understood: "You are the Messiah, the Son of the living God." And while Jesus never used these titles for himself, he praised Peter for recognizing this (Matthew 16:13–17). He also ordered his disciples "not to tell anyone that he was the Messiah" (Matthew 16:20).

Besides his casual use of the term, Jesus almost always used Son of Man when talking about his future plans and his eternal mission. "The Son of Man is to be betrayed into human hands," he told his disciples, "and they will kill him, and three days after being killed, he will rise again" (Mark 9:31). Suffering was an essential part of the plan. But Jesus also borrowed Daniel's language of exaltation: "Then they will see the 'Son of Man coming in clouds' with great power and glory" (Mark 13:26); "You will see heaven opened and the angels of God ascending and descending upon the Son of Man" (John 1:51).

During Jesus' trial, the high priest asked him, "Are you the Messiah, the Son of the Blessed One?" Jesus answered,

The fiery prophet Elijah never died, according to ancient teaching, but was carried to heaven in a chariot of fire. So you might excuse some people for thinking that Jesus was a returned Elijah—confronting authorities and working miracles, just as the old prophet had done. It was Peter who dared to go further, saying that Jesus was the Messiah.

On trial before Caiaphas, the high priest, Jesus broke his silence to warn that he would someday appear in power at God's right side. He was clearly citing Old Testament visions about the messiah who would set things right forever. The high priest took Jesus' words as blasphemy.

"I am; and 'you will see the Son of Man seated at the right hand of the Power,' and 'coming with the clouds of heaven'" (Mark 14:61–62). Jesus accepted both titles the high priest mentioned, but he returned to his favorite phrase—Son of Man. In his statement, he alludes to Psalm 110 and quotes from Daniel 7:13, clearly applying them to himself. As far as the high priest was concerned, the case was then closed. Jesus was claiming to be divine, thus convicting himself of blasphemy.

But Jesus used another Old Testament image in his self-understanding, the anointed preacher-healer. "The Spirit of the Lord God is upon me," Isaiah writes, "because the Lord has anointed me; he has sent me to bring good news to the oppressed, to bind up the brokenhearted, to proclaim liberty to the captives, and release to the prisoners; to proclaim the year of the Lord's favor" (Isaiah 61:1–2). This is the passage Jesus read in his hometown as he began his public ministry, sparking a riot (Luke 4:16–30). The crowd heard the word "anointed"—meaning messiah—and when Jesus said, "Today this scripture has been fulfilled in your hearing," the crowd became angry. Jesus was calling himself this Messiah.

Jesus alluded to this same passage in his answer to John the Baptist's doubtful query (Matthew 11:2–6). Jesus saw this as his God-given mission: preaching good news, healing, overturning society from the inside out.

Another Old Testament image applied to Jesus is that of the suffering servant. In Isaiah 40—55, the prophet introduces a character whom God calls "my servant, whom I uphold, my chosen, in whom my soul delights" (42:1). Later, he's identified as "a man of suffering and acquainted with infirmity" (53:3). His suffering, it turns out, is on our behalf, the prophet says. "But he was wounded for our transgressions, crushed for our iniquities…and by his bruises we are healed" (53:5).

Jesus never claimed to be this servant, though he did talk about the sacrificial quality of his life and death. And comments he made at the Last Supper did make many connections to the Isaiah texts. But the gospel writers, especially Matthew, saw several parallels between Jesus' life and the Isaiah texts. The early Christians ran with the idea. The image of the suffering servant was crucial in explaining the humble, servile, sacrificial mission of the "Son of Man."

At the Last Supper, when Jesus declared that the Passover wine was his blood, "poured out for many for the forgiveness of sins," he was evoking the image of the suffering servant that Isaiah had foreseen. "He was wounded for our transgressions," the prophet had written (Isaiah 53:5).

HOW OTHERS SAW HIM

✦ ✦ ✦

Above: *The disciples were in their boat, weathering a storm, when they saw Jesus coming toward them, walking on the waves. Peter dared to walk out toward him and nearly drowned. The awestruck disciples hailed Jesus as "the Son of God." Facing page: Those who watched Jesus grow up had a hard time seeing him as anything but the carpenter's boy, even after he gained a reputation for wise words and wonder working.*

JESUS' NEIGHBORS IN NAZARETH certainly had a hard time seeing him as anything other than Joseph's boy, the carpenter's son (Luke 4:22). But Jesus' reputation grew. It helped to have John the Baptist, already revered as a prophet, providing Jesus with introductions. John was giving advance notice of "one who is more powerful than I," one who would "baptize you with the Holy Spirit and fire" (Luke 3:16). John called Jesus the "Lamb of God," and after Jesus' baptism by John, a voice from heaven called Jesus "my Son, the Beloved" (Luke 3:22). Jesus avoided the term Son of God but was called this most often by demons. The devil prefaced his temptations with, "If you are the Son of God…" (Matthew 4:3,6). And Mark comments, "Whenever the unclean spirits saw him, they fell down before him and shouted, 'You are the Son of God!'" (Mark 3:11).

We know that Jesus asked Peter who he thought Jesus was, and Peter's oft-repeated response, "the Son of God," was also used by Martha (John 11:27) and Nathanael (John 1:49). After Jesus walked on water, his terrified disciples "worshiped him, saying, 'Truly you are the Son of God'" (Matthew 14:33).

Two thousand years later, believers and nonbelievers wrestle with Jesus' identity. If he was not the Son of God, who was he? At his crucifixion, Jesus was jeered by passersby: "If you are the Son of God, come down from the cross!" (Matthew 27:40). These words echo the tempter's taunt to Jesus in the wilderness. But the last word belonged

*Differing opinions of Jesus'
identity continued up to his
crucifixion, and even afterward.
Passersby taunted Jesus on the
cross, assuming that a Son of
God would never endure such
mistreatment, but the same scene
convinced an attending centurion that Jesus was "truly…
God's Son."*

to the centurion who "stood facing him" at the crucifixion:
"Truly this man was God's Son!" (Mark 15:39).

Jesus was often called rabbi or teacher (Luke 10:25;
John 3:2). He also answered to the title Lord (Matthew
8:2,6,8), but this may be less significant than it seems. The
Greek word *kurios* (Lord) translated the Hebrew name of
God Adonai, but it also was used generically as we might
use "Sir" today.

Another title used occasionally for Jesus was Son of
David. Apparently some Jews were looking for a descendant of David to appear, to take the throne, and to bring the
fulfillment of God's prophecies. Various people shouted
this name as they sought healing from Jesus (Matthew

9:27), and the crowds sang it at Jesus' triumphal entry into Jerusalem (Matthew 21:9). Yet it was a title Jesus never used for himself, perhaps because of its limits.

After fielding a round of trick questions, Jesus asked the Pharisees a trick question of his own: "How can they say that the Messiah is David's son? For David himself says in the book of Psalms, 'The Lord said to my Lord, "Sit at my right hand, until I make your enemies your footstool."' David thus calls him Lord; so how can he be his son?" (Luke 20:41–44). The verse he quoted was Psalm 110:1, which shows God (the Lord) talking to the Messiah (my Lord). Jesus is saying that the messiah has to be superior to David—he has to be an eternal being, not merely an earthly ruler.

"I Am"

EYOND ALL THE TITLES, what did Jesus say about himself? We can start with the seven "I am" metaphors in John.

THE BREAD OF LIFE (JOHN 6:35)

Jesus had recently fed a crowd with a small amount of bread, and so bread was on people's minds. Jesus recalled how God had fed the wandering Israelites with manna—bread from heaven—and he called himself the "true bread from heaven" that "gives life to the world" (6:32–33). He went on to say that anyone who would "eat" of this bread would live forever. Later Christians saw a hint of the eucharistic meal in these words, but Jesus probably had a simpler image in mind. Partaking of Jesus, believing in him, would lead to eternal life.

THE LIGHT OF THE WORLD (JOHN 8:12)

This was probably spoken at the Feast of Booths (Tabernacles) in Jerusalem, where the torches of the tem-

Below: *"Daily bread" was not just a phrase to pray, but a basic need. Jesus won followers when he miraculously multiplied bread to feed the crowds that came to him, but he also called himself the "bread from heaven"—indicating that he could satisfy even deeper needs. Facing page: Jesus not only told stories about shepherds hunting for wayward sheep, but he pictured himself as one. Possibly alluding to Isaiah's prophecy ("All we like sheep have gone astray"—Isaiah 53:6), Jesus said the "good shepherd" would sacrifice his own life for his flock.*

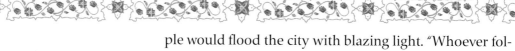

ple would flood the city with blazing light. "Whoever follows me," Jesus said, "will never walk in darkness but will have the light of life." Light was an image of righteousness and God's glory (see John 3:19–21).

THE GATE (JOHN 10:9)

Jesus paints a picture of a sheepfold, and he identifies himself with two parts of the picture: the gate and the shepherd. The Bible often compares the people of Israel to sheep (Psalm 100:3; Isaiah 53:6). As the gate, Jesus would be the only passageway for the sheep to "come in and go out and find pasture."

THE GOOD SHEPHERD (JOHN 10:11,14)

In the same picture, Jesus contrasts himself with the "thieves and bandits" who climb in and kill the sheep (probably a reference to earlier messianic pretenders who promised peace but brought only violence). In a scene reminiscent of Psalm 23, Jesus claims to be "the good shepherd [who] lays down his life for the sheep."

Jesus often backed up his words with mighty deeds. After declaring that he was "the resurrection and the life," he showed his power over death by raising his friend Lazarus. The man had been dead for four days.

THE RESURRECTION AND THE LIFE (JOHN 11:25)

Lazarus had just died, and his sister Martha was grieving. When Jesus promised that her brother would "rise again," Martha agreed that he would rise with everyone else "on the last day." Then, bringing her from vague faith to specific commitment, Jesus identified himself as "the resurrection and the life." Those who trusted him, he said, would live even if they died. He proceeded to bring Lazarus back from the dead as a foretaste of his future resurrection.

THE WAY, AND THE TRUTH, AND THE LIFE (JOHN 14:6)

In a quiet moment at the Last Supper, Jesus began talking about heaven, where he would be going soon. Thomas asked, "Lord, we do not know where you are going. How can we know the way?" (14:5). "I am the way," Jesus replied, "and the truth, and the life. No one comes to the Father except through me."

THE TRUE VINE (JOHN 15:1,5)

This is another extended metaphor. Jesus establishes his Father as the vine grower and himself as the vine, which nourishes the branches, his disciples. Those who "abide" in him will "bear fruit," Jesus said, but "apart from me you can do nothing."

Jesus made other statements about himself that reflect his humility. "Take my yoke upon you, and learn from me; for I am gentle and humble in heart, and you will find rest for your souls" (Matthew 11:29). On another occasion, he short-circuited a power struggle among his disciples by saying, "I am among you as one who serves" (Luke 22:27).

Jesus shocked his disciples by taking basin and towel and bending to wash their feet. This was servants' work, and Jesus was their master. But Jesus was teaching them humility—and urging them to follow his example.

As the disciples gathered for the Last Supper, Jesus washed their feet, the task of a slave. Afterward he asked, "Do you know what I have done to you? You call me Teacher and Lord—and you are right, for that is what I am. So if I, your Lord and Teacher, have washed your feet, you also ought to wash one another's feet" (John 13:12–14).

Yet this humility provides a fascinating counterpoint to the boldness of Jesus' "I am" statements. Elsewhere, Jesus told a crowd, "You are from below, I am from above; you are of this world, I am not of this world" (John 8:23). He clearly saw himself originating in heaven and headed back there—and he presented himself as the only way for people to get to heaven. That way would be through his own suffering and death. "When you have lifted up [crucified] the Son of Man," he said, "then you will realize that I am he" (John 8:28).

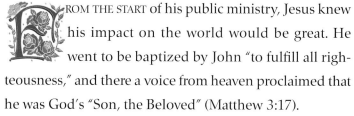

JESUS' SENSE OF MISSION

* * *

Above: *John the Baptist had shaken the nation, challenging the hypocrisy of the religious leaders and calling everyone to repent. He also announced that a greater prophet was on the way. When John was arrested, Jesus seemed to step into the gap, picking up John's call to repentance and adding his own rich teaching. Facing page: Jesus performed his first miracle at a wedding feast, turning water to wine.*

ROM THE START of his public ministry, Jesus knew his impact on the world would be great. He went to be baptized by John "to fulfill all righteousness," and there a voice from heaven proclaimed that he was God's "Son, the Beloved" (Matthew 3:17).

In the early going, he seemed cautious about public displays, as if he was fitting into some master schedule. Jesus at first rejected his mother's request to provide wine for the wedding at Cana, with the cryptic comment "My hour has not yet come" (John 2:4). But then he performed his first miracle (turning water to wine) anyhow.

Maybe the arrest of John the Baptist gave Jesus the green light for phase one of his ministry. "From that time on," Matthew tells us, "Jesus began to proclaim, 'Repent, for the kingdom of heaven is near'" (Matthew 4:17). His healing and teaching made him famous. But when a crowd responded to his miraculous feeding by trying to make him a king, he slipped away (John 6:15). As he told Pontius Pilate much later, "My kingdom is not from this world" (John 18:36).

So here was a king who turned down a kingdom, a Messiah who told people to keep his identity quiet. This was a healer who worked long hours, but still didn't heal everyone he met. He was a teacher who obscured parts of his message. Just what was he about?

As we've seen in his Sermon on the Mount, Jesus said he didn't come to abolish the Jewish law, but to fulfill it (Matthew 5:17). He went on to teach about a greater kind of righteousness. Was this his mission—as a reforming rabbi?

When the religious elite complained about Jesus' habit of eating with tax collectors, he said, "I have come to call not the righteous but sinners" (Mark 2:17). Was this, then, his mission—as a social reformer, extending the reach of God's favor?

At a couple of points in the middle of his ministry, Jesus sent out his followers to preach and heal (Matthew 10; Luke 10:1–12). Was this his mission—to train a generation of healers and preachers who would bring physical and spiritual wholeness to Israel? If it was, he knew it would fail. He warned these disciples that they'd be sheep among wolves, rejected, arrested, persecuted.

In this context, he demanded radical commitment. True disciples would put him above their own families. "I have not come to bring peace, but a sword....Whoever loves father or mother more than me is not worthy of me" (Matthew 10:34,37). Was this his mission—to prune the ranks of the faithful, creating a small group of unlikely saints totally dedicated to God?

Jesus took three disciples up a mountain, and as they watched, his appearance changed. He began to radiate with light—a symbol of God's presence—and suddenly Moses and Elijah seemed to be standing there with him. As at Jesus' baptism, a voice from heaven proclaimed that he was God's Son (Matthew 17:1–9).

A turning point seems to occur in Matthew 16, just after Peter confesses that Jesus is "the Son of the living God." As Matthew writes it, "From that time on, Jesus began to show his disciples that he must go to Jerusalem and undergo great suffering...and be killed, and on the third day be raised" (Matthew 16:21). All four gospels seem to note a shift here, somewhere between the feeding of the five thousand and the Transfiguration. As Luke puts it, "When the days drew near for him to be taken up, he set his face to go to Jerusalem" (9:51).

In Jerusalem, Jesus' enemies held power. Apparently Jesus was relatively safe in the northern region of Galilee, but Jerusalem held danger. Yet in this last stage of Jesus' ministry, he knew he had to go there and die. He regularly reminded his disciples of this.

In this period, Jesus focused more on his disciples and less on the crowds. He talked more about suffering than about righteousness. Even his parables changed—they were more about mercy and less about commitment. Quelling his disciples' dispute over their rank in his kingdom, Jesus said, "The Son of Man came not to be served but to serve, and to give his life a ransom for many" (Mark 10:45). Was this perhaps his mission all along—to open God's kingdom to everyone, offering wholeness through his sacrificial death?

THE VINEYARD

In the week before his death, Jesus told a parable that is perhaps the clearest picture of how he saw his mission at that point (Matthew 21:33–41). A landowner leased out his vineyard and moved away. At harvest time, he sent servants to collect his share of the produce—his rent payment. The wicked tenants beat and killed the servants. The owner sent more servants, who were similarly mistreated. Finally he sent his son, saying, "They will respect my son."

Wrong. The tenants killed the son, too.

Jesus asked the religious leaders who were listening to this story, "Now when the owner of the vineyard comes, what will he do to those tenants?" (This was a favorite device of his, getting his hearers to convict themselves.) The chief priests and Pharisees presumably remained silent because "they realized that he was speaking about them" (verse 45).

The vineyard was Israel (see Isaiah 5:7), and the wicked tenants were these leaders. Jesus accused them of reject-

The vineyard had long been an image of Israel, and Jesus had already told a striking story of vineyard workers who got paid the same for different amounts of work. But late in his ministry, Jesus depicted himself as a landowner's son visiting a vineyard to demand rent. In the story, the tenants killed him.

ing and even killing the prophets God had sent (see Matthew 23:35). Now they would arrange the death of God's Son, Jesus himself.

Here, as elsewhere, Jesus distinguished himself from prophets who had come before him. While aspects of his mission were prophetic, he had an even higher calling. He wasn't just "collecting rent"; his death would shake up the whole system.

After telling this story, Jesus quoted from Psalm 118, a processional song that had been used at his triumphal entry into Jerusalem the previous day. "The stone that the builders rejected has become the cornerstone" (Matthew 21:42; Psalm 118:22).

Note that Jesus was telling this story in the temple complex, which was in the midst of a massive rebuilding project. Jesus just had to point at stones that were being readied for this project. At another time, he had compared his own body to the Jerusalem temple (John 2:19). Here he was certainly making a similar comparison. This temple was the place where Israel went to meet with God, but Jesus himself would be the cornerstone of a whole new building project that would be "the Lord's doing." And his rejection (by the leaders) would be part of the plan.

The Last Supper was a Passover meal, with Jesus playing host. The "family" of disciples would have followed the traditional courses and prayers, including the blessing of the bread and the prayers over four cups of wine. But on this occasion, Jesus added new meaning to the meal.

THE PASSOVER

Jesus revealed something else about his sense of mission when he celebrated Passover with his disciples just before his death. The Passover, of course, commemorates the way God delivered the Israelites out of Egypt, with different parts of the meal carrying ritual significance. But midway through the meal, Jesus added his own meaning to it.

Jesus probably blessed the bread with the normal prayer: "Blessed art thou, O Lord our God, King of the Universe, who bringest forth bread from the earth." But

then he said to his disciples, "Take, eat; this is my body." After the blessing was said over the wine (probably the third cup of the Passover meal), he added, "Drink from it, all of you; for this is my blood of the covenant, which is poured out for many for the forgiveness of sins" (Matthew 26:26–28).

Suddenly the bread and wine of Passover had new meaning for Jesus' followers. As the blood of the lamb had protected the Israelites from the angel of death in Egypt, so Jesus' blood would protect his people from sin and death. As the Passover meal bonded Israelites together in a community of remembrance, so the participation in Jesus' sacrificial death would draw his followers together in a new covenant.

When Jesus told them, "Do this in remembrance of me" (Luke 22:19), he was asking them to understand their beloved Passover in a new way, redefining God's deliverance in terms of Jesus. This was gutsy, to be sure, but it was thoroughly consistent with Jesus' early mission statement: not to abolish the law, but to fulfill it.

The crossing of the Red Sea, depicted in this Sistine Chapel painting by Rosselli Cosimo, finally set the Israelites free from slavery in Egypt. Jesus and the early Christians explained his mission in parallel terms. He was freeing the slaves of sin and death. Just as Passover commemorated the escape from Egypt, the Lord's Supper would celebrate Christ's act of liberation.

THE UPSIDE-DOWN KINGDOM

❖ ❖ ❖

THE KINGDOM OF GOD was Jesus' favorite subject, but what did he mean by that term? And what did his hearers think when he used it?

Today we tend to think of the word geographically: A kingdom is a certain territory ruled by a king. But sovereignty was more fluid in those days. The Roman Empire—the kingdom of Caesar—had seeped throughout the whole world.

But many Jews faced a personal question of sovereignty on a daily basis. Whose rule are you really under? It was said that every time a man recited the Shema, the defining statement of Jewish faith—"Hear, O Israel, the Lord our God is one"—he placed himself under the sovereignty (the kingdom) of God.

Yet in Roman-occupied Israel, personal questions of sovereignty often intersected with national issues. This lay behind the highly charged question put to Jesus: "Is it lawful to pay taxes to the emperor?"

We have already seen the various expectations about the messiah—prophet, priest, or king. Itching under Roman rule, many Jews looked for God's climactic intervention. Would he raise up another Joshua, another Gideon, another David, another Maccabee brother to throw off the Roman yoke and cleanse the nation of Gentile abominations?

Various religious groups, including the Pharisees, thought God was waiting for Israel to get back to its spiritual roots. If the people would get back to keeping God's law, they asserted, then God's kingdom would come.

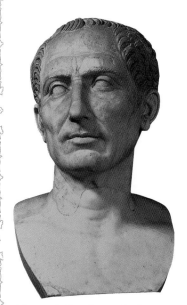

Above: *Julius Caesar had established a dynasty that ruled the Mediterranean world. When Jesus was born, Augustus Caesar was in power, and Tiberius Caesar was calling the shots in Rome as Jesus entered public ministry. To speak of God's kingdom was to challenge the sovereignty of Caesar, an idea most Jews would find tantalizing but dangerous. Facing page: The Jews had reestablished their own kingdom briefly (142 B.C.), after the Maccabees led a successful revolt against the hated Syrian ruler Antiochus IV (depicted here in this medieval manuscript). But within a century the Jews were under Roman rule.*

A la louenge de dieu tout
puissant nre crateur
et redempteur qui par
sa saincte miserico:de
voult en ce mortel monde
naistre homme de mere vierge ⁊ souffrir
mort et passion par les mains des
Juifz pour nous tous racheter denfer

au quel par le peche du premier homme
nous feusmes soubzmis et obligez
Et pour auoir entendement par
langage francois de listoire de la
destruction des Juifs et de la cite de
iherusalem ensemble de toute la terre diceulx
Juifs ce que plusieurs appellent la
vengence de la mort et passion de nre

John the Baptist gave voice to a popular notion that God was about to do something big in Israel, that God would soon be setting up his kingdom. Even the religious leaders could get excited about that. But what would this kingdom be like? When John, and later Jesus, criticized the leaders for hypocrisy, their tune changed.

Some looked for a Day of the Lord that would divide the present evil age from the glorious age to come. There would be upheaval, judgment of evildoers, and a total change of the system.

When John the Baptist appeared, preaching, "Repent, for the kingdom of heaven has come near!" (Matthew 3:2), he was of the same mind. That's why "all Judea"—including the Pharisees—went out to the desert to see him (Matthew 3:5). He predicted a new world order, the chopping down of the old forest—"the ax is lying at the root of the trees." Yet he alienated the religious leaders by criticizing them for their hypocrisy, and he threw his support to this renegade rabbi Jesus.

Jesus immediately picked up John's message (Matthew 4:17), but he explained more about God's kingdom. The kingdom wasn't just near, it was here! "Thy kingdom come," but it had come already. You may enter the kingdom someday, but will the kingdom enter you?

When Jesus spoke about God's kingdom, he didn't give coordinates. He didn't offer a systematic theoretical structure. He spoke of the kingdom as you might speak about a dear friend, less defining than describing, offering interesting details.

On at least one occasion, Jesus' disciples fought over who would have the highest position in the kingdom. They didn't understand. From the start, Jesus had said God's kingdom belonged to the poor (Luke 6:20), the poor in spirit (humble) (Matthew 5:3), and those who were persecuted for righteousness' sake (Matthew 5:10). In fact, the structure of the Beatitudes suggests that the kingdom is peopled with all these blessed ones—the mournful, the meek, the merciful, etc.

Who is the greatest in the kingdom of heaven? Children and those who are as humble as children (see Matthew 18:1–4; Mark 10:14–15). Put aside romantic notions of the purity of children. In that day, children were viewed as beneath the dignity of attention in religious matters. Jesus was offering a major shift in thinking, and those who thought they knew about the kingdom were in for a shock. Forget what you think you know and enroll in kindergarten once more, Jesus was saying. No one would even see the kingdom unless he or she was "born from above" (John 3:3).

Tax collectors and prostitutes—the dregs of society—would enter the kingdom before religious leaders would, and camels would get through the eye of a needle sooner than rich people would enter God's kingdom (see Matthew 19:23–24; 21:31).

In an age when children were considered religiously unimportant, Jesus welcomed them. When his disciples were turning children away, Jesus made it a point to bring them near, and he used children as examples of humble faith.

"Woe to you, scribes and Pharisees, hypocrites!" Jesus scolded. "For you lock people out of the kingdom of heaven. For you do not go in yourselves, and when others are going in, you stop them" (Matthew 23:13). Yet one scribe who affirmed that loving God and one's neighbor was "much more important" than burnt offerings or sacrifices was "not far from the kingdom of God," Jesus said (Mark 12:34).

Jesus even dared to suggest that Gentiles would also be included in the kingdom of God. Impressed by the faith of a Roman centurion, Jesus said, "Many will come from east and west and will eat with Abraham and Isaac and

Jesus praised the faith of the Roman centurion who requested healing for his servant. "In no one in Israel," Jesus said, "have I found such faith" (Matthew 8:10). Such high regard for a Gentile would have been shocking to the religious establishment.

Jacob in the kingdom of heaven, while the heirs of the kingdom will be thrown into the outer darkness" (Matthew 8:11–12).

The kingdom would defy all expectations. A repeated refrain in Jesus' parables was the "first will be last, and the last will be first" (Matthew 19:30). Everything would be topsy-turvy. Sinners were in; holy men were out. In God's kingdom, the rich man in Hell would be begging poor Lazarus for a sip of water.

In a curious passage, Jesus said, "The law and the prophets were in effect until John [the Baptist] came; since then the good news of the kingdom of God is proclaimed, and everyone tries to enter it by force" (Luke 16:16). Did he mean that the Pharisees (his audience at the time) were trying to earn their way into the kingdom by keeping the law, essentially forcing God to accept them? But Jesus had been preaching the "good news of the kingdom"—forgiveness, mercy, and grace. In the next verse, Jesus reminded his hearers how strict the law was. The Pharisees knew in their hearts that, while they appeared to keep the law, they fell short of its demands. Now if only they would accept

God's forgiveness and stop trying to force God's hand, they could see the good news as truly good.

But in God's upside-down kingdom, by clinging to their own goodness, they missed out on the goodness of God. The first were coming in last.

"Once Jesus was asked by the Pharisees when the kingdom of God was coming, and he answered, 'The kingdom of God is not coming with things that can be observed; nor will they say, "Look, here it is!" or "There it is!" For, in fact, the kingdom of God is among you'" (Luke 17:20–21).

Perhaps the Pharisees were looking for Jesus to predict a particular date for the world's upheaval, so they could prove him wrong when it didn't happen. Or perhaps they were giving him the benefit of the doubt. In any case, they appeared to be

On many occasions, Jesus rebuked the Pharisees for their elitism, pride, and inconsistent application of God's law. His idea of the kingdom of God was much different from theirs.

talking about this climactic Day of the Lord that would change everything. But Jesus said they were missing an important point about God's kingdom: It was already here, just as it is here in our day, also.

The message Jesus had given his disciples to share with others was, "The kingdom of God has come near you" (Luke 10:9,11). His miracles attested to the fact that God was ruling on Earth, stretching out his finger to exorcize the demons that had run rampant (Luke 11:20).

But Jesus and his hearers both knew that the job wasn't finished. Despite Jesus' healings, some people in Israel were still getting sick. The perfect kingdom of God had not yet arrived. Jesus himself taught his disciples to pray, "Thy kingdom come." Why pray for that if it was already there?

The secret lies in a group of parables Jesus told. God's kingdom is like a mustard seed, a tiny thing that grows big. It's like a handful of yeast that makes the dough rise (Luke 13:18–21). You can hardly see it, but it's there, and it's growing. God's kingdom is already here, Jesus was saying, but it's not completely realized yet. It's active, it's working, but slowly, not something to make you say, "There it is!"

This "already-but-not-yet" quality is crucial to understanding God's kingdom as preached by Jesus. It also helps us make the jump between the personal and the heavenly.

Just before his ascension, Jesus' disciples asked him, "Lord, is this the time when you will restore the kingdom to Israel?" They were looking for a national solution, perhaps political, perhaps spiritual, perhaps both. Jesus sidestepped the question—"it's not for

Above: *A field of yellow mustard plants in Israel.* Facing page: *In a medieval Russian representation, we see Jesus' ascension to heaven. Up to his last moments on Earth, he was talking about God's kingdom, promising that his Spirit would help his disciples spread the kingdom throughout the world.*

you to know"—but he commissioned them to "be my witnesses in Jerusalem, in all Judea and Samaria, and to the ends of the earth" (Acts 1:6–8). They got their answer, just not the answer they were expecting. The kingdom would be restored, but not just to Israel—to the ends of the Earth. They didn't need to know when or where God would break through the clouds to display his mighty power, but he'd give them power to tell people what they knew about Jesus, and thus the kingdom would flower in individual hearts.

THE DEMANDS OF DISCIPLESHIP

* * *

CCORDING TO JESUS, citizens of God's kingdom would be characterized by both radical commitment and pure joy. "Strive first for the kingdom of God and his righteousness," Jesus said (Matthew 6:33)—first, even above your daily food and clothing. But don't worry—it's "the Father's good pleasure" to give you the kingdom, and your daily provisions will be thrown in, too (Luke 12:31–32).

The one who puts his hand to the plow and looks back is not "fit for the kingdom of God" (Luke 9:62). Jesus sent his people out on a preaching mission with "no purse, no bag, no sandals" (Luke 10:4), but they came back crowing with joy (Luke 10:17).

Jesus called twelve disciples to travel with him, saying simply, "Follow me." They did, leaving their jobs and families behind. When Peter said, "Look, we have left our homes and followed you," Jesus replied, "There is no one who has left house or wife or brothers or parents or chil-

Right: *James and John were in a fishing boat with their father when Jesus asked them to join his team. They "left the boat and their father, and followed him" (Matthew 4:22). Total commitment to Jesus involved not only a separation from one's family, but also the loss of gainful employment.* Facing page: *Peter was one of Jesus' most loyal disciples, but sometimes he seemed self-centered. On one occasion he complained that he had left everything to follow Jesus—what would he get in return? But another time he affirmed that Jesus was "the Son of the living God" and was richly praised for his insight. Here Jesus grants him a symbolic key to God's kingdom (Matthew 16:16,19).*

dren, for the sake of the kingdom of God, who will not get back very much more in this age, and in the age to come eternal life" (Luke 18:28–30).

Following Jesus had its rewards, but it also had its price. While the twelve apparently stayed with Jesus until his arrest, there were other disciples who came and went. Unhappy about a number of fickle followers who had left, Jesus turned to Peter once and said, "Do you also wish to go away?" Peter's answer was classic: "Lord, to whom can we go? You have the words of eternal life" (John 6:67–68).

It was right at the turning point of his ministry that Jesus issued the strongest challenge to his disciples. Peter had just confessed his belief that Jesus was the Messiah. Jesus then explained that he had to go to Jerusalem, die, and rise again—a plan that Peter protested until Jesus retorted, "Get behind me, Satan!"

That's when Jesus said, "If any want to become my followers, let them deny themselves and take up their cross and follow me" (Matthew 16:24). What did it mean to "take up one's cross"?

The cross, of course, was a horrific symbol. There was nothing religious about it at that time—it meant what an electric chair or lethal injection would mean today, capital punishment of the most grisly sort. Was Jesus then telling them to commit suicide?

No. The image of taking up the cross is crucial. Think of the scene a few months later as the convicted Jesus carried his cross out of the city to be crucified. Yes, he stum-

Jesus bore not only the weight of his cross, but also the shame of carrying it through the city streets. He told his followers it would be necessary for them to "take up their cross," enduring ridicule and persecution for him.

bled, and Simon of Cyrene was forced to carry it—but this was the procedure: The condemned man took up his own cross. People along the way would stare and jeer as the criminal took his last walk. The cross was not only the instrument of his impending death, but also an emblem of his shame.

So Jesus was asking, "Are you ready to go with me on my death march? Are you ready to endure shame with me? Are you ready to endure pain for me?" He was not necessarily promising them death by martyrdom (though tradition has it that ten of the disciples died that way), but he was asking them to live in such a way that others would treat them as those on the way to be executed.

True disciples of Jesus would give up their lives—in one way or another—because that's the only way they would truly find life. Jesus gave up his own life, promising to rise to new life within three days.

The following verses explain it well: "For those who want to save their life will lose it, and those who lose their life for my sake will find it. For what will it profit them if they gain the whole world but forfeit their life?" (Matthew 16:25–26). Some translations use soul for that last word, and that's probably the meaning, but the Greek word for life throughout these verses is the same: *psyche*. Psyche can mean physical life or soul, outer life or inner. If you hang onto your physical life, he tells his disciples, you'll lose that part of you that gives you spiritual life—and that's worth more than the whole world.

THE PLACE OF THE OUTCAST

❖ ❖ ❖

ATE IN MATTHEW'S GOSPEL, we find a parable that stands out from the rest (Matthew 25:31–46). Most of the others involve simple stories of characters familiar to the common people. In this one, though, Jesus is clearly the central figure, and it is set in the future: "When the Son of Man comes in his glory, and all the angels with him, then he will sit on the throne of his glory."

As the story goes on, Jesus refers to himself as the "king," but this king is a shepherd. We see the king dividing the sheep from the goats.

We have already considered Jesus' use of the term Son of Man, but this picture fits perfectly with Daniel's vision of an end-time being. The shepherd-king was also a popular image in Israel, and had been since the time of David. Micah had foreseen a ruler born in Bethlehem who would "stand and feed his flock in the strength of the Lord" (Micah 5:2–4), and Zechariah had used the image at length. As for dividing the flocks, Jesus has already mentioned various separations—wheat from weeds, good fish from bad (Matthew 13:30,48). Make no mistake: Jesus was talking about a future judgment day, one that many of the prophets had promised.

On what basis, then, are the flocks divided? What are people being judged on? That's what Jesus' story tells us.

The sheep are welcomed into the kingdom, "for I was hungry and you gave me food," the king tells them. "I was thirsty and you gave me something to drink, I was a stranger and you welcomed me, I was naked and you gave

Facing page: Jesus portrayed himself as a "good shepherd" who cared for wandering sheep. But this same shepherd also separated the sheep from the goats. Picking up an Old Testament theme of the "shepherd-king," Jesus told this parable about the end-time judgment. In the parable, the good shepherd condemns those who neglected the needs of the poor.

me clothing, I was sick and you took care of me, I was in prison and you visited me."

"Great," the sheep are thinking, "but are you sure you've got the right animals? When did we ever do that for you?"

The king answers, "Just as you did it to one of the least of these who are members of my family, you did it to me."

The story goes on to the reverse image. The goats are condemned because they refused to help the king in his need. They are also confused: "When did we see you hungry…?"

And the point is made again: The way you treat the needy is the way you treat the Lord.

This is the last word of Jesus in the five sermons Matthew has recorded. Its placement suggests that it's a culmination of Jesus' teaching. In his previous words and actions, he had lifted the lowly, exalting the outcasts of society while shaming the well-to-do. But never had he put it so boldly: You will be judged for ignoring the needy.

In Jesus' parable of the good Samaritan, a priest and a temple assistant pass a robbery victim, perhaps fearing that he was already dead and would make them ritually unclean. But a despised Samaritan bends to salve the man's wounds. In a way, both were outcasts.

The leaders of Jesus' society were interested in perfection. They wanted the nation to have a clean slate so that God would deliver them. But in the process of promoting the letter of the law, they distorted its true spirit. Those who didn't get with the program—or who couldn't—were rejected. They didn't count. Prostitutes, tax collectors, lepers, debtors, foreigners, the woman with a bleeding disease who had been ceremonially unclean for 12 years, the bloodied traveler lying by the side of the Jericho Road—these people were the outcasts of society.

Jesus had touched lepers and healed them. He had dined with tax collectors, accepted worship from prostitutes, visited Gentiles, welcomed children, and taught women. Again and again, he had reached out to the outcasts.

In one parable, a king throws a wedding banquet for his son and sends his servants out with wedding invitations. One by one, those on the exclusive invitation list make their excuses and send their regrets. Some of them even mistreat the servants bearing the invitations.

Enraged, the king orders his servants to go to the main streets and invite everyone, good or bad, to attend: the blind, the crippled, the poor, and the lame. When there's still room, he sends his servants to the side streets to invite more people. His banquet will be crowded (Matthew 22:2–10; Luke 14:16–24).

This is yet another glimpse of the kingdom of heaven. The privileged ones had refused to come to God's party, and so the doors were thrown open to the common people.

On another occasion, Jesus taught, "When you give a luncheon or a dinner, do not invite your friends or your brothers or your relatives or rich neighbors, in case they might invite you in return, and you would be repaid. But when you give a banquet, invite the poor, the crippled, the lame, and the blind. And you will be blessed, because they cannot repay you, for you will be repaid at the resurrection of the righteous" (Luke 14:12–14).

In Jesus' teaching, the outcasts are God's family—and should be treated as such. He will repay their debts for them.

God's kingdom is like a wedding banquet, Jesus said. When the upper-class invitees send their regrets, the host brings in street people. The implication was clear: God was welcoming the outcasts into his presence. He wasn't shunning the privileged set; they were shunning him.

BETWEEN LAW AND MERCY

✦ ✦ ✦

SOME PEOPLE ENCOUNTER JESUS' rich teachings on love and assume that he was a feel-good teacher, all positive thinking and affirmations for the soul. But as we have seen, that's not the case.

Jesus spoke freely of God's judgment. Using the imagery of his day, he warned of eternal fire, the devil and his angels, and an outer darkness, "where there will be weeping and gnashing of teeth."

But Jesus' harshest words were reserved for the Pharisees and other religious leaders. He seemed to speak on behalf of the powerless against those in power, those who would "lock people out of the kingdom of heaven" (Matthew 23:13).

It's an odd mix of meanness and mercy. He sounds like a fire-and-brimstone preacher one minute and a self-help guru the next. It's "Come to me, you who are weary" in one chapter and "Cut off your hand if it offends you" in another.

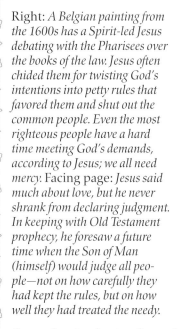

Right: *A Belgian painting from the 1600s has a Spirit-led Jesus debating with the Pharisees over the books of the law. Jesus often chided them for twisting God's intentions into petty rules that favored them and shut out the common people. Even the most righteous people have a hard time meeting God's demands, according to Jesus; we all need mercy. Facing page: Jesus said much about love, but he never shrank from declaring judgment. In keeping with Old Testament prophecy, he foresaw a future time when the Son of Man (himself) would judge all people—not on how carefully they had kept the rules, but on how well they had treated the needy.*

IMPOSSIBLE DEMANDS?

As we've already noted, Jesus demanded a great deal of those who would follow him. He asked for total commitment from the people closest to him, even following him to death. And his moral teaching set forth a code of conduct even stricter than the Pharisees' code.

"How come they got a day's wage for only one hour, and I got the same thing for working all day?" Most of us would agree with the disgruntled vineyard worker. But the shocking conclusion of Jesus' parable is this: God isn't fair. He shows mercy when it suits him. And that's ultimately a good thing for all of us.

He asked a rich young man to sell all he had and give the money to the poor. Generations of capitalists have cringed ever since. *How can we possibly do that?*

He told Peter to forgive an offender "seventy-seven times," a figure that in Hebrew numerology really means infinity. *Forgive and forgive and forgive? When does the offense become too great?*

He equated lustful looks with adultery. *Can't I look just a little? What's the harm in that?*

He said hateful thoughts and harsh words are tantamount to murder. *But what if the person really deserves it?*

"Love your enemies," he said. "If anyone strikes you on the cheek, offer the other also" (Luke 6:27,29). *But how does that work in international diplomacy, or labor negotiations, or with the bully who steals lunch money from my second-grader?*

Jesus' system may sound good, but it seems impossible. Millions of Christians have tried to live by his words and have had some success, but no one can do it all!

Maybe that was the whole point.

UNBELIEVABLE FORGIVENESS?

Two men went to the temple to pray: a Pharisee and a tax collector. The Pharisee bragged to God about his accomplishments, while the morally impaired tax collector humbly said, "God, be merciful to me, a sinner." Jesus said it was the tax collector who went home justified before God, not the Pharisee (Luke 18:10–14).

The listeners many have responded, "Are you crazy, Jesus? What about all the people the tax collector has defrauded? And look how good a citizen the Pharisee is. He gives ten percent of his income to charity, while the tax collector skims twice that for his own pocket. And you say the tax collector is the one who's justified? What's wrong with this picture?"

Jesus told another story that challenges our notions of justice. A vineyard owner went early in the day to hire workers, promising to pay them a denarius, the normal day's wage. But he needed more workers as the day went on, so he returned to the marketplace, where the workers hung out. He hired more at 9 A.M. and 12 noon and finally at 5 P.M., promising to pay them "whatever is right." When the workers all assembled at the end of the workday, the owner first paid those who had worked only an hour. He gave them each a denarius. In fact, as he went down the line, to those who had worked six hours, or nine hours, or twelve hours, he gave each worker a denarius.

Jesus once challenged a wealthy man to sell his possessions and give the money to the poor. The man had been eager to follow Jesus, but upon hearing the conditions, "he became sad; for he was very rich" (Luke 18:23).

As you might guess, the first ones hired were angry. "These last worked only one hour, and you have made them equal to us who have borne the burden of the day and the scorching heat."

But the owner replied, "Friend, I am doing you no wrong; did you not agree with me for the usual daily

THE TEACHINGS OF JESUS

The prodigal son returns home to his loving father. You can almost hear the older brother complaining to his friends: "Why should he get a party when he's squandered all his money?" And he has a point. Sinners don't deserve a father's welcome, but a loving father gives it anyway.

wage?…Am I not allowed to do what I choose with what belongs to me? Or are you envious because I am generous?" (Matthew 20:1–16).

It was the same complaint of the prodigal son's older brother: "Why are you treating him so well when I've been here all along?" The religious leaders had tried hard to keep the law, and now God was offering the kingdom to lawbreakers for free. It wasn't fair.

And for those of us in the modern age who believe in equal pay for equal work, it doesn't seem fair either. We like the idea that people get what they deserve.

But here's the rub. Even the Pharisees didn't deserve much. They kept most of the law, but they displeased God in some major ways. And by raising the bar—forbidding hatred, not just murder, and lust, not just adultery—Jesus guaranteed that no one had any claim of deserving God's kingdom. We are all prodigals. We are all tax collectors. The Pharisees who think they're right with God are in denial. Jesus called them hypocrites. We think of hypocrites as those who judge everyone else too much—and they do—but the basic meaning is that they judge themselves too little. They have no clue how much mercy they need. The prostitutes and tax collectors are closer to the kingdom because they realize they must throw themselves on God's mercy.

RESOLVING THE TENSION

There will always be a tension between law and mercy. Many Christians work hard to follow Jesus' higher standards. They avoid lust and hatred, they try to treat their enemies well, and they forgive those who offend them.

Others see these commands as impossible to attain, and so they don't even try. They know they need God's mercy, and they count on that to get them into God's kingdom.

The Apostle Paul developed a theology of righteousness and grace, acknowledging that all people have sinned and need God's free gift of salvation, offered through the sacrifice of Jesus Christ. No one can earn this salvation; it's a gift. Sin does not keep a person from qualifying for salvation. But once a person has received this gift, the Holy Spirit helps that person to live righteously. According to Paul, there is always forgiveness for sin, but those who are saved by faith in Jesus should continue to live by the spirit of Jesus, doing what is right.

Jesus' teachings present both demands and grace, keeping them in a tension that Paul and others have helped us to live with. But Jesus kept challenging people, showing them the life of the kingdom. He also kept offering God's mercy to those who would take it, opening the door for those who had been locked out of the kingdom.

The Apostle Paul, seen here in stained glass preaching in Athens, picked up Jesus' message about God's mercy. "All have sinned," Paul wrote, but "are now justified by his grace as a gift" (Romans 3:23–24).

SUMMARY

✦ ✦ ✦

YOU'RE IN FIRST-CENTURY GALILEE, buying a kitchen table from Joseph, that nice carpenter in Nazareth. You meet his son and apprentice, Jesus. Can you imagine that this gawky teenager will be remembered two thousand years from now?

People will date their checks with the number of years since his birth. Hundreds of millions of people will sing about him once a week, and many others will use his name as an oath on a regular basis. Some people will boycott companies because they think this carpenter would want them to, and through the centuries others will go to war for the same reason. Still others will stand courageously for peace, claiming the power that emanates from this young man who's handing you the bill of sale. He's helping you lug the chairs to your cart, and you have no clue that, within a century, people will choose to die rather than disown him.

This carpenter became a rabbi. He taught wherever he could, gathering a following. For three years he traveled

Right: *Jesus' childhood was a humble one; he learned carpentry from Joseph. His neighbors were astonished when he became a famous rabbi and healer.* Facing page: *The New Testament teaches that Jesus conquered death by rising from the grave. Guards were felled by dazzling light; disciples found the tomb empty. Within three days of his horrendous crucifixion, Jesus was meeting with, eating with, and speaking with his old friends.*

Jesus taught in synagogues, but also out in the open. His message was world-changing, but also deeply personal. As his fame grew, some wanted to crown him king, challenging the hated Romans, and some drifted away when he refused to go along with that plan. But he kept teaching about God's kingdom taking root in people's hearts.

the villages of Galilee, with occasional treks to Jerusalem, healing people and saying wise words. Some loved him, some hated him, many were indifferent. He seemed to be a prophet, but he claimed to be something more, the Son of Man, a humble servant-king. Would he overthrow the Romans, get their arrogant chariots off your village streets? No, that was not his style. His kingdom was from another world. Was this blasphemy, as the leaders were charging, or was this the answer you'd all been waiting for? Was he messiah or maniac, charlatan or shepherd?

His enemies killed him, but his followers claim he rose from the dead. You're sitting at your kitchen table when

you hear the news: He's risen! He's teaching again by the seaside. Peter's mother-in-law is going; do you want to come along?

Ironically, Jesus did overthrow the Romans. It took almost three hundred years, but his followers won their unarmed battle with the Empire and claimed it as their own. Ever after, Western civilization has been stamped "Christian." The rest of that history isn't always very appetizing. Christians did many things for Jesus' sake that would have made Jesus weep. But there were many good things, too.

From a purely historical perspective, few, if any, have had the impact Jesus had. Muhammad maybe, Buddha, Confucius, Alexander the Great. But after reading Jesus' teachings, you can't help but think that maybe history doesn't really see the true importance of Jesus. We have different "Pharisees" now, and different outcasts, but the good news of God's mercy is still as astonishing as ever.

Certainly Alexander the Great had a major impact on our world, as he spread Greek culture throughout the Mediterranean. And maybe a few other leaders could match the historical prominence of Jesus of Nazareth. But millions of Jesus' followers claim that he still lives.

INDEX